Ethical Empowerment

ETHICAL EMPOWERMENT

Virtue Beyond the Paradigms

by Arthur D. Schwartz

EMERGENCE BOOKS

ISBN: 978-0-9894671-4-8

Library of Congress Control Number: 2014916635

First Edition

Front cover design by Damonza

Published by Emergence Books, Box 398095, Cambridge, MA USA 02139

Publisher's Cataloging-in-Publication

Schwartz, Arthur D.
    Ethical empowerment : virtue beyond the paradigms /
  by Arthur D. Schwartz. -- First edition.
    pages cm
    Includes bibliographical references and index.
    LCCN 2014916635
    ISBN 978-0-9894671-3-1 (hardcover)
    ISBN 978-0-9894671-4-8 (paperback)

    1. Ethics, Modern--21st century. 2. Political
  science. 3. Social sciences. 4. Philosophy.   I. Title.

BJ320.S39 2014   170.9'051

This book is dedicated with gratitude
to my late mother, Lillian Levine Schwartz
and to my father, Herbert Schwartz.
Their love and support made this book possible.

The reasonable man adapts himself to the world; the unreasonable one persists in trying to adapt the world to himself. Therefore all progress depends on the unreasonable man.

— George Bernard Shaw

Contents

Contents

Preface

A fog of misdirection, formed by hardened perspective and preconception, confuses and obscures ethical thinking. Perennial philosophical questions of mental clarity seem even more urgent today. This book is concerned with the challenge of cutting through hypnotic-like misdirection in order to access the basic elements and conceptions that comprise the essence of morality and ethics. While general abstract principles are necessary gateways to wisdom and knowledge, greater wisdom may shine through when generalizations and preconceptions are untangled so that the unique essence of things can be appreciated without obstruction. Freed from habitual preconceptions that misdirect, ethical understanding may be deepened from the inside out. And the ethical deficiencies of some social and political institutions, including cultural norms and traditions, may be viewed from new perspectives. Hardened, inflexible thinking is common in the thinking of radicals, reactionaries, and all political persuasions. Accordingly, the present work is an ethical manifesto of non-doctrinaire perspective, and it can be as conservative as it is progressive.

There are many forms of hardened ethical perspective and they are characterizable in various ways and in different terms. They often overlap or exist side-by-side. I do not claim that the following list is exhaustive, or that it follows any formal or technical criteria. It might well be argued that some of the terms on the list are merely different expressions that refer to similar or, in some cases, almost identical types or patterns of thinking. But they are provided in this preface in order to convey a sense of the broad, interlinking subject matter of the book. Each form of hardened ethical perspective and its characterization may generally morph into one or more of the others and may, in turn, itself be viewed as a perspective concerning the hardening of ethical perspectives.

- conformism
- nonconformism
- social and cultural traditions
- political and economic institutions
- dogma and ideology
- hypnotic thinking
- perspectival myopia
- preconditioned belief
- habitual thinking
- "the conventional wisdom"
- paradigmatic thinking
- ideophobia (fear of new ideas)
- egoism (fear of being wrong)
- financial and political interests and biases

While the term 'ethical empowerment' could be misconstrued as a twisted entitlement to dictate right and wrong, empowerment actually suggests an opportunity to learn, to act, or to better oneself. In this book, ethical empowerment entails a process that goes beyond hardened ethical perspectives or rigid doctrines and seeks a grounding in ethical justification formed from the basic elements of morality that are the common denominators of ethical thought. Clearing confusions, blockages and misdirection away from the core or the basic essence of morality lays the foundation of ethical empowerment. The ethical approach that is adopted here does not presume a singular abstract principle that in itself can imply the solution of ethical disagreement, but seeks instead to understand the elements of morality. By means of casting this understanding into elemental principles consensus may be facilitated, developed and evolved. But how can we become ethically empowered when views on the nature of morality differ greatly between cultures, philosophies and ideologies? Ethical empowerment will, therefore, require an acceptance of moral diversity that is grounded by a broad underlying unity. Given a few moments of reflection, most individuals will acknowledge that there is a distinction between moral actuality and simple ethical rules of conduct concerning assessments of right or wrong and good or bad. After all, "God works in mysterious ways," and cultural or philosophical constructs are not likely to solve the mystery. Ethical empowerment requires a transcendence of rules and legalisms masquerading as morality itself when, in truth, they are merely ethical imperfections.

One of the key arguments of this book is that the basis of morality and its ethical conceptualizations concern nothing less than universal love. This is hardly a new idea, of course, as the Old Testament commandment to "Love thy neighbor as thyself" is also the "Great Commandment" of the New Testament and central to Christian teachings. Arguably, the sense of "Love thy neighbor as thyself" captures the spirit of most if not all of the great religions. However, philosophers have traditionally favored the concept of good or "The Good" as the essence of morality and, with a few exceptions (e.g. Joseph Fletcher's *Situation Ethics*), have shied away from the conception of love as the root of ethical thinking. I wish to submit, however, that the fused emotional and intellectual content of love as the source of morality is a truer foundation and analytical starting point for ethics than most conceptions of good. But absent an objective and consensually driven understanding that is specific enough to be used in difficult ethical deliberations, ethics will disappoint and leave us with little more than a heart full of emotion and a head full of wishful thinking. I suggest in this book that a rational, dialogical expression of love is in its essentiality a description of ethical empowerment.

Understanding universal love as the essence of morality empowers ethics because the free-spirited nature of love has the potential to heal human conflict. And in this regard, love is the best friend of philosophers and of audacious intellectual explorers who question traditional assumptions, or propose new or unconventional solutions to old and resistant problems. The power of universal love motivates the search for wisdom and new perspectives on truth, and so its power is also the power of truth and tireless questioning of inconsistencies, deficiencies and prevalent absurdities. The audacity of philosophy provides the luxury of critiquing entrenched institutions or submitting proposals for starting anew. It is not reckless to ask audacious questions or propose radical solutions; on the contrary, it is reckless for someone to acknowledge deep ethical or political questions but then to leave them be without much more than a shrug. But a less arrogant world will spiritedly subject itself to the joy of asking questions!

The word 'moral' often elicits a somber and all-too-serious tone! But Aristotle did not view the subject of morality in this way. His term, 'eudaimonia' or human flourishing, captures a truer spirit of living a moral life. Ethical empowerment and the purpose of ethics, i.e. the living of a moral life can also be stated as a process of self-realization or freedom to fulfill positive potential leading to individual and social flourishing. Nietzsche's "will to power" also suggests something more than the moralistic legalisms that have cast a dreary fog over ethics and its conceptions concerning the nature of morality. While moral do's and don'ts are most certainly a necessary part of any ethics, the conception of morality is vitalized when it is broadened and lightened enough to include more inspirational aspects of human flourishing in addition to its categorical imperatives. We are just as easily hypnotized into thinking that we are free when we are not, as into thinking that we are prisoners of circumstance when, once again, we are not. This is not to say that we are free or that we are not free. But ethical empowerment is the best guarantor of freedom.

In practice, the words 'ethics' and 'morality are nearly synonymous, but this book makes a simple but important distinction. Ethical opinions and conceptualizations are distinct from the moral states of affairs that they conceptualize. That which is ethically adjudged to be moral, i.e. 'right' or 'good' may be later reevaluated or reversed. This merely reflects human fallibility, and while some ethical beliefs or opinions are not likely to ever be reversed, in principle they can be. This is the same relationship that science has with physical reality: scientific knowledge concerning physical reality may be subsequently disproved or modified. And thus, ethical and scientific opinions, respectively, are always subject to fallibility owing to a deeper physical reality or a deeper morality. This distinction can be a helpful reminder of the pitfalls of bias and dogma.

PART I

Principles

I.1

Empowerment and Virtue

Virtue or moral excellence is in broad terms the goal of any ethics. To empower is to enable with power in order to perform, accomplish, create or influence and, therefore, while ethical empowerment cannot guarantee virtue it increases the potential for its realization. An archetypal example of empowerment and its relationship to virtue is education. While there is no doubt that the road to success is far more difficult for an individual who is poorly educated than for one who is highly educated, it may rightly be said that an uneducated person who begins life in a state of relative disempowerment may overcome deficiencies through self-motivation and self-empowerment. And, undoubtedly, overcoming obstacles is itself a central virtue. The unempowered individual may empower himself or herself and achieve great and unsurpassed virtue. Therefore, ethical empowerment facilitates virtue but does not guarantee it.

The old schools of philosophy speak of ideal virtuous men or sages who in all respects are the embodiment of virtue. This idealization, if taken too seriously is a mere fantasy. In truth, we are all works in progress from the moment of birth to our final breath. Even death, and perhaps death most of all, is a process of becoming; we all want to die virtuously. And our lives are a composite collection of actions and deeds, intentions and feelings in which we have sometimes more and sometimes less conformed to the demands of virtue. Conformity to virtue is by no means a black and white affair and it is, perhaps, more like an aesthetic judgment than it is a calculation, or perhaps it is a bit of both. Can virtue be taught without doctrine or specific creeds or systems of belief? And regardless of whether virtue is taught or inherited we need to ask, "What is virtue?" Lists of the virtues are not difficult to find. Here are a few virtues: Courage, Honesty, Trustworthiness, Resilience, Loyalty, Independence, Selflessness,

Perseverance, Wisdom, Compassion. However, is courage or loyalty in support of a brutal, despotic regime a virtue? Are perseverance, resilience and trustworthiness virtues when, in some circumstances, quitting a task, project or venture may be the wiser and more virtuous course? Is honesty a virtue when, in order to be honest, a promise must be broken? Is selflessness a virtue when the devotion to others is so strong that self-sacrifice leads to illness or personal ruination? Is independence a virtue if it thwarts greater accomplishment by blocking help or joint effort with others that would reap greater good and greater reward? Of course, wisdom is a virtue, but whose wisdom do we follow? And compassion is surely a core principle of morality, but even compassion can turn sour if it is blind to issues of justice or other moral imperatives.

Specific virtues are not autonomous gems but, rather, are expressions of a deeper morality to which they owe their truth. A virtue is a beautiful harmonic unity of good intention and action. Spontaneous acts of courage, unhesitating kindness or unwavering generosity are not only examples of the essence of virtue but also provide glimpses into its inner workings or process. We admire the clarity of individuals whose virtue seems to flow naturally from a purely good intention. Lao-tzu, in chapter 38 of the *Tao Te Ching* discusses how the higher or superior form of virtue is a quality that becomes second nature, whereas lower forms of virtue can involve a good deal of preconception that, for Lao-tzu, is indicative of an individual that has not yet achieved true virtue.[1] Lao-tzu's point is that true virtue must be completely absorbed by the one who is virtuous, and if the action is something that needs to be self-consciously enforced then it has not yet reached the status of virtue. Lao-tzu, who wrote about twenty-five hundred years ago, in effect acknowledges the subconscious component of virtue. Virtues share this quality with values: they are both examples of deep belief on both the conscious and subconscious levels. A value is a belief that has become an intrinsic part of a person's belief system and is reflected by the conditioned, reflexive response to favored or disfavored opinions expressed by others. Values become hardwired, and rewiring them requires a rare shift in long-held beliefs. Similarly, virtues are also deeply embedded on the conscious and subconscious levels, often reflecting behavior patterns that are focused on values. An act of virtuous courage, for instance, is motivated by a desire to defend something of great value or greatly loved such that it appears almost instinctual and perfectly ingrained in the psyche as a swiftly orchestrated and beautifully realized moral harmony. Another example is the virtue of perseverance, which is motivated by the high regard for the object that is being kept or acquired. Or consider friendship, one of the most esteemed values, and excellence in the art of friendship is also among the most important virtues. Further examples showing the connection between virtues and values are plentiful and are easily observed to be products of deep subconscious belief and conditioning.

> You love your virtue as a mother her child; but
> when has a mother ever wished to be paid for
> her love? Your virtue is what is dearest to you.[2]

Virtue itself may indeed be the highest form of value, as the practice of virtue continually adds value to life in a world that craves value and longs for virtue.

Subconscious belief is deeply and intricately involved in our ethical judgments and conceptions of moral value and virtue. A fundamental function of philosophy is to reexamine both conscious and subconscious preconception concerning value, virtue and all belief in the spirit of Socrates whose words perfectly express the value of virtue, "The unexamined life is not worth living." And an empowered ethics, therefore, must be charged with the responsibility for reexamining our beliefs. And this is our task, to break through the hardened layers of belief that may have outgrown their usefulness or perhaps were never useful. Let us begin by being mindful *and* critical of our values and our virtues. Let us become familiar with the hypnotic character of our beliefs and develop the virtue of reexamination and the courage and the will to exercise it. Virtue requires an ease with which one lets go of his ego, or of building up the ego so that it may be let go. Thus, virtue involves an ability of the self to both loose itself from affiliations and attachments, but also for valuing them and knowing when to remain attached and giving them all due credit. Virtue involves an ability to know when an apparent value is only a false value, i.e. not a moral value. In other words, virtue requires that we become unfazed by the detours of egoism and selflessness, attachment and detachment and, most of all, preconception.

The ordinary ethics of everyday life has its challenges and conundrums in conflicts between promise-keeping, truthfulness and honesty that emerge in the variety of human relationships. However, so-called ordinary ethics works fairly well, and when it seems not to work it may be because there is no ethical problem or conflict *per se*, but only an avoidance of ethics that is due to weakness in the hearts and minds of people who in everyday life choose personal advantage over doing what they know to be right. Here we see a legitimate place for "virtue ethics," which focuses on building the self-esteem of virtue in individuals by deepening conscious and subconscious conviction and action in accordance with what is believed to be right. However, the outlines and divisions of ethical conflict more clearly surface in the form of political, socio-economic, cultural and religious issues. The line between the individual and society is not always clear. Perhaps the line may be clearly perceived by the example of asserting your "right to vote." It is sometimes said, "everyone should exercise their right to vote." However, should someone who is thoroughly ignorant of the political positions held by the different candidates, and has made no assessment of their character, and in general has paid little attention to the issues of the election campaign or the merits of the candidates decide to exercise his right to vote? One of the characteristics of virtue is in knowing when action is indeed virtuous, or if its exercise would be wrongful. Acting virtuously is not a simple knee jerk, and choosing *not* to vote can be a virtue: Lao-tzu's idealistic conception of virtue cannot go so far as to exclude Socratic reexamination. On the contrary, to knowingly cast a vote based on ignorance would be a vice. I recognize that I have made a great oversimplification here because probably very few voters think of their vote as an exercise of ignorance, but how many voters simply vote the party line without knowing anything more about the candidates other than their names? An ethically empowered society is one that effectively empowers its citizens with opportunities to become virtuous; but is the exercise of ignorance a virtue? The empowerment of individuals is no guarantee of virtue, and empowerment that is abused disempowers society.

The abuse of the voting privilege is an important issue for anyone who believes that democracy is the most empowering of political forms. We would like to think that the greatness of democracy rests in the hands of its citizens but, certainly, virtue is not a product of the mindless following of rules such as "you should *always* exercise your right to vote." Ethical and social empowerment is very much a mutual function shared by the individual and society. Socialists emphasize the role of society while libertarians place the onus on the individual and self-empowerment. But it is all too clear that both extremes are extremely incorrect in their imbalanced assessments. Egoism and altruism, self-interest and compassion for others, individual habits and behaviors mandated by law all play critical roles in ethical empowerment and in the virtuous flourishing of both the individual and society. A low moral status of the social environment will generally lower the moral status of its members. We each benefit and suffer from the quality of the moral environment. But of what does the environment consist? Is it not individuals and their decisions that collectively determine the quality of their environment, and is it also not true that one person can make a difference? Indeed, man is a social animal but he is much more than that! Moral excellence or virtue flourishes when there is a harmony between strong individuals and a strong society that cultivates virtue and never weakens in its commitment to greatness.

Empowerment by itself is not destiny, but it is the creation of potential for what could be a positive destiny. While a glorious outcome may be made possible through empowerment, it is by no means inevitable or certain but is dependent upon the realization and exercise of virtue.

I.2

Moral Actualities and Ethical Formalities

Is not the philosophical equation of actuality and reality a great presumption? A critical distinction may be made between the uses of the two terms, and while the terms may sometimes be used interchangeably a distinction of sense must be made. 'Reality' more generally denotes existence, whereas 'actuality' generally denotes a perspective or set of beliefs about existence or what is existent. For example, it might be said that, "In actuality the jury was wrong because evidence was later discovered that exonerated the innocent man who was convicted of a crime." But it would be awkward to say, "In reality the jury was wrong…" because 'reality' refers to the unalterable truth conditions of the case and not merely the jury's verdict concerning those facts. The jury decided what it decided and, for all we know, the consensus of opinion regarding the verdict could be reversed yet again! However, there is no awkwardness in stating that in *actuality*, the jury made a bad decision because it was later proved wrong. Typically, actuality is the accepted belief of what is the case, whereas reality refers to that which is the case independent of belief or knowledge. Reality is that which is transcendent of beliefs and human fallibility, whereas actuality is, ultimately, merely what is believed to be real.

It is not important whether or not this ordinary language distinction between 'actuality' and 'reality' is accepted, but the distinction—even if it is thought to employ *un*ordinary language, is important because it has been an enormous source of confusion. The confusion seems to have its philosophical origins in Aristotle's use of the terms 'actuality' and 'potentiality'. Counterintuitively, Aristotle says that actuality precedes potentiality. An actual thing is its form fused with formless matter. Actuality is the existent thing, e.g. a man, a boy, a home, a stone, any *thing* and, as such, is distinguished from its potential form as, for example, a boy who has not yet actualized his potential in becoming a man. The form of a thing is immanent in the thing itself and combines together with formless matter to produce the actuality of the thing. Paradoxically, all potentiality is also actuality in itself but it is distinct from the actuality of the existent things that precede it and in which it is immanent. From where does the actuality, which precedes every material thing, come? Pure actuality, which precedes and is the requisite condition of all actuality both present and future is the pure actuality of the Unmoved Mover (God). Aristotle does not argue for a Platonic World of Forms, but rather for a God principle that is the immaterial pure actuality he also describes as pure thought or "thought thinking itself." The Unmoved Mover has also been described as "God thinking itself." Pure actuality is pure thought. An actual thing is its immanent form combined with matter and delimited by the actual forms of its potential existence. Therefore, actuality equals reality. And from this equation a long philosophical tradition was initiated that was to conflate actuality, reason and reality.

The conflation of actuality and reality probably reached its pinnacle with Hegelianism. Hegel liberally used the term 'actuality' to interpret historical reality in terms of his divination of the evolution of consciousness; for Hegel, actuality was whatever he justified by his dialectical logic. Ultimately, for Hegel, right thinking in accordance with actuality reflects the deepest nature of reality in its unfolding. In contrast, modern science trends in a very different direction as new scientific theories that create broadly new perspectives may themselves get replaced like old eyeglasses (or paradigms) whose prescriptions no longer fit; science is or should always be looking for better eyeglasses. And yet paradigms of right science can resemble Hegelian actuality by the authority not of Hegelian logic but by the authority of the ruling paradigm. Paradigms "shift" sometimes with Hegelian-like slowness, but if it is true that "justice delayed is justice denied," is not the thwarting of truth also a thwarting of justice? In truth, reality is filled with secrets, mystery and uncertainty and thus there can be no monopoly on the truth, and the modern world may in part be defined in terms of its relative comfort level with uncertainty.

An actuality is created by accepted opinions concerning factual or moral states of affairs, but as understanding deepens actualities can change. It may be said that actualities are *believed* realities. It is important to be mindful of changing actualities or emerging new actualities. There are moral actualities as well as physical actualities. Here would be an example of someone predicting an emerging moral actuality: "You think that Mr. Smith's behavior was reprehensible, but in actuality he acted nobly and in the best interests of everyone; his motives will become apparent soon enough!" However, generally, we have tended to think of actuality more in terms of matters of fact, such as in the natural sciences or in sociological and behavioral statistics, than in terms of moral actuality. An actuality can be a simple fact of which there is no warrant for reasonable doubt. Indisputable facts are actualities, bearing in mind, of course, that objections might later emerge that cast doubt on the facts so that the actuality becomes unclear or doubtful. An actuality can also be a product of a broad class of accepted beliefs such as history, the details of one's own life or facts concerning other persons. Science is built upon the actualities of accepted theory and experimentation and the basic premises of scientific method. Paradigms, and scientific paradigms in particular may be viewed as a subspecies of actuality: they are intellectual architectonics or blueprints of the perceived states of affairs that seek to explain the accepted scientific actuality. Although scientific actualities concern intellectual paradigms and broadly based practices such as scientific method, as well as some biases that shape perceived realities, they may not be universally accepted. Actualities and paradigms are in a continuing process of change and adaptation. For example, the theory of relativity dramatically changed the actualities for the everyman as much as for scientists, as did the theory of Copernicus and as have other revolutionary theories and discoveries throughout the history of science. However, scientific actualities are not shared by all as, for example, the actuality of biological evolution is accepted by most scientists but not by creationists and, therefore, actuality is not uniform in the community but is relative to belief and perspective.

Ethics is the study and practice of morality. But what is morality? And what is moral actuality? Perhaps the best approach in attempting to answer these questions is to show clearly what morality is not. Morality is not reducible to the simplistic following of rules or injunctions. Immanuel Kant, in a little essay entitled, "On a supposed Right to Lie because of Philanthropic Concerns" states that, "To be truthful (honest) in all declarations is…a sacred and unconditionally commanding law of reason that admits of no expediency whatsoever."[3] And accordingly, if a known murderer asks a homeowner whether the man he is pursuing is hiding in his house, Kant believes that the only possible right decision is to tell the murderer the truth! The great philosopher's opinion is so outrageous that the first impression on hearing it is that he was probably joking or, perhaps, it was a misstatement of what Kant meant or intended. Unfortunately, it is neither. He rationalizes the absurdity: if we do not obey our duty to always tell the truth then the foundations of ordinary morality and contract law will fall apart at the seams. Or it could open up a Pandora's box of unintended consequences for which the one who lied to protect the innocent victim may become legally liable. Kant's philosophy seems, at times, to be an exercise whose primary function is to justify its own burdensome terminology. Philosophy at its best, however, uses language as a means to overcome its limitations because, while understanding may be given birth by using words, words cannot by themselves account for wisdom and understanding. Moral actuality is profoundly deeper than Kant's cold expression of moral duty. Kant's defense of telling the truth without regard to the violence or mayhem it might cause is difficult to fathom but Kant had, by the time he wrote the article, already admitted his penchant for dogmatic slumbering.

Principles and ethical rules, inflexible virtues and fixed values are shorthand *formalities* that we regularly abandon when they are inapplicable. We assume many things to be true through convention or habit but it is not infrequent that we are surprised when our assumptions turn out to be false. But the breakdown of ethical rules such as truth-telling or promise-keeping does not undermine morality, and exemplifies the truism that "rules are made to be broken." While troubling at times, inconsistent ethical rules do not destroy ordinary or everyday morality. Faith in the general utility of formalities such as truth-telling and promise-keeping has not been shaken by their fallibility, in fact, exceptions and extenuating circumstances that preclude their application are likely to be taken in stride. It is tacitly recognized that morality is deeper than rules, maxims and preconceptions. These exceptions are accepted because it is understood by all except the adorers of legalism that the rules and maxims that guide everyday life are only formalities or guideposts that are supervened by the greater authority of moral actuality.

The critical issue, of course, concerns the basis of morality that shapes assessments of moral actuality. If moral actuality is not comprised of unworkable ethical rules or standards such as the utilitarian standard or Kant's "categorical imperative," or values and virtues that beg the question of moral rightness or goodness when they are detached from the concreteness of actual situations, where is the true essence of morality to be found? Actualities regarding the facts of the physical world are formed on the basis of experience, observation, and empirical justification; do not moral experience and ethical observations provide the basis of moral actuality with a degree of depth and assurance that mere formalities cannot? Do observations of moral experience pertaining to right and wrong, good and bad, desirability and benefit and their contraries provide a basis to escape the presumption and contrivance of abstract standards and highly fallible rules? Are ethical observations of morality any less revealing than scientific observations of physical facts or phenomena? If morality can be observed, might it not also be described? I propose that morality can indeed be described, and moral actuality may be discerned not by the arbitrariness of rules or maxims and other formalities but by observations of what is preferable or praiseworthy, beneficial or helpful, supportive to others as well as to the self. The goal of ethics is not to prescribe on the basis of rusty old rules that may be useless when it counts the most, but to *describe* the moral actuality that is presented to us. Ethical formalities such as maxims, rules, and even ideologies and "philosophies of life" have a role and can often illuminate and bring us closer to wisdom by assisting in the description of moral actuality, but they can also obscure and confuse like a heavy fog. While ethical formalities should be taken seriously, even very seriously, they simply do not always apply because they are imperfect reflections of moral actuality. Factual truths are not prescribed but are accepted as true based upon sufficient description (observations, controlled experiments, evidence, eyewitness accounts, etc.); similarly, degrees of "moral truth" conceived in terms of rightness or wrongness and goodness or badness are also matters for description (of intentions, results, consequences, benefits, fairness, and etc.)

G.E. Moore argued that good is an unanalyzable, non-natural property.

But it is argued here that good and all moral predication are highly analyzable, and while they are indeed "non-natural" they are not properties. Moral actuality like physical actuality *is* non-natural because they are both products of reason and rational perspective. David Hume and Adam Smith were describers of morality. Even Nietzsche was as well. But while Hume's ethics is characterized as "naturalistic" I submit that this is a poor and inaccurate characterization. Truth and good are both expressions of rational opinion and are, ultimately, on a level with novels, scientific treatises and works of art because fiction and non-fiction alike are non-natural. Everything is a perspective, and in this Nietzsche would certainly agree, and the distinction between science and ethics is not that one is "natural" and the other is "non-natural" but only that they involve different species of rational perspective. In the case of, say, a scientific paper, arguments may be presented in which certain facts are said to exist, i.e. to be true. But a scientific paper cannot establish absolute truth but only rational reasons for believing that some things are true. And, of course, in science it has not infrequently occurred that what was once thought to be true later turns out to be false (and vice versa). Is not ethics much the same with respect to rational perspectives but within the confines of its specific domain? Is it not quite common to think that something is good but only later realize the mistake in judgment, and then reverse opinion? Examples would be endless, Oh ye of broken vows!

Moral actuality is no more or no less non-naturalistic than physical actuality, and it is best to dispense with terms that have no meaning. Physical and moral actuality are different simply because ethics and science represent two very different species of reason. But it remains to be shown how good (and morality in general) is analyzable and describable without resorting to rigid definitions or claims that they consist of physical properties. The knowledge of science is ever increasing, and one of the many areas of enormous growth concerns the various branches of atomic and nuclear physics. And there is ample reason to believe that the description of the different atoms and their compositions will continue to change and evolve as knowledge in the atomic and nuclear sciences grows. Ethics is not nuclear physics, but problems in human conflict have stubbornly persisted throughout history. And in the case of ethics, Moore argues that there is nothing that can be learned about the anatomy of good. Good is, he says, a simple and unanalyzable quality: "x is good" for no other reason that it is good. Thus, saying that pleasure is good, or happiness is good, or justice is good is to beg the question because while they provide examples of things or properties that are good they do not deepen the understanding of *why* something is good other than it *is* good. The emotivist argument (e.g. that of A.J Ayer or C.L. Stevenson) that came along years after Moore published his *Principia Ethica* (1903) produced an even more radical subjectivism. The emotivists agreed that good is unanalyzable, but not because it is non-natural but, rather, because it is a subjective mental quality, an "I like" or an "I don't like" so that, in the final analysis, ethics is reduced to something like taste testing in an ice cream factory. Moore's "naturalistic fallacy" and the arguments of emotivism are false because moral predicates are not properties of anything, natural or non-natural, but are simply a means and a species of rational affirmation. There are reasons, based upon fundamental rational principles, for affirming something to be more or less good or bad and right or wrong. But the failure of ethics has been a failure to adequately analyze and describe the basic rational elements and principles that account for the morality of intentions, actions and their consequences that are the stuff—the describable "phenomena," of morality. A successful analysis and description of that which constitutes moral actuality could empower affirmation or denial in terms of good, right, value, and virtue or in terms of relative degrees of moral coherency.

*   *   *   *

Ethics, like any discipline of study, can only form conceptions of its subject. The only alternative would be a claim of direct intuition or mystical clarity, but even that would have to be filtered by the perspective and the constitution of the perceiver. We owe this basic realization to Kant, who says that our perceptions and our understanding are structured by transcendental conceptions of the human mind, and that knowledge of reality (or "noumena") beyond these confines and limitations is, therefore, unknowable. But while Kant avoided any claim to absolute knowledge of physical reality by his acknowledgement of the unknowability of noumena, his transcendental concepts and categories are themselves absolutes and, therefore, constitute a virtual contradiction. Kant's ethics is similarly immodest in his assertion of absolute ethical principles amid his acknowledged mystery of freedom. A spirit of philosophy and knowledge can always benefit from Socratic humility. It was Kurt Gödel who, in his incompleteness theorem, set the bar by concluding, at least with respect to mathematics, that it is impossible to prove the truth of a proposition or set of propositions without using propositions borrowed from other systems, thus leading to an infinite regress of unending justification.[4] Therefore, it would follow that Kant's categories are not provable (indeed, it can be argued that some have already been disproved) and any ethical conception of morality—if we were to apply the Gödelian perspective, is unprovable on its own terms or its particular "system" of thought. The best we can do is to develop principles and theories that, in the case of science, are empirically demonstrable and can be put into practice and, in the case of ethics, that achieve rational coherence in theory and practice that might ultimately lead to consensus. Consensus is a difficult issue because mere consensus in any field may be fleeting. However, without consensus most if not all value is lost. In ethics, in particular, there is no methodology more worthless than one that has no adherent other than its author; of course, its worth may yet be resuscitated or discovered at a later time. Therefore, ethical consensus is not only a part of any ethical deliberation, it also helps determine whether an ethical theory will help shape moral actuality.

The syntax of 'ethics' and 'morality' corresponds with the syntax of 'actuality' as distinguished from 'reality'. The flexible use of the terms should not conflate ethical *conceptions* of moral actuality with morality itself, much as scientific *conceptions* of physical actuality should not be conflated with physical reality itself. And the mindful distinction between ethical conceptions of morality and the ultimate unknowability of what is conceptualized is a protection from the pitfalls and dangers of dogma. Ethics can progress with an open attitude that avoids dogmatic preconception by describing elemental concepts of morality as they are expressed in the diversity of situation and in the flow of history, but perhaps the surest path to the attainment of ethical empowerment is the recognition of fallibility and the constant need for self-correction. It is difficult to acknowledge error if the defined purpose of one's path is to assume the self-conscious burden and presumption of defining what is right.

I.3

'True,' 'Good,' 'Right'

Truth is a paradox. Excepting definitional truths, any statement "It is the case that *p* is true," holds the potential for later disproof. Thus, any statement of truth could be later determined to be false. The universe has a deep and myriad capacity to contradict assumptions, premises and conclusions concerning physical reality. Truth statements concerning facts can only reflect actuality, not reality. (§I.2) Stating anything at all about physical reality can never be more than a perspective on the truth, and any perspective may be false. We are unable to say or write anything about physical reality with theoretic certainty. When something is said to be true we may want to mean that it is "absolutely true" but there are no absolute statements of truth concerning physical reality. And if a statement of fact is not absolutely true, what is it? "Relatively true?" "True but not absolutely true?" Perhaps. We often talk about truth in exactly these terms, but in these cases it is unclear whether we are really talking about the truth or only using "relatively true" as a euphemism for falsehood. Truth and falsehood are often supposed to be a duality, but if 'truth' includes that which is relatively true then we will have to discard the notion of duality here and simply accept that there are only shades of truth and shades of falsehood.

There are two primary meanings of 'truth.' The first meaning of truth may be called *pragmatic truth* and is conventionally used to signify that there is sufficient reason to assert or affirm that something is or is not the case. "It is raining" is said by someone to be true when, for example, she looks out the window and sees that it is raining, or has been told by someone whom she has no reason to doubt that it is raining. Of course, "off the wall" scenarios can be concocted for cases where the assertion that it is raining is false, e.g. the person conveying the information has an ulterior or malicious motive to derail another's plans for the evening. Nonetheless, the person who on good faith accepts the word of someone who says it is raining correctly uses the word 'true' because there is no good reason to believe otherwise. Using the word 'true' to affirm something does not require a Congressional investigation; standard criteria suffice. However, it remains the case that it is theoretically possible for the most ordinary assertions to be disproved, and this ubiquitous possibility directs us to the second primary meaning of 'truth,' which we shall call *absolute truth*. Absolute truth signifies *that which, given a specific context, can never be falsified.* The statement "Scott is the author of *Waverly*," which was famously used by Bertrand Russell in his theory of descriptions, does not denote an irrefutable fact simply because it is theoretically possible that Sir Walter Scott did not write *Waverly*. Any statement of authorship and any statement of fact can, in theory, someday come into question. There is no reasonable doubt that Scott is the author of Waverly—even though he had denied his authorship for over ten years—however, as is the case with any factual assertion the statement of Scott's authorship is falsifiable. On the other hand, absolute truths of reality are not falsifiable and, therefore, they cannot be stated. Reality simply *is*. Wittgenstein's remark in his closing of the *Tractatus* is very applicable: "Of that which cannot be spoken, one must remain silent."

Ethical assertions, much as assertions of fact and science (i.e. pragmatic truth) may be characterized as pragmatic and grouped together under the broader rubric of *pragmatic belief*. Collectively, pragmatic beliefs are the assertions that constitute perspectives of physical and moral actuality. The primary terms for moral assertion and denial are 'right' and 'good' and they concern both intentions and actions. There are also other moral attributes that are used to affirm ethical propositions; e.g. "She is a virtuous person!" affirms that the woman referred to is in particular ways a very good person, or "Education is the most valuable possession a person can have" affirms that education has great moral significance. Generally, 'right' is the ethical analog of 'cause,' and 'good' is the ethical analog of 'effect.' A 'right' action is an action that is affirmed to be the *cause* of something good, and something that is affirmed to be 'good' is the *effect* or result of actions or events that can be intended, unintended or the result of natural occurrences. The rightness or goodness of actions are assessments of intentionality and effectuality, respectively.

When considered from the standpoints of intentionality and effectuality the moral arena is far too uncertain and unstable to be reduced to a simplistic pass/fail grading system of right and wrong. In order to decide the ethicality of action we need to determine not only the rightness of intention, but also consider the consequences and overall effects of actions that follow the intention. Consider the situation of a jobseeker who is weighing employment with Company A or Company B. After extensively researching both companies she elects to work for Company A. The new hire feels confident that she has made a 'good' decision, and the 'right' decision for herself. After beginning work she tells friends that she now has a great job and works for the best company in her industry. The use of 'good' and 'right' suggests the belief that sound reasoning went into the decision, but also that positive consequences and a happy state of affairs will be the end result. The judgment to accept employment with Company A was made because of the likeability of management and staff personnel, future career opportunities, corporate health, the company's reputation concerning its ethical and social responsibility and, of course, issues of financial compensation and job security were all decided affirmatively after a process of good due diligence. By all measures Company A seems to have had Company B beaten. There was little doubt that choosing Company A was the 'right' decision. As it turns out, however, Company A soon became embroiled in a maze of controversy. The government took action on a litany of serious environmental violations, and the chairman and other corporate officers came under criminal investigation for various alleged misdeeds. Our new employee never saw it coming. Worst of all, the charges turned out to be true. Subsequently, it was Company B that rode to the top of its industry! Was the jobseeker's decision 'right'? If we accept the premise that there was no realistic basis for discovering the impending crisis, then there would be no basis for criticizing the decision to join Company A. And if the decision itself cannot be criticized, then how can it be characterized as a 'wrong' decision? If good decisions can produce bad results and bad decisions can produce good results, what is the point of ethical deliberation? In what sense might it be said that the 'right' decision of the jobseeker was a 'bad' decision? More than likely, the jobseeker would have just said that she made a bad decision even though in hindsight it doesn't seem that there was a rational basis for deciding differently. There can be an asymmetry in the form of good choices and bad results, or bad choices and good results.

A description of the relative symmetry between intentionality and effectuality is at the core of any descriptive ethics.

Hegel's dialectical philosophy egregiously forces an acceptance of what is unacceptable in history, but he deserves credit for forcing an appreciation of the broader currents of morality. Morality encompasses the interplay of broad causative influences between the individual, the state, culture, ideas and history. If we cease with the imposition of contrived concepts, and instead view history in terms of interacting multilinear dialectical threads it may be possible to reconcile moral intentions, actions, and consequences in the context of the moral holism. Our moral status is as much a product of our own creation as the product of dynamic interactivity between individuals, cultures, institutions and the world at large. Our individual and collective moral status evolves. So, in following through with these ruminations, let us return to the unfortunate and unlucky jobseeker who made a bad choice, even if not a wrong choice, in her acceptance of job offers. Her intentions were good and, let us assume, that her due diligence exceeded the norm. Therefore, her decision must be considered to be a right decision because, should similar situations arise in the future, it does not seem that a bad outcome could be avoided. At the same time, it is also correct to describe the decision as a bad one because surely the outcome was not good.

While our jobseeker was not responsible for the mess she found herself in, her situation was at least partially a product of circumstance. The good or bad of the situation was more than a matter of unforeseeable results because those results will now, in turn, produce other good or bad opportunities for the jobseeker that could result in her becoming more successful than would have been the case had things gone according to plan. Conversely, the aftermath of the misfortune may be one of falling into a state of prolonged and self-destructive despair. Who is to say if there is not some guiding hand in the course of personal destiny? Destiny clearly is shaped by the challenge and struggle of difficult circumstances by creating opportunities for the expression and the conduct of virtue. And from this dialectical perspective there would appear to be at least some lessening of the incoherence between 'good' and 'right' respective to intentionality and effectuality. Success and failure both present moral challenges. A success may have hidden potential for bad, and a failure may have hidden potential for good. A success may lead to failure, and a failure may lead to success. And while disappointments are not to be desired, the potential for good is always waiting to be realized.

I.4

Hypnotic Thinking

"According to nature" you want to live? O you
noble Stoics....For all your love of truth, you
have forced yourselves so long, so persistently,
so rigidly-hypnotically to see nature the wrong
way, namely Stoically, that you are no longer
able to see her differently. And some abysmal
arrogance finally still inspires you with the
insane hope that *because* you know how to
tyrannize yourselves—Stoicism is self-tyranny
—nature, too, lets herself be tyrannized: is not
the Stoic—a *piece* of nature?⁵

Friedrich Nietzsche

We are hypnotized in the present and conditioned by the past.
Moral actuality for a child begins to form almost with the
inception of language. A small child cannot articulate the reasons for its
displeasure other than to cry or conduct a tantrum when its wants have been
denied. By the time the child has grown enough to express *why* it is
unhappy, not in terms of "I want it!" but in more complex terms of "I want
it and *should* have it because..." the rudiments of its moral actuality have
begun to form. Progressively, from early childhood, the basis for justifying
what a person wants becomes more deeply couched in basic moral concepts
that are learned and are a part of the commonly accepted language of ethical
justification about good or bad, right or wrong. While ethical reasoning in
pre-adolescent years may be limited to uncritical acceptance of concepts to
support wants or needs, adult reasoning on ethical matters frequently has a
knee-jerk quality as well! With hypnotic-like acceptance, basic ethical

concepts are accepted and are then conditioned by formalities and the moral actuality that they help form. To a significant degree, of course, this conditioning is completely necessary; basic precepts and formalities should always be accepted unless the weight of ethical reasoning overrules them. And, of course, there is no other way to teach children but, at some point, should not adults be capable of questioning particular applications of accepted moral presumptions?

The present is much more than sensory data but also includes beliefs, ideas, perspectives, values, memories, emotions, emotional pleasures and emotional pains. The present is not only the "Now," a supposed pure awareness of the moment stripped of all thought and language and all manner of distraction. The silence of the Now, shouts of arguing ideologues, and all forms of distraction are in competition to capture the conscious and subconscious attention of the mind. Any of the myriad aspects of the present can capture the mind's focus and, in turn, can set in motion behavior and thought patterns that profoundly condition the future. A thought pops into our head, fads develop overnight, advertising creates wants and perceived needs and even determines our choice of elected political leaders. From where did that thought originate? From a movie, or a conversation with a friend or a stranger, a conversation with oneself, a book recently read, an advertisement? The present sometimes just grabs hold of us and directs us along new paths in life. But each present immediately turns into the past and new patterns may become old patterns that become the basis of self-identity. A new pattern, habit or belief may begin in the present in a moment of subliminal intensity or form gradually, but ultimately it is the follow-up reinforcement of the past that is most powerful. The process of blind acceptance and reinforcement applies both to individuals and to the social collective. Formalities harden beliefs and behaviors and much like stubborn habits can be extremely difficult to change even when change is in the best interests of the individual or of society. But while a vehicle rushing downhill benefits greatly from momentum, it is highly advisable to avoid the ride if the vehicle does not have workable breaks. Our conditioned habits of thought and behavior are no less in need of a good breaking system; it is important to stop, question, reflect and examine lest we risk rushing headlong into an avoidable fate. Habits and conditioned behaviors are created by us to serve us, not the other way around. The familiar refrain comes to mind: "I have always done it this way and I am not going to change now!" Why? A habit is slave of reason, and when it stops serving our purposes we should be done with it!

While hypnosis can involve entering "trance states" that are quite similar to meditation states, its uniquely distinguishing characteristic is what is referred to as the "critical factor" that allows the critical thinking of the conscious mind to be bypassed. This bypass penetrates the normal tendency of the conscious mind to edit, filter or block suggestions that run contrary to preexisting belief. The highly influential hypnotist, Dave Elman, writes that the bypass of the critical faculty is a product of selective thinking that has blocked out competing thoughts or opinions. As an everyday example, Elman describes a superstitious individual who believes that Friday the thirteenth is unlucky and accordingly organizes his schedule for the whole day around the superstition. Selective thinking has self-hypnotized the acceptance that any Friday the thirteenth is somehow different than any other day by that distinction alone.[6] Our beliefs have different levels of depth or mental penetration. Overcoming the critical factor in hypnosis generally concerns the bypass of beliefs, both conscious and subconscious, that the rational, conscious mind very much wants and desires to change. For example, we generally want to be pain-free, break bad habits, perform better, etc. However, in areas of belief in which there is some level of intellectual confusion the task can become far more difficult. And where there is conscious confusion there is also likely to be subconscious confusion as well. Deep beliefs can possess hidden schisms for a variety of reasons including mixed allegiances or uncertainties or conflicting belief systems that may clash with other beliefs that are conscious or subconscious, and articulated or unarticulated. In general, ethical beliefs have the potential to stir a wide range of confusion and conflict in which deep moral feelings may conflict with ethical deliberation. Broad social and cultural changes or pressures can also produce confusion and uncertainty in the social collective that challenges the critical factor and, perhaps, the need for overcoming it.

Elman elegantly defines selective thinking as "whatever you believe *wholeheartedly.*"[7] Wholehearted thinking is not necessarily a good thing, just as the word 'hypnosis' or 'hypnotic' may or may not entail a positive mental state of affairs. Selective thinking, in our present context, means uncritical acceptance without interference by the critical faculty.

Wholehearted acceptance is evidence of a critical bypass and while, ultimately, all belief must get through the critical faculty its negative significance is that it is also the gateway to the selective thinking of ideology and dogmatism. In his claim that "truth is the agreement of content with itself," the philosopher Georg W.F. Hegel seeks a philosophical hypnotization. By selectively forcing history to fit the terms of his selective thinking (or dialectical logic) Hegel makes the preposterous equation that truth and his particular conception of truth are the same. The concept is in the truth, the truth is in the concept. For Hegel, every event or action in the world "agrees" with the dialectical unfolding of Ideas through the process of world consciousness. Hegel's philosophy is the great philosophy of rationalization by providing ultimate justification of all that is, all that was, and all that may come to be. The phrase, "God works in mysterious ways" would be quite Hegelian were it not for the fact that Hegel thought that he had explained away the mystery through the "unfolding" logic of dialectical necessity. He famously presented the argument of the "master-slave dialectic" in his *Phenomenology of Spirit* but its blunt consequences (specifically regarding the African slave trade) appear in his lectures on the philosophy of history:

> ...existing in a State, slavery is itself a phase of advance
> from the merely isolated sensual existence—a phase
> of education—a mode of becoming participant in a
> higher morality and the culture connected with it. Slavery
> is in and for itself *injustice*, for the essence of humanity
> is *Freedom*; but for this man must be matured. The
> gradual abolition of slavery is therefore wiser and
> more equitable than its sudden removal.[8]

"Wiser and more equitable?" The proper question is *who* was in need maturation: the slave or the enslaver? To dismiss Hegel's logic as merely "a product of its time" to some degree can be accepted as a simple fact, and it can be unfair to judge thinkers in terms of thinking that evolves generations later; however, it can also be argued that this sort of acceptance becomes just another Hegelianism that rationalizes the present and avoids the duty of deep moral reflection. Are we all *merely* a product of our times, intractably stuck in the quagmire of the prevailing ignorance? Hegel argues that there is no escape from history's dialectic and therefore it was necessary that slavery be tolerated until consciousness evolved; however, by accepting one of history's most heinous institutions as unavoidable and necessary and failing to resist it is to knowingly cave into a moral actuality known to be wrong on the deepest of levels, indefensible on the basis of love, and defensible by no means other than a love of dogma.

Hegel implied that someday slavery would be abolished, but when would its abolishment become dialectally justifiable?

> *Thesis:*   The essence of humanity is freedom.
> *Antithesis:* Maturity is necessary for freedom.
> *Synthesis:* Slavery is necessary for the slave's maturation.

Hegel's dialectical logic is, essentially, Aristotle's syllogism applied to historical change. The synthesis (or conclusion) is necessarily implied by the thesis (or major premise) and the antithesis (or minor premise). However, the application of syllogistic reasoning to social change forces interpretation to masquerade as deductive certainty. Hegel's project was to force the flow of history to follow an utterly contrived and fallacious logic. Nonetheless, it is possible for dialectical thinking to be restructured so that it may be a useful tool for creating or assessing multiple perspectives. For example, both Hegel's thesis and antithesis imply that the absence of freedom constitutes a state of existence that is something less than human. The thesis posits freedom as the "essence" of humanity, and the antithesis posits that "maturity" is the essential requirement of human freedom. The slave is trapped between a rock and a hard place: s/he doesn't possess what is the essence of being human (i.e. freedom), and in order to acquire it s/he has to be declared as mature by none other than by the enslaver himself! But if the thesis were changed to "Human freedom is desirable," those human beings who are not free could be seen as no less human than those who are free. While freedom certainly flourishes with maturity, the desirability of freedom is only a reason to free the slaves, not perpetuate their enslavement! The only separation between the freeman and the slave is freedom, not the status of their humanity. The revised thesis sets off the possibility of a multiplicity of alternative perspectives to slavery, all of which are multilinear dialectical threads guided by the desirability of freedom. Three such possibilities for a revised synthesis or conclusion follow:

1. Actions should have been taken to
    eliminate slavery.
    (Slavery is a contradiction of the major
    premise that human freedom is desirable.)

2. The European nations should have let Africa
    develop on its own accord.
    (Economic exploitation is not a moral
    imperative.)

3. The Europeans should have become partners
    with the Africans, and educated them so that in
    time mutually beneficial trade relationships could
    develop.
    (Enlightened self-interest dialectally empowers.)

The encouragement of intellectual freedom is arguably the primary goal of philosophy, and tools like the multilinear dialectic are useful antidotes for myopic mentalities such as the conventional wisdom, "rigidly-hypnotic" adherence to accepted paradigms and, worst of all, blind acceptance of the morally unacceptable. Relatively few people today may see themselves as dialecticians in the nineteenth century Hegelian mode, but most of us to some degree possess prejudices of conventional thinking that constrain thought too much along the lines of the knee jerk. Hypnosis is a metaphor for strength as well as weakness. As much as we may be prone to knee-jerk thinking we can also become "hypnotized" to the strong mentality of open-mindedness, self-correction and, indeed, truth. There is a natural tendency to interpret experience and events so that in neo-Hegelian fashion it agrees with our own "truths" and, to be fair, sticking to our own truths, provided that we do not descend into obstinacy, arrogance and dogma can be a profoundly moral exercise and a mark of strength. Indeed, sometimes being true to oneself and to our own truths can mean having the courage to defend convention and the existing actuality. It is perhaps not too gross an oversimplification to say that most of intellectual life can be expressed as the problem of knowing when to conform to convention and prevailing actuality, and when to break away in order to forge new paths.

Perhaps we *want* to be hypnotized. Ideologies posit formal answers to the ambiguities and uncertainties of life. And it is easy to look at the ideologies and totalitarianism of the twentieth century and of the present century and see the indoctrination and unquestioned and unchallenged "answers" to all matters of life, and then find satisfaction in believing that we in the liberal democracies are protected from the mindless adherence to authoritarian and totalitarian dogma. However, no one is free from the conditioning of habit and no society can ever be free from the threat of inhuman repression that is rooted in dogmatic thinking. The threat is quite real and ubiquitous and can be seen even in the likes of Schopenhauer, a philosopher who based his ethics on pure compassion. Schopenhauer despaired of the short-term pleasures and imperfections of life and believed that contemplation of otherworldly Platonic-like Ideas—which for him were best expressed in art and music, were the only source of solace. And, thus, he advocated the abnegation of life in favor of a quiet life of contemplation. The Will or nature's life force for Schopenhauer is only a cause for pessimism; far better to be mesmerized by metaphysical Ideas than to look for meaning in the fleeting intangibles, the *samsara* of everyday life. The renunciation of life in favor of abstract concepts is a dangerous model because life is nothing if not imperfect, and thus an artificially imposed order of fantasized universal harmony is the perfect excuse for the repression of the real in favor of the unreal.

Philosophy shares with hypnotism the informal assignment of distinguishing appearance from reality. As previously discussed, reality is unknowable and philosophy, like science, deals with inherently fallible actualities that are sometimes consciously and sometimes subconsciously confused with reality. Hypnotherapy, psychology and all disciplines that deal with the subconscious mind seek to create a sort of reality that distinguishes subconscious fears, habits, compulsions, etc. from other behaviors that may be considered to be rationally determined. The goal is that the conscious and subconscious might coexist in rational and healthful harmony. With regard to those subconscious demons, some grandiose dreams may be dismissed as delusional. Or a patient is assured that fears of impending crisis have no basis. Are these dreamers and visionaries irrational? No one can truly know what within ourselves comprises our deepest truths. And how many obsessions that have paid enormous dividends to humankind would—if they had been therapized or "treated," be lost to posterity!

I.5

Self and Other

A hypothetical, purely selfless mind is probably inconceivable in human terms. To deny that humans are born with many selfish desires more than stretches credulity. While some studies may suggest that human beings possess innate kindness, a deeply selfless mind must first *become* selfless by overcoming many self-interested and selfish dispositions. Ironically, a purely selfless mind would require self-interestedness to overcome itself by self-correcting any temptations that might sway it from its unswayable path. Self-interestedness is not inconsistent with virtue but is, on the contrary, the basis of the self-correction that all virtue requires. Self-interest in becoming more selfless is necessary for developing the virtue of selflessness.

Consciousness requires a dichotomous relationship between *Self* and *Other*. The Self evolves from a process of self-correction. It is a process of differentiation between Self and Other in which there are accretions of self-identification and self-correction in the form of modifications, corrections or rejections. Self-correction both builds and humbles the ego. With each positive self-correction there is a build up of a sense of self, but at the same time there is a humbling experience that the ongoing evolution of oneself is in large part a result of interactions and learning from others. Even if some learning is claimed to be purely self-learned, we are humbled by the realization of the enormity of what remains unknown or is unknowable. Learning from others is most humbling because as our self-image changes and evolves we become, at least in some ways, less like our former self and more like others. The issue is cast in an interesting light in Roland Barthes' article, "The Death of the Author." What is the true identity of an author when it is impossible to determine the source of his or her ideas, and when language itself is like an intoxicating flow of energy that brings in dimensions of meaning of which the author is as much a creator as a responder:

> ..a text is... a multi-dimensional space in which a
> variety of writings, none of them original, blend and
> clash. The text is a tissue of quotations drawn from
> the innumerable centres of culture.[9]

The most personal question of all is "Who am I?" But it is not at all clear that this question can ever be answered by anyone. Language can force us to respond much like an audience swept away by the skills of a talented orator, and the response is oftentimes subconscious. The meanings and metaphors that are attached to language do not come with advance notice. Our self-identity is for us the chief actuality in our lives, but if the actuality of the Self is cast into doubt then what are the ramifications for our self-identity and its actuality? The question of authorship and the continuing change and evolution of the ego naturally bring to mind Descartes' Cogito, "I think therefore I am." But if we can ask, "Who is the author?" can we not just as easily ask, "Who am I?" Barthes states, "the author is never more than the instance writing, just as *I* is nothing other than the instance saying I."[10] What exactly does Descartes prove when he says, "*Cogito ergo sum?*" It can be argued that if we are not the author of our own thoughts then they do nothing to establish the reality of our existence. What sort of existence of self is demonstrated by our thoughts if their origin is itself a question? Even if we assume that the structure of Descartes argument is logically sound, once we accept the public and multi-textured nature of language we might say that while it proves that something exists, that something might only be a phantom of something or someone else.

    I remember a few years ago a conversation in which I was told that cursive or "script" handwriting had fallen out of favor in the grammar schools and that, generally, only "print" was currently being taught. I was surprised to hear of this change and remember saying, with a bit of pride in my voice, that I still wrote cursively. I was a "script person," I thought. And I continued to think of myself as a script person until years later I had the occasion to review an old notebook that I had compiled between some 25 and 30 years prior and noticed that it was indeed written almost entirely in script. And then, out of curiosity, I compared the old notebook to more recent notebooks and to my great surprise discovered that my handwriting was now almost exclusively in print! Years ago I had stopped writing cursively but was completely unaware of the change. A change had taken place but it had not consciously registered with me. I changed and yet I was not aware of it. Other than being a somewhat striking display of my own obliviousness, I think that it is also indicative of what can be an unawareness of gradually changing belief.

The changing Self is tied to challenges and adaptations of its beliefs. Beliefs are key ingredients of the ego's self-identity and are naturally resistant to change. We require a foundation upon which to build premises and if our beliefs change with each whim we would be intellectually helpless. Beliefs define how we see ourselves in relation to others and to the world as a whole. Challenges to self-identity and self-image are buffered by the quieting foundation of rock-solid belief. Self-identities, however, formed by national, cultural, religious and political beliefs can tend to divide as much as they unite. Dividing camps hunker down into their hardened positions for little more reason than preconditioned habit or intellectual myopia. Muslim, Jew, Christian, Socialist, Libertarian, Conservative Republican, Liberal Democrat, pro-life, pro-choice, environmentalist, pro-growth. These labels are like banners that tell us as much as they tell others who we are or who we think we are. The ideal and the ego are in close alliance. Together they form a psycho-philosophical edifice that holds fort against inevitable tides of change. But the edifice is an illusion that seeks to withstand change even as change inevitably occurs.

Jean-Paul Sartre proclaims, "You are nothing else than your life"[11] and seeks to anchor the ego with actions rather than ideals or unfulfilled potential. A person has

> no reality except in action...he exists only to the extent
> that he fulfills himself; he is therefore nothing else than
> the ensemble of his acts, nothing else than his life. [12]

For Sartre, each man must invent himself because he is not born according to a prefabricated ideal of what it is to be human. We are all works of art in progress. A human life is like a work of art, and there is good art and there is bad art. The existentialist ego is a gallery from which one may admire his past. The glory of artistic creativity may indeed have much to tell us about morality and of what heights it may be capable of, and ethics may ultimately be a kind of art but in the absence of ethical rules different criteria become necessary. Sartre finds the essence of morality in action, and attempts to save existentialist ethics from the insignificance of arbitrary action by recasting Kant's "categorical imperative":

> When we say that man chooses his own self, we mean
> that every one of us does likewise; but we also mean by
> that in making this choice he also chooses all men. In
> fact, in creating the man that we want to be, there is not
> a single one of our acts which does not at the same time
> create an image of man as we think he ought to be.[13]

Compare Kant's categorical imperative: "I should never act in such a way that I could not also will that my maxim should be a universal law."[14] Sartre replaces "maxim" with "act" but the universal intent is essentially the same. Whereas Kant thought that he had solved the dilemma of the asymmetry between moral intention and moral action by unifying free will (or intention) in accordance with moral rules, Sartre similarly tries to solve the asymmetry by unifying will and action under a universal "image" of the good man. Both Kant and Sartre telescope morality into a perspective of particular actions that they claim holds for every rational being. A heavy burden, indeed! Both Kant and Sartre reject the possibility that there may be more than one possible right action that can produce different but perhaps equally good results. Existentialist and Kantian ethics have different metaphorical qualities: for Kant, it is dutiful submission of free will under the categorical imperative and for Sartre, it is duty to the authenticity of the self. Kant's ethical system imposes rules or maxims for every action, whereas Sartre's ethics holds that individual actions must be intended to be a universal model for all. Kant's assertion of a universal maxim for every action is arbitrary, and Sartre's imposition of the burdensome universality of each action is subjective and illusionary. Both are equally impossible.

Bertrand Russell showed that a class is not a member of itself. And if individual minds, as members of a logical class referred to as Mind, are also aspects of a continuum of Mind, then the only self-interest that the greater Mind has with respect to individual minds is that they be consistent with it; therefore, the interests of individual minds and the greater Mind are shared even if not equal or the same. Putting the metaphysical or quasi-metaphysical question of a greater Mind aside, the notion of a universal and transcendent moral pretext that underlies ethical principles suggests a counterargument to the likes of Kant, Sartre, Mill and all propagators of unitary ethical principles that are supposed to function as universal arbiters of ethical disagreement. The absolute standards are, in fact, only misplaced wishes that misdirect ethical theory away from the substance of morality, which defies definition and deductive logic. The quest of ethics is greater harmony with the moral unity whether that unity consists of a greater transcendent Mind or only the workings of many minds.

Morality exhibits both other-regarding and self-regarding character-istics. The speculation that individual minds are expressions of a greater Mind suggests that the differences between Mind and minds may be reconciled within the context of interests shared with the whole. Ethics is ultimately about figuring out how the appearance of differing self-interests can be resolved in terms of 'good' and 'right' within the context of the unity of the dichotomous relationship between Self and Other. The conventional approach of ethics in attempting to resolve or mediate the schism between the self-interests of Self and Other consists of rule-based systems. In general, ethics is thought in terms of rules and rulemaking. Even a pure utilitarianism ("act utilitarianism") that eschews ethical rules and that seeks to justify actions situationally in terms of the utilitarian principle of "the greatest happiness (or pleasure) of the greatest number" inevitably resorts to rules. It is impossible to quantify pleasure, happiness or good as one would count the number of beans in a beanbag. While ethical rules will always be pragmatically important, the more fundamental challenge for ethics is a depth analysis of the basic elements of morality. *The basic moral intention is love*. Love has the uncanny capacity to be conceived of as either the clearest manifestation of a transcendent Mind or as the most powerful and beautiful result of individual and separate minds binding together. Regardless of whether a transcendent Mind exists, love bridges the gap between Self and Other. It is only through loving intention that conflict between apparently self-interested minds can be resolved, i.e. by means of the interest that the Self has in the Other and that the Other has in the Self. But without further analysis, the power of love is as ineffective as the use of any raw, misunderstood or untamed energy. We will need to look much more closely at love, and at how this fundamental moral essence might explain the complexity of the moral universe.

Love involves the overcoming of self-interest and the identification of one's own interest with the interests of others. But love also includes self-love. By bridging and harmonizing the dichotomy between the interests of Self and Other, pure love does not distinguish between interests that are self-regarding or other-regarding. Love chooses from the perspective of that which is in the best interest of all. The meaning of love is often confused by a focus on romantic love. And while romantic love does involve aspects of love *qua* the essence of morality it is also easily corrupted into a vehicle of simple self-interestedness if not selfishness. Romantic love sometimes bridges the interests of the Self to the interests of the beloved merely as a sort of egoistic expansion. Clearly, much romantic love is purely self-interested. The basic interests behind romantic love are both sexual and non-sexual companionship, financial security, domestic comfort, and the desire for procreation and family life. But another interest of romantic love *is* love. In romantic love exists the formative kernel of the pure love that is the essence of moral life, which is nothing less than overcoming the divisions between Self and Other. In purely logical terms the phenomenon of love is not comprehensible. Logic may, for example, turn a matter into something utilitarian that rationalizes the greater good in such a way that a minority must repress its own needs for no other reason than that they are a minority. Logic requires, love desires. Love transcends utilitarian calculations and *desires* nothing else other than what is best for all that it encompasses. A parent does not act or feel in a utilitarian way when she gives up her meal to feed her child. This sort of loving self-sacrifice is common when action is demanded by love's desire. As with romantic love, familial love is easily corrupted. Among the most corrupt variants of "love" is, as is oft observed, the "good family life" of certain crime families that do not hesitate to obliterate the families of others by torture and murder out of subservience to monetary greed. This sort of rationalization cuts to the core of the corruptibility of love and how it is easily perverted as a vehicle for egoistic expansion. The corruptibility of love is shown in groups, large and small. The morphing of love of country into a grotesque self-interested expression of jingoism is a danger of which democracies and all nations must continually address themselves. Love of country may indeed be an expression of a higher love. But a pure and unadulterated love is as much a self-love as a selfless love.

I.6

Love and Morality

Romantic love possesses some of the qualities of the universal love that comprises the essence of morality. But when we think of love we often think of emotion and feeling, and if morality is based on love we need to ask the question, "Are emotions and feelings a basis for ethical decision?" And, conversely, we also need to ask, "Is there any basis for an ethics devoid of emotion?" The Stoics claimed that the extirpation of emotion can clear the mind for dispassionate reasoning and is in harmony with nature, however an emotionless ethics is patently unnatural for human beings, and perhaps for any rational being. Nonetheless, most everyone would agree that emotions need some taming before they can consistently accord with reason.

In stating that, "reason is the slave of the passions" Hume acknowledged the intimate connection between emotion and reasoning, most especially ethical reasoning. Hume can hardly be accused of taking the Stoic position. The passions, he argues, are the drive and purpose of reason; we reason because it helps us to satisfy our passions, emotions or sentiments. While human beings have many needs, morality is only one category of need that needs fulfilling. If we need food or shelter we use our ability to reason to procure it. If we desire material possessions for entertainment or security or social status we use reasoning to acquire them as well. Hunger motivates efforts to procure food, and the emotional, psychological and physical aspects of the sex drive motivate that it also be satiated. And secondary needs such as intellectual curiosity or imagination motivate more curiosity and imagination. Hume reasons that without the passions the faculty of reason would lay dormant. But morality is also a need of civilization as, e.g., a disregard of the need for moral or ethical restraint in efforts to satisfy needs for food or sex is a deep perversion.

Hume's immediate predecessors in British philosophy began referring to the *moral* feelings or emotions, in combination with reasoning concerning them, as the "moral sense."[15] Hume's ethical work was the culmination of this line of philosophical development and, thus, while the intellect may be the slave of the passions the moral sense argument indicates that at least some of the passions or sentiments are intrinsically moral by nature. Our five senses do not provide us with knowledge but only raw data which must be augmented, supported and confirmed before we award them the mantle of knowledge. And even when that mantle has been awarded it can be taken away if the knowledge should later prove to be false. The only knowledge we have is that of pragmatic truths. (§I.3) Sense perceptions provide a basis upon which information about the universe may be built, but without an intelligent and continuing reprocessing and reevaluation our knowledge remains immature and speculative. Acquiring knowledge often requires experience and study. The natural "laws" of science are the result of intensive investigation and theory backed by the confirmation of equally intensive experimentation. Even then, scientific theories and laws are only pragmatic truths that are always subject to rejection or modification. Science depends upon a rational *empirical sense* that matures with experience. On the other hand, the rational *moral sense*, upon which the stipulation of ethical "laws" ultimately depend has not matured nearly as well as has the rational empirical sense.

The impotence of ethical reasoning as compared with scientific reasoning is due to the fact that traditional ethical theories have proffered only definitions of morality, not principles that help explain it. For example, the utilitarian standard is serviceable as a provisional definition of morality provided that we recognize that it does little to help us out of the morass of difficult ethical decision-making. Thus, if by "the greatest good for the greatest number" is meant that every person should have his or her interests weighed and reconciled with those of everyone else then we would all be utilitarians! Of course, that is not what utilitarianism means; both "act utilitarianism" and "rule utilitarianism" ultimately fail because there is no self-enforcing principle of reconciliation, only defined rules that try to force a consensus that may not be inherent in the moral actuality. But consensus transcends rules, and the more we delve into moral conundrums the more lacking and inadequate ethical rules become. Commonly accepted scientific principles predict and explain, but commonly accepted ethical rules do neither: they are mere talking points. Kant stated that the human will is autonomous, but a free and good will is in Kant's view the will's conformance to duty in following ethical rules. However, while Kant may deny that rules are made to be broken, acting with good moral intention not infrequently requires that they must be. In both Kantian ethics and utilitarianism you need to be a good philosophical lawyer. Ethics and morality have often been viewed legalistically, but can rules ultimately decide moral issues? Intuitionists, for their part, cannot describe what is good or what is right but they say that they know it when they see it. Objectivists or egoists express concern for self-interest and they believe that they can enlighten it, but they ultimately beg the question concerning the essence of morality in the dogmatic—not to mention oxymoronic—rejection of altruism. Religious-based morality begs the question of ethics because "so it is written" is not a philosopher's creed. Let us look more closely at the moral sense. The passions may be the initial motivators of reason, but like the combustible fuel that powers a machine, the intelligent design of the machine tames the combustion like a trainer tames a stallion. *Passion is as much a slave of reason as reason is a slave of the passions.* Hume chose the wrong metaphor to describe the relationship between reason and emotion because reason is not the slave of the passions if by working together they achieve freedom. Emotion and reason are teammates working together. The alternation between emotion and reason in assuming positions of leader and follower is the true harmony that the Stoics sought but failed to realize. Within the harmony of emotion and reason, the guidance for ethical decision-making and the path to ethical empowerment and virtue may be found.

The moral sense is a useful metaphor, and emotions are the "raw sense data" of the moral sense. Consider the case of a person who is born blind. If physical problems preventing sight are corrected much later in life sight is likely to remain profoundly impaired. Sight is more than the straightforward introduction of visual sense data into a neural processor and the representation of images on the "screen" of consciousness. Sight needs to be learned. In *An Anthropologist on Mars* neurologist and author Oliver Sacks recounts the story of a man named Virgil who had been almost completely blind for nearly his entire life. Then, after 45 years of blindness an operation became available that restored Virgil's physical ability to see; however, without any prior experience of seeing his vision had almost no meaning as his brain struggled to make sense of impressions that were suddenly flooding his mind. Sacks describes how the orderliness of Virgil's existence before sightedness was suddenly transformed into a state of near chaos.[16] Let us conduct a thought experiment in which a person is born with all emotions shut off. We'll allow physical pain and pleasure because the five sense organs are in good working order, but this imaginary person would be incapable of experiencing anger or hate. Nor would he have any emotional response relating to fairness or compassion. He might react when struck but without anger or other emotion. But, now, imagine that as a mature adult our subject's emotions are suddenly turned on! It seems almost a certainty that his response would be quite analogous to Virgil's. He would have to learn for the first time how to use his emotions and, like Virgil, it is quite likely that he would have severe difficulties in managing and understanding the new "phenomena" that would be cascading into his consciousness. If emotions are the motivating impetus of human moral feelings and behavior, then we may perhaps be justified in describing our subject's state of being as one of moral blindness. Before our subject has his emotions turned on he can conceive of right and wrong but only in a cold, logical manner. After the emotions are turned on his "moral sense" would become chaotic and filled with unimaginable conflict. A purely intellectual morality is the only possible morality for a purely emotionless being. Human beings may be rational beings but they are also emotional beings and, as such, reason and emotion are inseparable in human morality. Persons with normal eyesight learn to use their vision at a very young age. In the case of morality, on the other hand, learning to use the moral sense is a process that is continuing and never-ending.

The emotions, when activated, provide raw data for ethical deliberation. Emotions are autosuggestions by our subconscious mind to our moral consciousness that signal a need for reflection or appropriate action that may stand in need of still further modification by the intellect. For example, an emotion such as anger that is untouched by the intellect produces situations that are fraught with danger, but through the engagement of the moral sense and further ethical deliberation the anger may be subdued and even transformed. The balancing of emotion and reason *is* the moral sense in action. I can hear objections that a criminal or a tyrant might finely coordinate his emotions with his reasoning for horrific purposes, but such an example only demonstrates a highly imbalanced relationship between the emotions and reason in which negative emotions and amoral thinking dominate. The finely tuned balance of non-loving emotion and amoral intentionality do not disprove a solid foundation of morality and for ethics but merely create the perfect picture of what the moral sense and morality are not. The moral sense is in some ways comparable to the physical senses, but it also compares to the "musical sense" or the "artistic sense" in which sustained development is vitally important. In the beginnings of moral awareness loving intention is a faint glow sparked by innate emotions or sentiments such as those of compassion. But through the course of experience loving intention, like a beacon, is made brighter by ongoing inner ethical dialogue and experience in using the moral sense. Love and morality evolve together and are inseparable. Even the Stoic's extirpation of emotion implies that there must first be emotion before it may be stoically removed! If emotions are like the sense data of morality, then Stoicism is an ethics that has lost its vision.

Morality concerns human self-realization individually and collectively and, as such, *both* self-regarding emotions and other-regarding emotions are moral feelings. The basic statement of the meaning of philosophical or spiritual love is found in *Leviticus (19:18)*: "Love thy neighbor as thyself," which is also the Great Commandment of Christianity. No statement has more clearly expressed the essence of love and morality. Love of others and love of self are put on an even pedestal. Many have recognized the power of this biblical statement. Schopenhauer discusses it in *On the Basis of Morality* but he misinterprets or fails to understand love's self-critical dimension; for Schopenhauer the basis of morality consists solely and exclusively of compassion and compassion alone.[17] However, if compassion is viewed dualistically such that it can be applied to the Self as well as to the Other then the dualistic nature of "Love thy neighbor as thyself" applies also to self-compassion as well as to a self-regarding dimensionality of the other moral sentiments. Ralph Cudworth, a seventeenth-century British philosopher, posits love as the source of all morality as framed in New Testament passages.[18] And Joseph Fletcher made love the central moral principle in his *Situation Ethics*. Love is almost always treated in the most platitudinous of ways, but if it is more than a mere platitude then it should be capable of being expressed concretely in ethical deliberation. A love-based ethics—and this is redundant because *all* morality is love-based, is largely impotent if it is not expressed in the concrete. Echoing Fletcher, morality is situational and universal, relative and non-relative, abstract but also sublimely concrete. There is an important place for inspirational language and poetic expressions of morality and virtue, but it is essential and imperative for ethics to move beyond the merely inspirational on the one hand and a mechanistic allegiance to rules on the other.

Is the moral sense, rooted in loving intention, a purely anthropocentric notion that would likely not apply to intelligent life on worlds other than earth? How would a different emotional makeup influence an alien species' understanding of morality? The emotional nature of humans varies greatly yet variation has not inhibited the formation of distinct beliefs about the universality of morality. Let us imagine a particular species possessing what might be described as a hive mentality and a communistic social structure ruled by a "queen bee" with worker bees and drones robotically in toe. Would a moral sense have any place in such a society? If the fracture between ruler and the ruled is endemic in the very nature of these beings such that the notion of equal rights is impossible, then we would have to conclude that this hive society is endemically amoral. Love, as the expression of love thy neighbor as thyself and the essence of morality, is a relation between selves and others who possess equality in their moral agency even if not in their virtue. However, it may be speculated that even the emotional makeup of rational beings from other worlds would eventually converge much as earthly systems often do. Totalitarianism, the human analog of the hive and its crushing of individuality and self-interest, is a ghastly archetype of moral incoherency, social dysfunction and disharmony. However, moral forces inevitably lead towards convergence. We can see this happening today as Communist and democratic countries have converged to some degree. China and Vietnam, for instance, have developed economies that possess far more capitalistic characteristics than was imaginable a generation ago. Can further democratic developments be forestalled over the long term? As individuals acquire more responsibility a sharing of power becomes inevitable over the long term; the major question is whether it will occur peacefully. Higher consciousness is incompatible with moral incoherency. The moral expression of loving intention is the *reunification* of Self and Other based on the recognition that the ostensible differences in the world are fractal manifestations of its underlying unity. Some form of reunification is an inevitable outcome of the self-corrective consciousness that seeks to bring existence into accord with underlying unity. Morality is, therefore, a function of existential self-realization. And a mind that would profess to reject the function of morality would, by rejecting love, reject itself.

Wittgenstein's remark that "an 'internal process' stands in need of outward criteria"[19] suggests the critical importance of subjective "inner" processes such as emotion and its conformance or nonconformance with ethical criteria. If we are to untangle confusions between moral feelings and moral actions, then a greater understanding of the diversity of moral expressions will emerge. Singular perspectives dominate the mind and they have dominated philosophy, and when they harden into formalities they become the proverbial trees that hide the forest. We allow particular perspectives like those of egoism or objectivism or relativism to hypnotically control thought by blocking the myriad and subtle contradictions that do not fit the prevailing paradigmatic perspective. The history of thought is as much a record of continuous forgetting as it is one of remembering as one intellectual trend is swept away by another. The love-based nature of morality transcends the perspectival myopia of the paradigm. Love values the glory of the individual as much as the glory of the collective, and the glory of the union of both. Self-sacrifice is at times required, but the sacrifice of oneself can also be a submission to the false idols of ideology. And self-sacrifice for the sake of the group can be brave but can also be weak if the comfort of group acceptance takes priority over a repressed acknowledgement of a more fundamental moral actuality. There are great acts of self (egoism) and great acts of selflessness (altruism), but there is reciprocity in either case because an egoistic act that is moral benefits the Other just as an altruistic act that is moral benefits the Self. There are no purely selfless acts because the beauty of pure selflessness inevitably becomes a deserving object of pride that one has in oneself. It is paradoxical that selfless persons want to escape egoistic motives that are inescapable. And self-interested acts can also benefit others; yes, a self-interested act can be thoroughly consistent with altruism.

A love-based ethics entails that means and ends are as inseparable as intentions and consequences. Every action or means to an end has a particular set of consequences. A young man wants to study at the university but does not have the money. Let's say that the obtaining of a university degree is his "end" and that there are three discernable choices: a) He borrows the money, b) His parents or another benefactor gives the money to him, or c) he steals the money or obtains it in some illegal and unethical manner. Does the means chosen in any way affect the end? The standard response is that, if the end is defined as the attainment of a university degree then, provided that the student is successful in receiving the degree, the "end" is not affected. But this answer boxes us into a narrow definition of ends. Differing means have differing consequences. Obviously, the consequences of criminal behavior, such as theft, are fairly transparent. However, questions concerning financial options are also quite significant. Let's say that the student's parents would have no problem in paying for the education but that they want their child to have the responsibility of repaying a large loan when she finishes school. A parental decision one way or the other would have a powerful effect on the student's life for years to come. What if fear of the ability to repay the financial debt causes the student to change his mind about enrolling or causes him to drop out of school? On the other hand, perhaps the student who knows that he will need to repay the loan after graduation will prompt a more serious and studious approach to schoolwork. It is clear that *the actual* ends may be dramatically affected by the means chosen and, therefore, the end is in significant part a product of the means used to achieve it. Therefore, ends and means are effectually inseparable: *a difference in means equals a difference in ends*.

Love is both means and ends. An ethics that is based on love rather than on formalities imposes its power on intentionality as well as on effectuality. As is the case with ends and means, the evaluation of intentionality and effectuality blends together. For example, a demonstration of good intention such as asking permission or consulting with an interested party may be all that is necessary to make an action effectual. Ethics is learned. We learn how to become more ethically effectual by experience and this process of learning is not amenable to a simplistic approach of assigning 'right' and 'wrong' as if ethics were a pass/fail system. A descriptive, love-based ethics allows for relative degrees of rightness or wrongness, goodness or badness in the diversity of situation. Existentialists, pragmatists and other architects of our so-called modern relativism have correctly recognized the tentative, relative and ineffectual nature of the traditional foundations of ethics. However, while we do not have the luxury of looking backward to simplistic rules of the past, we are in need of a middle way between pure relativism and pure non-relativism to guide ethical decision.

*   *   *   *

It is often acknowledged that love transcends difference. Obstacles and barriers between people are created by differences concerning what is thought or believed, or of what is possessed or what is thought to be possessed or should be possessed. Differences exist between the haves and the have-nots. Mistrust develops between believers and non-believers. Animosities develop between members and non-members. Anger, jealousy, envy, greed, and feelings of superiority or inferiority are some of the names given to the negative emotions, and they are the emotive indicators of moral strife and of a world that has failed to adequately understand the underlying unity that binds it together. But it is often said that in love we find the ability to forgive. In love we joyfully share with loved ones. In love we have the compassion to help the downtrodden or the unfortunate. In love we are able to experience the incomparable joy of giving. In love we are capable of letting bygones be bygones so that while the past is not forgotten we nonetheless grow because of it. In love we are inspired to achieve greatness because it provides us with the vision to see beyond our own mortal insignificance *and* to see the miracle, wonder and potential of our own individual existence. And yet, how tragic it is that these words generally remain only words except in the intimate connections between friends and loved ones or in the deeds of inspired benefactors. The transcendent force of love as the essence of morality has routinely escaped the province of ethics in everyday life in all its facets and, as a result, ethics is often un-empowered and can itself, at times, become part of the very problem it is unable to resolve.

Morality is the dialogical expression of loving intention. Ethics must interpret this dialogue, but the integration of love in the methods of ethics requires a better understanding of the dialogical complexity between the elemental dualisms that form the basis of morality. A love-based ethics would transcend the oversimplifications of egoism and altruism or the artificial disconnection of ends and means. Morality is the unfolding of good intention and its project is the evolution of conduct that better realizes or effectuates this intention. This does not involve the discarding of rules or ethical formalities; doing so would surely be as absurd and foolish as it is impossible. It does mean, however, that we need to know when to let go of ethical formalities when they do not improve moral actuality but merely impede or interfere with it. Morality deeply reflects both intentionality and effectuality. "You reap what you sow" (Galatians, ch. V1, v. 7) states the case well although I think that this biblical reference is specifically concerned with actions and their consequences rather than with the intentions that precede them. We need to delve deeper into motive and intentionality. How can we be sure that behind a kind smile does not lurk the evil intention of a fiend? But the relative rarity of the extreme moral imposter gives us faith in the character of others, even if we grant the capacity of a skilled actor to fake kindness. There is a need, however, for a thorough examination of the external and behavioral accompaniments of moral intention in both its self-regarding and other-regarding dimensions. Failure to recognize the balanced role between self-regarding and other-regarding intentions distorts and confuses moral understanding. We reap what we sow and the seeds of evolving moral actuality are the intentionality of our actions. The good life may truthfully be described as the collective and individual reaping of the benefits of good intention. Changing course or modifying actions after assessing their consequences are more likely to be greeted with forbearance when they have been undertaken with good intention. Bad intentions or the perception of bad faith poison the moral atmosphere. Positive intentions, however, cultivate an atmosphere of cooperation that is more forgiving of mistakes; honest error, after all, is part and parcel of learning to live the good life. Intentionality, effectuality and the world of opinion that surrounds them interact dialogically, adapting and evolving in a self-corrective process by which the seeds of wisdom grow in the rich soil of uncertainty.

I.7

The Basic Ethical Dualisms

What are the basic elements of morality? Without understanding its components love, as the essence of morality, is just another platitude that can be used to justify almost any action. "I did it out of love!" "I did it for love of country!" What does love mean? I take cover in the limited scope of my ambitions; this section only consists of some theoretical dabbling in an initial foray into describing the core elements of universal love which, as I have argued, is the basis of morality and ought to be the foundation of ethics. This disclaimer aside, I also argue that the basic premise that love is the motivational and evaluative core of morality is a reality that emerges all too clearly whenever rule-based ethics and ethical preconceptions reveal themselves as paper thin and unfit for the task.

A life devoted to helping those suffering from disease, impoverishment, war or natural disaster is a life that may be characterized as other-regarding in its display of virtues such as generosity and compassion. On the other hand, a life dedicated to achievement in the business world may be characterized as self-regarding and is often viewed as largely motivated by desire for material wealth. The desire for fame, similarly, while it may well result in enormous benefit to others is most generally thought of as self-regarding and egoistically motivated. Either of these distinctions between self-regarding and other-regarding motivations, when they are used to dismiss or minimize the other, is an ethical myopia. Any moral perspective that is purely other-regarding or purely self-regarding is headed down a slippery slope without exit. A purely selfless mind, if one exists, would first need to overcome its own self-interestedness in being selfless. It may also need to overcome self-interested temptations before true selflessness is attained. Self-interest and selflessness are two sides of a coin, and while it is true that a *selfish* self-interestedness is intrinsically amoral and unethical in its lack of any semblance of loving intention for others, it is also true that the *selfless* individual can never completely escapes his own self-interest. Self-regarding and other-regarding qualities, in a moral context, are largely chimeras produced by over-analysis. Morality is in its essence both self-regarding and other-regarding. Loving intention injected into the myriad of life situations determines a balance within a continuum of self-regarding and other-regarding forces. The balance is not arbitrary or predefined. Morality is a constant tension within the duality of Self and Other.

The three basic elements of ethics—from the standpoints of both intentionality and effectuality—are *fairness*, *beneficence* and *compassion*. I first became impressed with the intrinsic duality of moral concepts through working with my hypnotherapy and philosophical counseling clients who were dealing with difficult self-esteem problems. These individuals often tend to treat themselves with far less respect than they accord others, but objectively they may be successful in professional and personal life and are well regarded by everyone but themselves. I found myself telling clients that the relationship that a person has with himself is or should be much like the relationship that he has with others. We should be kind to others and, likewise, we should be kind to ourselves. We should be helpful to others, and we should be helpful and supportive to ourselves. We want to be encouraging of others, and we should seek self-encouragement from ourselves. We do our best to keep promises that we make to others; should we not keep the promises that we make to ourselves? The importance of honesty is as important when communicating to oneself as when communicating with others. The avoidance of negativity or needless criticism is as appropriate to inner self-dialogue as it is in dialogue with others. The pain of those suffering from low self-esteem and depression and various related anxieties began to appear to me as an interior reflection of ethical difficulties and of the moral or ethical dilemmas in society and the world as a whole. I began to tell my clients that the failure to treat yourself with the dignity and respect that you accord to others should be raised to the level of the ethical, because the relationship that you have with yourself is equally as much a moral concern as the quality of your relationships with others. You would never treat others with the same sort of negativity and disrespect that you routinely show towards yourself! "Love thy neighbor as thyself" is a definition of morality that has never been surpassed, and while there are multiple definitions of morality that help to achieve some diversity of perspective, none is more logically compelling or universally applicable. If you fail to love yourself you are in the wrong. You have denied yourself the respect and ethical treatment that you have no difficulty showing others. When basic fairness, kindness and compassion have been denied it may justifiably be said that a wrong has been committed regardless of whether the denial is to the self or to others. And in either case, the result is ethical disempowerment.

The distinction between 'duality' and 'polarity' has been exaggerated. Western philosophy has been accused and chastised by some for favoring dualistic opposition over scaled gradation or continuum. Good and bad (or evil), for example, when viewed as a duality may be said to be in polar opposition. It is similarly the case for freedom and slavery, truth and falsehood, mind and body, being and non-being, etc. The East, on the other hand, as typified by the magnificent *I Ching* and its perspective of *yin* and *yang* that favors a continuum of forces in which extreme polar oppostions are only markers of relative degrees of intensity. However, there is no serious disagreement between Eastern and Western philosophy concerning duality and polarity. Plato and Aristotle both viewed the multiplicity of the world as ultimately a manifestation of a monistic metaphysical principle, e.g.: 'Good' (Plato) or 'Unmoved Mover' or 'Nous' (Aristotle) and, for the most part, Western ethics has celebrated moderation as an integral part of the good life. But there is an important linguistic role for dualistic opposition. If opposition framed as polarity is always conceived in terms of gradiating dissimilarity it would become nearly impossible to think! Thought is dependent upon differentiation, and the establishment of dualistic oppositions facilitate the process of creating further differentia. The truth is that both 'dualism' and 'polarity' have their uses. In physics, for example, a positive charge is the opposite of a negative charge and there is no in-between. If we were to use electric charges as a model for human thought we would find ourselves in an absolutist universe that would be too horrifying to imagine. In his categorical rejection of duality Nietzsche, like other overenthusiastic dualism bashers, adopts the generalization that all dualism is bad. While I may be largely in agreement with Nietzsche and with the view of the *I Ching* that good and bad are aspects of a continuum, the dualistic representation of good and bad makes for a necessary road map that we would be ill advised to discard. Let us look at how absurd it would be to completely dispense with dualisms. The duality of Self and Other is the originating principle of the basic ethical dualisms that we are about to discuss. What if we were to rigidly insist that Self and Other do not comprise a 'duality' but are, in fact, a 'polarity'? While it is fair to say that our sense of self or ego is highly interrelated and do, indeed, converge, to call them merely two poles of a polarity but not *also* independent physical entities would be a laughable form of philosophical extremism that would end up making me you, and you me. The terms 'duality' and 'polarity' have a difference in emphasis, and it is useful to refer to the basic ethical dualisms as 'dualisms' rather than as 'polarities' because it is useful to fix their differences before we begin qualifying them because *without difference there is no meaning*.

William James wrote that, "The elementary forces of ethics are probably as plural as those of physics are."[20] Modern-day physics understands the elemental forces of nature as far less plural than James believed, and I submit that it is likewise the case that the elemental forces of morality are also few. The question concerning 'plurality' in both cases has not so much to do with the absolute constitution of 'force' which may well be monistic but rather with the practical and intellectually effective breakdown of a monistic principle into to the fewest comprehensible and usable parts. Too many elements may create complications to an extent that only confuses and increases difficulty, but too few elements may take away necessary anchors and points of reference that make analysis and solutions possible. The traditional theories have almost no practical use outside the classroom because they do little to enlighten the actuality of moral contexts that are strikingly and notoriously resistant to theoretical explanation. The non-ideological and non-dogmatic truth is that emergent moral actualities transcend rules and preconception. The three basic dualisms proposed in this section can certainly be formulated in ways different than as described herein, and I have no doubt that they are ripe for criticism. But from my point of view, it is important and, indeed, vital to emphasize the dualistic nature of the fundamental ethical principles and their implicit and ubiquitous presence in ethical reasoning so as to stimulate meaningful discussion, debate and inquiry. The descriptions of the basic ethical dualisms that follow are closely interconnected and reflect differing aspects of the unifying moral essence; each dualism entails the other two. And the three dualisms are effectively six because each pole may be thought of as a distinct principle: self-regarding fairness, self-regarding beneficence, self-regarding compassion, other-regarding fairness, other-regarding beneficence and other-regarding compassion. Each dualistic pole is a focal point for analysis. While I may interchangeably refer to these principles variously as, e.g., "the basic ethical dualisms" or "the basic ethical principles" they are used equivalently and refer to the conceptualization of the elementary moral forces that now follows.

~ *Fairness* ~

It is thought to be unfair when a perceived prerogative or right is denied. Property, territorial and economic prerogatives are often viewed as rights. There are standards of income and standards of life that some view as everyone's right to enjoy. But fairness is also at the core of the simplest moral precepts. Telling the truth and keeping one's promises fall within the province of fairness. If someone is lied to about reasons for a prospective action that will adversely impact him he may feel that he as been treated unfairly when the deception is revealed. There are rights to know, and if that perceived right is violated it will be deemed to be unfair. Much the same holds for promise-keeping; after all the promise is the essence of a contract in its simplest form, and if a promise is broken it will be deemed unfair especially if conduct was undertaken under the assumption that the promise would be kept. Telling the truth, keeping promises and staying true to agreements, and the "right to know" constitute a significant share of fairness issues. The belief that legitimate prerogatives hold in a given state of affairs is at the heart of the principle of fairness. But fairness also crisscrosses the entire moral landscape, and *any* perceived ethical violation may be construed as unfair to the victim of unethical conduct. There are many elements involved in the ethical assessment of a moral actuality, but any form of unethical treatment will likely also be viewed of as unfair. Why? Because to be denied ethical treatment is to be denied what is rightfully yours and is thus unfair. And, arguably, the right to ethical treatment is the most valuable of possessions.

Dialogic Fairness

Much unfairness has been committed in the name of fairness. And unfairness can be directed against the self as devastatingly as it can be directed against others. Fairness, in one form or the other, has accounted for most of the traditional concern of ethics.

Deception is intrinsic to the dualism of fairness and to its pursuit. The very effort to be fair must always contend with possibilities that self-regarding interests masquerade as other-regarding interests. Your claim of being fair may, perhaps subconsciously, be a self-deception that disguises self-interest as other-regarding interest but that in actuality unfairly benefits yourself. Self-interested deceptions can appear intractable. The intransigence of the deception is likely caused by confusion over moral and non-moral motivations. Disagreements over property, territory, rights to know, etc. may be disagreements that are non-moral in nature and come down to the power to force one's will over that of another and, if viewed as such, the controversy is not moral in nature but purely one of self-interest that disregards the interests of others. If we grant that *non-moral motives* are at the bottom of many putative moral issues, then the ability to separate them from *moral motives* would be a valuable tool for the resolution of *ethical* disagreements by acknowledging the non-moral nature of some claims.

A majority of persons may well be of the opinion that they are in possession of a good will, i.e. a will that is guided by loving intention, when in truth they may not be. The source of this deception can be ethical confusion rooted in ideology and preconditioned thinking, extreme moral relativism without any anchors, and much confusion over the very foundation of right and wrong. How can an individual have mental clarity respective to his or her moral intentionality if it has been preconditioned and unexamined? A clearer perspective on the constitution of moral and non-moral intentionality and action is essential.

And what is the correction for unfairness that is inflicted by the self on itself because the self-infliction is viewed as just? These inflictions may be deceptions of justice.

~ *Beneficence* ~

Who could argue with the popular, contemporary maxim that encourages people to "Practice random acts of kindness and senseless acts of beauty." Be kind. Help others. Volunteer one's time and energy. Contribute money to those in need. Offer one's services and ask for nothing in return. But other-regarding beneficent impulses can become self-defeating as happens when, in extreme cases, an intention to be fair to others can result in unfairness towards oneself. And dialogically, the principle of beneficence is as vital for the flourishing of the self as it is for the flourishing of others and the greater collectivity. Similarly, the expression of beneficence by means of unrestrained giving to others can ultimately sabotage both self-regarding and other-regarding deeds by an exhaustion of physical, emotional or financial resources. The principle of beneficence, much as is the case with each of the three basic ethical dualisms, is an expression of the fundamental Self-Other duality that applies to oneself as well as to others. Fairness is primarily dispassionate, while beneficence is intrinsically passionate. Is beneficence a mere "extra" that is not ethically required? While fairness is more about leveling the playing field, beneficence is motivated by a more expansive attitude for creating opportunities, encouraging knowledge and progress and, yes, actively promoting fairness and justice. The basic ethical dualisms converge. Can a person be fair but not beneficent at the same time? Each aspect of morality entails others as expressed by the underlying and unifying essence of morality, which is universal love. The validity of Humean passion as the driver or master of reason is clear on this point and an ethics absent emotion or passion is a cold legalism without real motive: its dictums could be easily broken. Beneficence is not merely a subjective flourish or an act of moral panache but a required cofactor along with fairness and compassion. And without beneficent motive fairness can sour with age and degrade into selfishness, jealousy and greed.

Dialogic Beneficence

Ayn Rand and advocates of "rational self-interest" rant against altruism as an illogical perversion of reason because in their minds the only rational basis for making choices is individual self-interest. If one chooses to beneficently make a contribution to a particular charity, it is deemed justifiable by the Randian only if greater social stability or other personally advantageous result also benefits the giver. Rand says that self-interest is in the interest of "life" and, therefore, if you make a charitable contribution that it is not in your rational self-interest you are acting irrationally. Rand argues that the only interest of life is to act to the benefit of one's own life and therefore, good and right (I would assume) are for the Randian only that which benefits the moral agent. Rand calls her credo "the virtue of selfishness."

Rand's argument has semantic, ethical and metaphysical implications. #1, Rand's semantic argument is peculiar. She makes selfishness a moral concept to fill the void left by her vilification of altruism. The ordinary language definition of 'selfishness' very simply means self-interestedness combined with a rejection of any countervailing altruistic motives or concern for others. Rand could have been consistent in her own terms if she said that the "virtue of selfishness" is the following self-interest without any necessary linkage with helping others. "Rational self-interest" is a redundancy because, quite clearly, a purely selfish individual would never knowingly take any action that would damage his or her self-interest. Therefore, Rand and her supporters can argue without self-contradiction that selfishness and greed are good without rationalizing that they can collaterally help others. If others should benefit indirectly from acts of unloving self-interest they could at least cease with the rationalization that rational self-interest could be beneficial to the greater good—even if that is not their goal—in an effort to camouflage their ideologically based near complete disregard for others. Then they can rejoice in returning 'selfishness' to its rightful place of utter disregard and unconcern for others and thereby represent themselves without distortion. #2, Rand's ethical argument is amoral. What would be more ludicrous than a practitioner of the 'virtue of selfishness" practicing random acts of kindness. The powerful resonance created by beneficent actions deeply connected with loving intention is laughingly dismissed by the Randians as far too *selfless* to be ethical. Doublespeak? Indeed! An ethics devoid of other-regarding love is an ethics detached from morality and, as such, is a twisted and perverse conception of ethics. Beneficence begins with the notion that helping others and the greater community is ethically justifiable for the very reason that ethics is concerned with the interests of both Self and Other. #3, Rand's substitute for a metaphysical love of God is the love of self. Many philosophers have rejected metaphysics, but most who have done so create an offsetting aesthetics in recognition of a deep human need even if the metaphysical or spiritual explanation is replaced by physical or scientific reasoning. In Rand's case, however, life is in its essence a gluttonous satisfaction of pure self-interest or selfishness.

The so-called "positive" version of the golden rule, "Do unto others as you would have them do unto you" is perhaps the ideal expression of beneficence. Beneficence is a powerful emotive force that overwhelms the practical. Morality is too often construed as a set of universal don'ts. And, indeed, don'ts are clearly needed. But the spirit of beneficence is a calling that urges us to go beyond ourselves, to continually redefine ourselves by helping others and, yes, by also helping ourselves. And the spirit of beneficence is also the spirit of greatness.

~ *Compassion* ~

Compassion is the emotion of caring through feelings of deep caring and commonality with all conscious beings. Unlike fairness and beneficence, compassion lacks explicit exteriority. The outward criteria for compassion may be reducible to undetectable behavioral expressions of feeling. On the other hand, a relatively uncomplicated computer program could provide instructions to *act* fairly or beneficently. Fairness, for example, may involve the give and take of compromise, sharing information, following through on promises and agreements and a whole spectrum of conventional behaviors. While beneficence possesses emotional qualities associated with giving it is distinguishable from compassion because, unlike compassion, it entails demonstrable actions and behaviors of giving or helping. While fairness and beneficence certainly involve emotional expression *compassion is itself an emotion.* In principle, a computer could go through checklists of potential actions to determine a particular person's legitimate interests and decide fairness or produce a list of potentially beneficent acts that are doable and worth doing for no other reason that they benefit the parties concerned. The computer's potential to calculate lists of fair or beneficent actions by no means excludes the importance of emotion respective to fairness and beneficence, but well-programmed emotionless computers could nonetheless make at least some of these ethical determinations. However, is a compassionate computer even imaginable? In order to imagine a compassionate computer we will also need to imagine a conscious computer. The far greater ease in imagining a fair and beneficent computer than a compassionate computer highlights an essential distinction that separates compassion from fairness and beneficence because the sublime significance of compassion is that it is a fundamental aspect of morality that is in its essence emotional feeling and nothing more.

It is quite conceivable to imagine unconscious computers that act with rational self-interest or other forms of rational decision-making, however, pure compassion is nothing other than the sentiment of concern for others, sympathy with the needy, and the plight of those who suffer. The paradox of compassion is that it makes a certain type of non-rational behavior rational. Logic requires, love desires. Specifically, love desires by means of compassion that might not be logical. The basic principle of compassion *commands* because morality commands, and compassion is the emotion that connects our feelings of emotional and physical suffering with the plight of other conscious beings. Emotions form a nascent moral imperative in the form of subconscious autosuggestion. Anger is often a negative emotion, but it can also trigger its own transformation that, through ethical reflection, allows the self to profoundly improve itself. Once the dance between reason and the passions begins any emotion may rudely butt in. But compassion provides love's primary emotive force. By attempting to extirpate emotion the Stoics drained themselves of the creative moral power that inspires the harmony with nature that they claimed to seek but that, without compassion, produced only a coercive harmony of uncompassionate self-denial and rigid conformity.

Dialogic Compassion

Perhaps the dualistic nature of compassion can best be understood through the lens of its poor sister: pity. We might be tempted to say that pity and compassion are similar, but the fallacy in this thinking is quickly apparent when compassion is turned inward as self-compassion. Self-compassion is self-empowering while self-pity is self-demeaning. Self-pity is the pathetic mood of surrender to one's plight and one need only think of the many stories of those who in the most hopeless of situations managed to maintain hope. Nothing is more pitiful than he who is mired in self-pity! Perhaps there is no more inspiring documentary on the power of self-compassion and resistance to self-pity than Viktor Frankl's memoir of his experiences in one of Hitler's concentration camps in *Man's Search for Meaning*. Persons suffering from depression and low self-esteem are often victims of self-pity. And much as self-pity is a negative emotion, pity towards others is also destructive. Unless the disparagement is purposeful and justified, feelings of pity are generally best avoided and replaced with compassion to aid, assist and empower. Pity, even if not mean-spirited, has intrinsic negative content whereas compassion is always positive.

But morality is far more complicated than simple compassion, as is shown in this naïve passage from Schopenhauer's *On the Basis of Morality*:

> Boundless compassion for all living beings is the
> firmest and surest guarantee of pure moral conduct,
> and needs no casuistry. Whoever is inspired with it
> will assuredly injure no one, will wrong no one, will
> encroach on no one's rights...[21]

If we are compassionate we are beyond moral error? It is quite ironic that the philosopher of pessimism is also the philosopher of compassion, and his claim that "violating the duty of self-love" is impossible (§I.6) may have allowed him—at least philosophically if not in practice, to dismiss self-compassion and hope. Nietzsche, on the other hand, was acutely aware of the grave danger in ignoring self-regarding aspects of compassion even though he, like Schopenhauer, failed to adequately appreciate its dualistic nature and swung far in the opposite direction by generally equating most other-regarding forms of compassion to pity.

> ...the value of the 'unegoistic,' the instincts of pity,
> self-abnegation, self-sacrifice, which Schopenhauer had
> gilded, deified, and projected into a beyond for so
> long...at last ...became for him "value-in-itself," on
> the basis of which he *said No* to life and to himself.

> But it was precisely against *these* instincts that
> there spoke from me an ever more fundamental
> mistrust, an ever more corrosive skepticism![22]

We must come to grips with the lack of compassion for the self. Lack of compassion for the self can come in the form of Nietzschean hardness or Schopenhauer-like self-pity.

Are Schopenhauer's philosophical pessimism and advocacy of retreat from the world and towards a life consumed with the contemplation of fine art and Platonic Ideas the disguise of an unabashedly king-sized ego? After all, he claimed that the ego needs no prompting to treat itself with self-love. Perhaps Schopenhauer showered himself with too much compassion! Was Schopenhauer's "pessimistic retreat" a form of narcissism? I am not a critic of the thoroughly contemplative life; contemplation is a decidedly admirable way in which to spend one's life provided one does not bash the efforts of others attempting to make sense of the hectic activity of the world. Incidentally, before the contemplators of fine art enter meditative reverie, do not artists first need to actively work in order to create their art? It should perhaps be noted that Schopenhauer, like many philosophers, did not practice what he preached as he appears to have earnestly enjoyed life particularly after he finally acquired some fame; was his pessimism only intellectual?

I take this to be Nietzsche's truest sentiment: "Saying Yes to life even in its strangest and hardest problems...Not in order to get rid of terror and pity...but in order to be oneself the eternal joy of becoming, beyond all terror and pity..."[23] But his fervor at times pushed him into uncompassionate-sounding remarks about those suffering from self-pity, and the withholding of compassion towards others is no less justifiable. Is not compassion a preferred emotion? Here Nietzsche pities those who are mired in self-pity, but would not self-compassion dramatically reframe the mood of those who cry:

> If only I were someone else...but there is no hope of
> that. I am who I am: how could I ever get free of myself?
> And yet—I am sick of myself!...Here the worms of
> vengefulness and rancor swarm; here the air stinks

of secrets and concealment; here the web of the
most malicious of all conspiracies is being
spun constantly...[24]

Nietzsche also rants against the "weak" and "born failures" and reveals a Social Darwinism that is as terrifying as it is wrongheaded, but the need to celebrate strong-willed achievers is nonetheless a vital antidote for mediocrity to counter the influence of the herd mentality against which Nietzsche frequently rails. The issue of self-pity cuts across the psychology of individual persons to society and issues worldwide. It is self-pity that is the foundation of scapegoatism because self-loathing can morph into hatred of others by "calling into question...our trust in life, in man, and in ourselves."[25] "Vengefulness," "rancor," and the spinning of "malicious conspiracies" eerily brings to mind what was to be Germany's Nazi future, and also the Nazi effort to fallaciously claim Nietzsche as a philosophical cousin. And in our own day the turmoil of the world is fueled by uncompassionate perspectives and attitudes held by the politically or economically downtrodden who suffer also from self-pity. Poor and frustrated peoples strike out against the Western powers. Is this ressentiment? But do the great powers act on only their national self-interest? When does national self-interest morph into a repression of the interests of others?

Compassion acknowledges the interests of both Self and Other and by so doing imparts the energy of loving intention. Morality is the re-unifier of the polarization or dualistic separation that is Self and Other. Pity stands in stark contrast to compassion. In pity, the strong and ungrateful separate themselves from others less fortunate, and in *self-pity* a man separates himself from the very bond of humanity that inspires in him the uplifting spirit of compassion that lends hope and the motivation to carry on.

~ *Moral Coherence and the Moral Equipoise* ~

Morality is a dialogue that concerns a harmonic unfolding of the elements of loving intention. 'Love' and 'morality' are words that are used quite differently and have very different connotations, but ultimately morality is nothing other than the expression of loving intention both personally and in terms of the greater social and institutional collectivity. The proposed ethics conceptualizes oscillating moral forces in terms of the basic ethical dualisms that express the diversity of moral situations and contexts. The goal of the ethics presented herein is the understanding and the facilitation of moral coherence between intentionality and the effectuality of actions. One of humanity's great tragedies is its love of complex ideology, but the tragedy is not in the ideologies or philosophies themselves—because ideological beliefs can provide penetrating insights not otherwise possible; the tragedy of ideology is that it has too often made humanity blind to the inner unity of its purpose. Morality, as is the universe as a whole, cannot be described in terms that are absolute or, conversely, that are purely relativistic, but it does possess an emergent intentionality that can fill all variety of moral exigency. Moral expressions are not in conflict if they are moral, but degrees of coherency certainly occur and some moral actualities are better than others. While there are differences of opinion about what is best or what is most right, there is also an inevitable convergence towards what is most coherent.

Questions about appearance and reality have filled the mind with wonder. Plato's cave of shadows and his Theory of Forms in which a perfect metaphysical order is counterposed to the pale and imperfect world of human experience are philosophic icons of appearance and reality. There have been other great paradigms of the schismatic relationship between fundamental, underlying truth and confused conceptions of everyday life such as theories of the unconscious developed by Freud (who was closely anticipated by Schopenhauer), Jung and others that help to explain how motives and intentions can lay hidden or repressed from conscious awareness. To some degree the basic ethical dualisms can likewise be hidden from conscious awareness: not only by subconscious repression but also by intellectual blocks such as formalities, abstract values detached from concrete realities, preconceptions and also by the variety of selective hypnotic thinking. Selective thinking obscures moral actuality by creating clouds of abstraction that misdirect ethical focus away from the essence of morality, which is nothing less than the expression of loving intention. The essence of morality becomes obfuscated when secondary principles of far less importance assume positions of authority made "true" by redundancy, repetition or ulterior design. If any persuasion is needed with respect to the illusoriness and common misapprehensions of morality all one needs to do is to allow his or her consciousness to form around the lowness to which our species has too frequently fallen.

In the context of this work, moral coherence is defined as overall harmonic resonance of the basic ethical dualisms with moral intentionality and effectuality. More broadly, 'the basic moral forces' may substitute for 'the basic ethical dualisms' because the latter are only a particular conception of the moral forces that are postulated in this book. Prospective or hypothetical actions may be thought of as resonant or dissonant, but moral coherence refers to an evaluation of moral actuality, i.e. concerning actual contexts, situations and states of affairs. Perfect coherence would mean a perfect balancing of the complex array of moral forces that, of course, is impossible or unknowable. But the lack of perfection does not prevent continuing efforts to achieve greater moral coherence in the ethical life of individuals and of the greater collectivities of the world's societies. The basic dualisms are ethical resonators that assist in this ongoing process as conceptual tools used to help determine or assess their relative resonance with both intentionality and effectuality respective to actions, methods, behaviors, institutions and consequences. Perfection is not required for doing well in life and ethical life is no different. A singer learns to hold a tune, but superior vocal performance and brilliant harmony require more training and, perhaps, further skill development; the development of virtue (moral excellence) requires the same. Achieving moral coherence involves the never-to-be-realized search for "perfect ethical harmony" by locating optimal positions within the oppositional flux of moral forces. A schematic representation at this juncture is beneficial. Let us call this hypothetically perfect harmonic state a *moral equipoise* (ME). Let F=Fairness, B= Beneficence, C=Compassion and let x equal a numeric value from 1 to 100 in which 1 equals an action that is assigned pure self-regarding status and 100 equals an action that is assigned pure other-regarding status. The moral equipoise varies as each dualism is assigned a value that reflects a different self-regarding or other-regarding status that changes in accordance with the situation. A moral equipoise (or optimal coherency) may be stated as ME= FxBxCx. Lesser or more imperfect configurations (i.e. most if not all cases) could then be compared. The moral equipoise is only a hypothetically ideal state of moral coherency, but it can help to gauge the moral state of affairs and may, further, help to suggest when a particular judgment requires reexamination or additional deliberation. Certainly, there may be more than one optimal condition of moral coherency and, therefore, there may be more than one possible moral equipoise found in a given situation. However, while the possibility of multiple fixations of the moral equipoise suggest ethical pluralism, it contravenes unbridled moral relativism.

The question naturally arises whether a theory such as the one proposed provides any basis for ethical agreement. It will be said, "Rules in ethics as in law are essential." I do not disagree! However, ethical rules are ultimately ignored when they come into irreconcilable conflict. Ethical empowerment cannot come from limited rules that generally have little utility for resolving deep and novel conundrums. In the midst of a genuinely taxing ethical conundrum, philosophical lawyering will simply not do. A rule will not uncover the contextual meaning of love's desire. The basic ethical dualisms are ethical resonators that help describe moral actuality. In combination with a diversity of perspectives, and by applying the basic ethical dualisms to at least some of those perspectives, which are then finally combined with consensus it is possible to arrive at deeper understanding and solutions that are discovered or, perhaps, uncovered, but not ethically litigated. Our focus now turns to the diversity of ethical perspective.

I.8

Changing Perspectives

Philosophy is the search for rational perspective. This statement is suggestive of a particular philosophical perspective on philosophy, and its self-referential nature reflects one of philosophy's perennial preoccupations, the question "What is philosophy?" Certainly, asking questions and challenging convention comprises much of the value in doing philosophy. The dualistic and oscillating nature of the basic ethical dualisms is intrinsically multi-perspectival, and the dualistic Self-Other perspective is only an initial perspective on ethics. There is no knowable absolute truth, and empowerment cannot be gotten in conflicting rules or nice maxims. In place of ethical legalism and dogma, it is necessary to establish a methodic perspectivism that is also a plural perspectivism that not only tolerates and accepts a diversity of opinion and perspective but also actively and aggressively seeks new and alternative views of actuality. Diverse perspective is a practical therapy for absolutism to help clear the cobwebs of preconception, sharpen the view, or even resuscitate perspectives that may be lost, buried or forgotten.

~ *Plural Perspectivism* ~

Philosophical pluralism and philosophical perspectivism are fundamentally similar but also quite distinct. Pluralism is an acceptance of a diversity of beliefs, and by that acceptance it entails some measure of validity to a multiplicity of divergent viewpoints. Perspectivism, on the other hand, tends to place more emphasis on the uniqueness of each and every perspective. My perspective is my truth even if my justification of what I hold to be true is a matter of my own selective, self-limiting judgments. Generally, perspectivism, unlike pluralism, rejects any form of underlying or transcendental unity even if it appreciates different perspectives that add to the multitude of perspectives that constitute the storehouse of knowledge. Therefore, pluralism's emphasis is on diversity and a sort of unity that may or may not be thought of as transcendental, whereas the emphasis of perspectivism is on the uniqueness of perspective even while it is quite capable of acknowledging and appreciating perspectival diversity. There is a synergistic and a paradoxical relationship between pluralism and perspectivism: the more deeply unique perspectives are understood, the deeper and richer pluralism becomes. And the richer the culture of pluralism, the more value is placed on unique perspectives that fortify the pluralism. Fundamental to both pluralism and perspectivism is that there is no monopoly on truth, and there is no greater defense against dogma than a plural perspectivism that aggressively seeks and welcomes new perspectives.

Nietzsche, who is generally considered the founder of philosophical perspectivism, also recognized the tension between a radical perspectivism that may appear more subjective and strident in denying truth, and—in the case of Nietzsche I wouldn't use the word 'transcendental'—a more coherent perspectivism that embraces a wider collection of alternative perspectives. His radical perspectivism:

> There are many kinds of eyes. Even the sphinx has
> eyes—and consequently there are many kinds of
> 'truths,' and consequently there is no truth.[25]

But Nietzsche also acknowledges the necessary balance between a multiplicity of perspectives and selective, more egoistic belief:

> There is *only* a perspective seeing, *only* a perspective
> 'knowing'; and the *more* affects we allow to speak
> about one thing, the *more* eyes, different eyes, we
> can use to observe one thing, the more complete will
> our 'concept' of this thing, our 'objectivity,' be. But
> to eliminate the will altogether, to suspend each and
> every affect, supposing we were capable of this—what
> would that mean but to *castrate* the intellect?"[26]

The castration of the intellect, Nietzsche is saying, would result from a diffusion of focus by assisting more and more "eyes" to have their say and thereby weaken unique impressions by which the will to power might make its mark on the world. But clearly Nietzsche is torn in two directions in which he recognizes that the seeking of a multiplicity of perspectives, or what I call a *plural perspectivism*, can help make concepts "more complete"; at the same time, however, he deeply values the uniqueness of individual belief and perspective. Any pluralism would, indeed, be *castrated* without the passion and the power of unique perspective and belief. There is no real conflict for Nietzsche here, and the tension he sees between radical and more moderate perspectivism echoes remarks he makes elsewhere concerning the struggle of "instincts" within the mind for dominance or power. Each perspective challenges others, and the greater power and brilliance of some perspectives ultimately makes knowledge and wisdom more complete, even while it is always susceptible of being toppled or replaced by more powerful beliefs or perspectives. From our perspective, ethical perspectives that seem contradictory or even hostile to each other may be ultimately compatible if they are grounded by the perspective of morally harmonic and coherent basic ethical principles that express the essence of morality.

Isaiah Berlin, in his argument for "value pluralism," says that moral values are incommensurable and in intrinsic conflict:

> ...values can clash...They can be incompatible
> between cultures, or groups in the same culture, or
> between you and me. You believe in always telling the
> truth, no matter what; I do not, because I believe that it
> can sometimes be too painful and too destructive....Justice,
> rigorous justice, is for some people an absolute value, but
> it is not compatible with what may be no less ultimate
> values for them—mercy, compassion—as it arises in
> concrete cases.[27]

Berlin could, in his basic expression of value pluralism, be described as a type of radical perspectivist. But is a value intrinsically beyond criticism simply because someone values it? Any underpinning of morality, as has been argued in this book, (§I.7) will need to make sense of the morass of values and other ethical concepts such that commensurability is possible to the extent that they fall within the spectrum of morality. Moral diversity and value pluralism are not equivalent to moral incoherence. *Moral* values are commensurable just because they are moral, and if it is not possible to make values coherent then, while they may be values they are not moral values.

Berlin's view on the incommensurability of values such as justice, for example, "with what may be no less ultimate values for them—mercy, compassion—as it arises in concrete cases" is a confusion that results from his failure to distinguish concrete values and abstract values as differences in kind. There is a critical difference between justice as valued in the abstract and justice that is valued in terms of its expression in a particular, concrete situation. For instance, hard work, honesty, mutual respect, self-respect, going to church, friendship, a safe neighborhood are only a few examples of what can be considered values. But conceiving of a value abstractly or *extra-contextually* is quite different than conceiving of it *contextually* in the concrete. Consider what happens when honesty, hard work, etc. are particularized and put into context. Let us look at each case: 1) Hard work for two individuals can mean quite different things. One may value physical labor more than mental effort, and what one sees as working hard another may disparage as working foolishly or not "working smart" and, indeed, if too much energy were to be expended it would be evaluated by the critic as a negative value. 2) Honesty is a concept that simply means someone who tells the truth. But Kant's absurd argument that truth-telling or honesty means informing a known murderer of the whereabouts of his intended victim would not be accepted as a value by most individuals. There are myriad other examples that are commonplace, such as when honesty would betray another's trust and confidentiality. Here again, most would not agree that the value of honesty has universal acceptability when considered outside of concrete situations. 3) Mutual respect can be misunderstood when the nuances of behavior and communication are considered, and a showing of respect by one person might be judged by another to be something less. 4) We can all agree that self-respect is important, but if someone derives self-respect from conduct that another finds abhorrent then, while "self-respect" as an abstract value will be valued there will be disagreement about whether the particular case represents a person's respect or disrespect of himself. 5) Going to church might be considered a strong value by two persons, but if one of them believes that the other uses his churchgoing as a front by which to present himself to the community while his life away from church is an unsavory one, the critic will likely feel that the unsavory person's churchgoing should not be considered something of value. 6) Surely friendship is a value, but a particular friendship may be considered wrong and destructive for any number of reasons; it would not be viewed as a value, but the ending of the friendship would be greatly valued. 7) A safe neighborhood is surely adjudged to be a value; but what does one say of the extreme but not unheard of cases where the safety of the neighborhood is the result of extortion by a criminal gang? Perhaps the latter example would not be truly described as "safe" but the point being made here is clear. Values that are expressed contextually in the concreteness of a situation and values that are stated or defined extra-contextually in the abstract are entirely different. Consider how different the entire issue becomes when values are considered in the concrete. Abstract values in apparent conflict such as justice, on the one hand, and mercy and compassion on the other may appear incommensurable and irresolvable, but incommensurability can vanish if adversaries living and working together should find that justice, mercy and compassion have common ground. How could this be possible? Moral values are valueless when they are not viewed as reflections of transcendent morality or, at least, the broader moral actuality.

A pluralism that is overly preoccupied with extra-contextual abstract beliefs gets stuck in incommensurables. This is particularly true when beliefs or values are embedded in cultural and religious differences. And yet, the world is filled with stories of enemies and staunch opponents who become friends after they have been afforded the opportunity of getting to know one another as human beings rather than as abstractions. It is one thing to be indoctrinated by religion or ideology, it is quite another for individuals to experience for themselves their shared humanity. Justice, mercy and compassion are abstract principles until a concrete situation develops. William James writes about situational uniqueness:

> ...every real dilemma is in literal strictness a unique
> situation; and the exact combination of ideals realized

> and ideals disappointed which each decision creates is
> always a universe without a precedent, and for which
> no adequate previous rule exists.[28]

It is obvious that we could not get along without abstract values, but in the end they can only be validated by the broader and deeper actuality of moral coherency that is the substratum of all ethical valuation. Abstract ideas of democracy, *any* abstract value, can be easily corrupted. In their abstract form values have the value of generalization and beneficent emotive affect, but if not also backed up with concrete actions, behaviors and institutions they can distort as much as they may inspire.

If value pluralism celebrates the full expression of values, then the toleration of repressive political regimes and other forms of conduct that run counter to the standards of Western liberal democracies would seem to be condoned. Berlin was forced to find some unifying principle lest his value pluralism was to descend into a degenerate sort of moral relativism permitting the most unthinkable and horrific of "values." It clearly was not Berlin's intention to protect Nazism or terrorism by the umbrella of value pluralism. In "Two Concepts of Liberty" he proposes "negative" liberty as the minimum standard of liberty:

> What then must the minimum be? That which a man
> cannot give up without offending against the essence
> of his human nature. What is this essence? What are the
> standards which it entails? This has been, and perhaps
> always will be, a matter of infinite debate...But whatever
> the principle in terms of which the area of non-interference
> is to be drawn, whether it is that of natural law or natural
> rights, or of utility or the pronouncements of a categorical
> imperative, or the sanctity of the social contract, or any
> other concept with which men have sought to clarify and
> justify their convictions, liberty in this sense means liberty
> *from*; absence of interference beyond the shifting, but always
> recognizable, frontier.[29]

Negative liberty, which seems to echo Spencer's "law of equal freedom" and Mill's *On Liberty,* defends any action provided that it does not interfere with the activity of others. However, Berlin's principle is even vaguer and more ambiguous than are Spencer's and Mill's. Berlin simply acknowledges that human decency does not permit unfettered freedom of action and that there is a basic principle that takes precedence over pluralism. Value pluralism requires a foundation in order to prevent its application in the political sphere from degenerating into something that condones the very sort of absolutism it is intended stop or inhibit. If value pluralism—in self-contradiction, protects the violations of the personal freedoms it holds to be essential, then it has the potential of running full circle to justify absolutist regimes such as those of Hitler or Stalin. Berlin thus reveals a transcendental pluralistic side to his philosophy by attempting to create a floor beneath which his value pluralism and the incommensurability of values cannot sink into self-negation. But Berlin's balancing act is itself, ultimately, a genuine incommensurable. Since it is a *reductio ad absurdum* to argue that pluralism can exist only if it justifies the existence of that which would lead to its self-destruction, it became necessary for Berlin to formulate the principle of negative liberty, but by so doing he acknowledges that incommensurables are secretly or implicitly commensurable. The resolution of the problem is a conceptualization of the basic moral forces. The basic ethical dualisms—a conceptualization of the basic moral forces, are implicit in ethical discourse and permeate the breadth of morality, and prevent incommensurability by encompassing the broad spectrum of moral coherence. The perspective of justice and compassion as incommensurables reflects a myopic definition of values that commingle and produce intellectual offspring as effectively as horses and elephants mate. Ethical commensurability occurs through the adaptations and transfigurations of the basic ethical dualisms; we can also speak of "complementary incommensurables" as a wink and a nod to the superficial paradox of conflicting abstract values. A justice that rejects compassion is an inferior and endangered justice over the long term, and a compassion that rejects justice is deeply flawed and incoherent. A compassionate person with no sense of justice would be a moral schizophrenic unworthy of ethical defense, though still amenable to a cure.

                            *   *   *   *

Plural perspectivism and its corollary proposal involving the basic moral forces or principles may find informal support in Gödel's Theorem. Searching outside of a system of thought is the best tester and sharpener of opinion. A system itself may not prove its own propositions, and while going outside the system is—admittedly—open to an infinite regress of seeking never-ending justification, the effort can only sharpen and improve understanding. The basic moral forces (and their conceptualization as, e.g. in the basic ethical dualisms) cannot be formally proved, but the diversity of perspective that plural perspectivism invites can build an ethical foundation grounded in the consensus of many "systems."

~   *The Basic Ethical Dualisms and the* I Ching   ~

The essential attitude of plural perspectivism is one of mindfulness and alertness to different perspectives that both reinforce and challenge existing belief. Here we discuss an experimental methodology that adapts the ancient Chinese *Book of Changes* (*I Ching*) presented primarily to graphically illustrate the oscillating perspectives of the basic ethical dualisms. Innumerable oscillations occur in the three basic ethical dualisms respective both to their resonance with intentionality and the effectuality of action. The oscillations may be represented by the configurations of hexagrams of the yin-yang duality in the classic Chinese work, the *I Ching*, and are adapted to our purposes in order to depict the diversity of ethical perspective necessary for a methodic plural perspectivism. The elemental components of the hexagram are two monopoles that each account for half of the yin-yang dualism: an unbroken line (yang) monopole and a broken line (yin) monopole. For the purpose of our adaptation, let 'yang' = 'self' and let 'yin' = 'other'. There are eight trigram configurations:

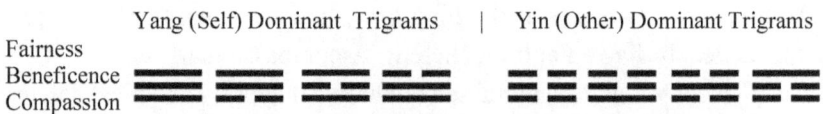

	Yang (Self) Dominant Trigrams		Yin (Other) Dominant Trigrams
Fairness			
Beneficence	▬▬▬ ▬▬ ▭▭ ▬▬		▬▬ ▬▬ ▭▭ ▬▬
Compassion			

Fig. 1 (see Appendix, fig. 2 for reference)

For our purposes, a trigram is considered dominantly yang (self) or yin (other), respectively, if yin or yang lines occupy a majority (two or three positions) on the trigram. Four of the trigrams are yang (self) dominant, and four are yin (other) dominant. Each of the three basic ethical dualisms is represented by their fixed position in each of the two trigrams that together comprise the upper and lower components of the hexagrams (see Appendix, fig. 2) as follows: *fairness* holds the top positions (1 and 4), *beneficence* holds the middle positions (2 and 5) and *compassion* holds the bottom positions (3 and 6). Thus adapted, the hexagrams represent sixty-four configurations of the basic ethical dualisms, and a great diversity of ethical perspective is achieved when they are applied to moral situations and contexts. For our purposes, sixty-four configurations are more than adequate, however, if we were to practice the *I Ching* in its traditional form it would generate a total of 4096 possible perspectives (64 x 64 = 4096) because each of the 64 hexagrams has 64 possible couplings with other hexagrams and would, thereby, produce a virtually endless supply of ethical perspectives for situational engagement. Each adapted hexagram helps form a distinct perspective of the oscillations of self-regarding and other-regarding forces and their degree of resonance in the moral situation. The hexagrams are considered "major dominant" in favor of Self (yang) or Other (yin), respectively, when a majority (two or three positions) is held in both the upper and lower trigrams. The hexagrams are "minor dominant" when yang or yin lines, respectively, dominate the upper trigram but not the lower. These assignments are arbitrary; the purpose of this scheme is only to generate a multiplicity of configurations so as to foster a plurality of ethical perspective.

The representation of sixty-four configurations or perspectives of the basic ethical dualisms (or thousands more when utilizing the traditional "changing" combinations of the *I Ching*), is offered here as a speculative tool for a methodic and plural perspectivism. (It may be noted that other hexagrams can serve the same function, as e.g. the Star of David, which is comprised of two equilateral triangles consisting of six lines).[30] Ethical decision-making is generally a product of individual deliberation and reflection and consensus with others. Consensus is clearly a powerful force in ethics, but it is not necessarily the most significant factor in decision-making because consensus may itself be resolvable or negotiated by the harmonic resonance or coherence of moral actuality. The vast quantity of perspectives facilitated by the *I Ching* helps pinpoint the oscillation of the dualisms that are resonant or dissonant in moral states of affairs. It could also help locate optimal moral coherency or equipoise, of which more than one could emerge.

The philosophy of the *I Ching* and also of Taoism is in some ways harmonious with morality viewed dualistically (and as a polarity) and, specifically, with reference to the basic ethical dualisms. However, the view of morality presented here is one of an overarching existential project to influence and to some extent shape the understanding and the shaping of moral actuality. The traditional view of Taoism, while it may be argued that the moral project is contained in the Tao as part of its natural flowing, is probably at odds with the notion that morality is a project. The view that morality is a project, which may perhaps be thought of as a more traditional Western view, suggests some sense of struggle between coherent and non-coherent moral forces that is more directed and perhaps more confrontational than in the abiding and universal flow of the Tao.

~   *The Moral Dialectic*   ~

Dialectical reasoning, or the effort to impose logical resolution between oppositional ideas or concepts has been described as a form of sophistry or fraudulent argumentation. But most of the dialecticians were sincere in their belief that dialectic is a process of thought by which didactic certainty is achieved. Plato and, by tradition, his mentor Socrates developed dialectic as a form of argument in which conclusions are shaped and predetermined by the skillful definition of its premises. Establish a defined truth such as "Truth" or "Justice" and many things that follow in the discourse can be demonstrated to be true or not true, or just or unjust by premises that have been defined by the dialectician. Plato's dialectic is meant to reveal those beliefs or actions that are consistent or inconsistent with his Theory of Forms. This method is also called the "Socratic Method" and lawyers are trained in its use so, not surprisingly, Socratic Method is a notorious deceiver of the truth. Ultimately, Socratic Method is a form of sophistry because ideas are defined in such a way that competing points of view are ignored or distorted. It might (perhaps) be justifiable for a lawyer to use dialectical reasoning because he may be more interested in winning his case than in upholding the truth. However, sophistry is not welcome as a method of ethical deliberation or philosophical analysis and reflection. Nonetheless, dialectic has an odd appeal and while we have no need for sophistry in ethics, the dialectical play of ideas is not without value.

Even Aristotle, an empiricist, scientist and historian of philosophy, and a philosopher who may perhaps also be viewed as a classical precursor of pluralism, viewed his syllogistic logic as the formal essence of Plato's dialectic. Both the dialectician and the practitioner of syllogistics, says Aristotle, "argue syllogistically after stating that something does or does not belong to something else."[31] But William James quite accurately articulates the blunt truth about classical dialectical logic:

> Intellectualism in the vicious sense began when Socrates and Plato taught that what a thing really is, is told us by its *definition*. Ever since Socrates we have been taught that reality consists of essences, not appearances, and that the essences of things are known whenever we know their definitions. So first we identify the thing with a concept and then we identify the concept with a definition, and only then, inasmuch as the thing *is* whatever the definition expresses, are we sure of apprehending the real essence of it or the full truth about it.[32]

The fiction of classical philosophy, and much of the hypnotic nature of everyday preconception from economics to politics to science and just about everything in-between is that the world is subordinate to language. Hegel brought dialectical thinking to new levels of absurdity by drawing absolute conclusions concerning world history merely from the interplay of language. Still, dialectic-like thinking through creative and metaphorical suggestion can produce glimpses of hidden truth. And while few major philosophers have produced a greater mass of nonsense than Hegel, it is difficult to deny that his nonsensical thinking has been a remarkable stimulus for further thought. But if dialectic or, at least, dialectic-like thinking is restrained and modified so that words and language are vehicles that bring us closer to the truth without being the truth itself, then the stimulatory effect of dialectical thinking can play a useful role that is complementary with plural perspectivism.

As an experimental free play of ideas, dialectic could help to open up the mind to the possibility of new perspectives. Traditional dialectical thinking, particularly as used by the likes of Hegel, Marx or Mao to interpret history, is nothing less than a method used to exclude diverse currents of history in order to misdirect focus to the selective thinking of the ulterior dogma. Basic truths of economic injustice and exploitation recognized by Marx are overwhelmed by other truths of repression and extreme moral incoherence that are all too clear when viewed with a breadth of ethical perspective. If dialectic contrived to support ideological obsession is left in the dustbin and is replaced by a multilinear dialectic that embraces multiple threads of opposition (§I.4), then dialectic will find its place not as a theory but as part of a methodology of plural perspectivism. The dynamic interchange between forces that tug in opposing directions—each revealing and deepening the understanding of the other, is a perspective that is worth pursuing.

Truths and untruths reside in many perspectives and in many traditions, and promiscuity in entertaining new or different ideas is not unfaithful. You cannot be a lover of truth without acquainting oneself with the thinking of other beliefs and different perspectives. When it comes to the love of truth, it is dogmatism and ideological rigidity that are unfaithful. Dialectical partners, like partners in a marriage or in any *loving* relationship share the best of what each has to offer, and in recognition of how a loving relationship may at times become stale, dialectical relationships are well built for rebirth and reinvention. The dialectical "interpenetration of opposites"— a term coined by Friedrich Engels—is perhaps not too far off key as a quasi-sexual metaphor. The metaphors of sex and dance as expressions of dialectic are not without merit because relationships between persons and between beliefs are infused with possibilities, hopes, disappointments, temptations, fears, offers, rejections, unions, disunions, connections and interconnections. Two people can fall in love even if one sees the other as far from perfect; each finds positive qualities that compensate for perceived imperfections. And we can also fall in love with philosophies or ideologies without embracing them completely. The moral requirement in both amorous and intellectual love is their grounding in loving intention. A morally bankrupt philosophy, no less than a morally bankrupt individual, is not worthy of love. Intellectual honesty requires and demands some intellectual promiscuity if only because we should know something about ideas before we reject them. Consider the outrage that is the scorning of a child merely because she is of a race different than oneself! And is this outrage in essence much different than arbitrarily rejecting a belief because of prejudice against the philosophical or cultural tradition from which it originates? All the mindless, knee-jerk denigrating by "liberals" or "conservatives" by one or the other is a common example of prejudice that only serves to poison political discourse. A beautiful child born of an interracial couple is a "union of opposites" that can be viewed as a metaphor for the natural "synthesis" of dialectic. Hegel and Marx tried to artificially force dialectical synthesis, but the evolving coherence of moral actuality derives in part from a dialectical dance whose outcome cannot be predicted with certainty even if it may, with insight, perhaps be anticipated.

The source of dialectical influence is the inner dynamics and ethical expression of love. The moral dialectic, which really is the only dialectic, is perpetually working through the deepest essence of the rational mind to move rational beings in the direction of love. There is no escaping the influence of the moral dialectic, which is not to say that the success of the moral project is inevitable; clearly it is not. But love and the strivings to realize it represent the positive destiny of all rational beings. The moral dialectic is the only real dialectic because it represents an intellectual process that is in some sense directed by the nature of what is being intellectualized. Definitional implication (deductive logic) reveals only that which its definitions imply, and a falsely defined material fact will imply things about the world that are also false. If one of the necessary qualities stipulated in a definition of 'human being' is 'rationality,' such that its absence would disqualify a being from being human, then surely 'human' has been falsely defined because, as we well know, not all humans are rational. We could call logic dialectical because in its watered down sense 'dialectical' and 'logical' are sometimes used synonymously, but would it not be better to just call definitional implications 'logic' and leave it at that? Science and other rational practices and behaviors require formal and informal rules for determining what are and what are not facts, but facts do not determine themselves but are determined by agreed and applicable rules of fact-finding. But science and other types of fact-finding are very unlike dialectic because they are driven by observations that are guided by objective empirical standards, while dialectic is a product of myriad strains of ethical consensus. Ethics is not about definitions but it is, like science, dependent upon facts. Ethics is about understanding the intentions behind rational actions and the relative coherency of their consequences and their effectuality. There is no certainty in the direction of ethical deliberation. The processes of ethical judgment and evaluation undergo dialogical expressions of underlying dualistic tensions between multiple threads of self-regarding and other-regarding forces, and the ultimate moral unification of differences cannot be defined but only resolved in accordance with facts and under the guidance of love. Morality is the rational struggle to bring the world in accordance with love. But this process does not happen autonomously or in isolation, but through a combination of personal reflection and consensus with others exposed to plural perspectivism and the diversity of differing and seemingly discordant perspectives. There is no dialectally predetermined outcome to the moral dialectic, which is largely a consensual movement that is part of a convergence that also includes the chain of cause-and-effect and the involvement of free will. But amid diverse forces of convergence, the multilinear dialectic—which *is* the moral dialectic—has a critical role in the unfolding of human destiny.

One would like to pronounce that dialectic is the irresistible force of moral reason, but it would be more accurate to say that it is a force that struggles to be irresistible but settles for just being listened to. There are many distractions to the rational mind besides the moral sense; the moral sense is, really, only but one of the Nietzschean "instincts" that seek to emerge as dominant. I am understating; morality is humanity's most noble instinct, but it could still fail in the end. The unity of opposites, in the case of the moral dialectic, is a harmonization of oppositional tensions that are conceptualized through the use and application of the basic ethical dualisms. However, the moral project could fail, and if it does fail it seems most unlikely that humanity would survive for the very basic reason that morality is the primary, existential functionality of the rational mind. Morality is, in the final analysis, a matter of human survival if not the survival of *any* rational species. A positive, beautiful and morally coherent destiny is not preordained but, rather, is the gradual ascendancy of mind through the actions of its collective moral agency. And the interplay between coherent moral forces and those that are less coherent, or are morally incoherent, is the nexus of dialectical change.

I.9

Relative Freedom

A bsolute freedom for human beings is as nonsensical as the idea of absolute human intelligence. Freedom and intelligence are both relative, non-absolute concepts. Absolute intelligence would require that a being in possession of it would never make a mistake, but s/he would also have no need to ponder solutions because solutions to all problems would be knowable from the start. There are some very intelligent people and others less intelligent, but none are remotely close to possessing absolute intelligence. Freedom is equally non-absolute. The so-called "free will," much like intelligence, is relative. There is no human being who is absolutely intelligent or absolutely free, but a human mind can become more intelligent and it can also become more free. The fact that we do not possess absolute freedom does not mean that we are not free or that we are incapable of developing our free will. And if science should someday prove that there is more than one possible future, then it would provide empirical verification of freedom because an indeterminate future would necessitate undetermined and unnecessary actions.

There can be hardly any doubt concerning the importance of external circumstances. Whether a person is born rich or poor, in the twentieth century or the fifth century, has loving parents or abusive parents are circumstances that will have enormous influence on the course of his or her life. Are internal factors that influence a person's individual character as causally determined as external events, even while recognizing that external events are themselves influenced by the intentionality and character of the individuals who are part of the events that unfold? When someone asks, "Why did you do that?" a reason or cause for the action will likely be provided, and if a deeper cause or explanation is sought another reason will be provided, and so on but ultimately the questioning will come to an end, perhaps with the answer of "I don't know" or "I did it because it was the *right* thing to do." There can be little doubt that long causal chains precede and determine much of our action. Free will often has little to do with our actions; I can personally attest to its absence each time that I tell myself that I will take a different route on my drive home than is my custom, but then fail to make the turn and only some minutes later realize that my *free* will has surrendered to habit (and I then proceed to cuss myself out accordingly!) My familiar drive had conditioned me by dozens or hundreds of earlier trips. Habits or subconsciously conditioned behaviors occupy a very large part of the mental activity that accompanies everyday activity. If I were in a state of perpetual freedom I would never miss my turn because I would always do exactly what I profess to myself as my intention barring coercion by external restraints that are outside of my control. Much of behavior perfectly reflects the causal chain of determinism. But consider the more significant situation of two individuals, Mary and John, who are applying for the same job. It so happens that Mary has a friend who is eager to help her in any way he can. Unbeknownst to Mary, this "friend" communicates *false* information concerning John to the company's personnel director in order to influence his decision in favor of Mary. Unlike her friend, Mary is exceptionally ethical and when she learns what her "friend" had done she immediately reports the matter to the personnel director. Mary clearly is a woman of noble character, and it is her good character that has interrupted the causal chain that had been set in motion by her "friend" that if left unchecked would have almost guaranteed her the job. While her hire may now be in doubt, it is possible that the personnel director may still hire Mary because of the integrity that she displayed when, all things being equal, John may have otherwise had the edge.

Freedom and reason are intimately aligned. Once we accept the mantle of reason we are not free to reject it. The paradox of freedom is that, in the context of rational and ethical life, a life guided by reason will likely have narrowed choices as compared with a life that is lived without ethical or rational restraint. An interesting aspect about freedom is that rationality limits the range of free choice. The more 'free' we are in one sense, the less 'free' we are in another. If an individual conceives of himself as always acting rationally it would be impossible for him to *willfully* act irrationally while maintaining his self-conception of rationality. If an individual consciously chooses to stray from his self-conception, then he admits that he is guided by something other than his rational intellect. The concept of free will is completely dependent upon rationality and ethical reasoning in particular. We cannot be free unless we are in accordance with the dictates of our reason; otherwise, our actions are merely determined by the casual chain. Kant argues that every rational individual acts "under the idea of freedom"[33] and, as such, in a "practical" sense we are freely obligated to abide by duties as reason commands. Kant says this even though he believes that in a purely theoretical sense "freedom is only an idea of reason whose objective reality in itself is doubtful."[34] Kant's conception of practical freedom in absolute terms is a contradiction and needs to be turned on its head. Belief in absolute truth and absolute good and other forms of absolute unknowability may be entertained as a matter of faith provided that we also grant that our practical applications are always uncertain and fallible. Kant unconvincingly claims practical moral certainty by claiming autonomy for the will to freely and unyieldingly conform itself to the false certainty fabricated by his categorical imperative and other fallible principles. The allegiance to reason does not mean as Kant believed that in order to be free we must categorically follow an abstract principle.

Kant, however, is correct in claiming that there can be no notion of freedom that is unconnected to reason. Without the ability to at least *in some measure* step outside of the causal chain of determinism there can be no freedom. Individual freedom mandates a dedication to conduct oneself in accordance with reason as best we comprehend it and the duty to strive always to improve our ethical reasoning. The overriding question then becomes, what shall determine the application of reason once contrived absolute standards such as the categorical imperative are discarded. It is the intrinsic weakness of absolutism in all of its forms to insist that its principles are far more clear and certain than there is any right *with all due modesty* to assume. The methodology by which we might approach this goal is to creatively discover ways to escape old habits and formalities of thought when they no longer serve us or fit the exigencies of the situation. Plural perspectivism, with the guidance of loving intention, creates freedom or, more exactly, makes us freer. If the free will may be said to exist in any meaningful sense it must be capable of escaping the legalistic maze of ethical rules. Rules have significance only in a context. What is it in the context or in the situation that gives ethical rules their significance? Conflicting ethical rules are irreconcilable by a hierarchy of other ethical rules that are hardened into incommensurability. Ethical reconciliation can result when deliberation and consensus is focused on the basic elements that are implicit in any ethics that accepts love as its basis and only source. The source of morality is also the source of freedom.

If commingling between free will and determinism occurs there is no absolute freedom and there is no absolute determinism. Is gold that is adulterated with copper pure gold? Obviously not. If determinism is adulterated with even a particle of freedom then determinism is false, because one "free" action disrupts the causal chain and the entire deterministic process. Likewise, if free will is adulterated with even a particle of causal determination then free will is false because the grounding of choices and options would be partially shaped by a determined chain of events. The free will asserts itself in a struggle with deterministic forces, and determinism generally wins. But freedom is an ever-present possibility and its emergence constitutes what are perhaps life's most valued experiences.

> [Hegel] never cares to point out how the man's
> hair's-breadth of choice gives all its significance
> to human art and human conduct.[35]

The above comment asserts the theater of freedom. Freedom is a rational choice, and it is morality that in large part creates the *potential* for freedom. Yes, we must first choose to be free by identifying choices and creating the potential for freedom before we may become free. Human beings are not, as Rousseau believed, born free, but we create freedom through intellectual and ethical advancement. And contrary to Rousseau, it is necessary to create political, social and cultural environments that both support and encourage not only political freedom but also free thought and intellectual freedom. Ironically, a hypothetical state of nature would be about the least free of any situation that is imaginable short of overt imprisonment.

If freedom exists, i.e. if it can be created, it must require an initial exposure to randomness before it becomes realized. The human mind is most likely seeded with gaps of randomness that are, I believe, the birthing of freedom. The adaptation of the *I Ching* hexagrams (§I.8) illustrates an example of randomness that may be analogous to random presentations of choice for the mind. Rather than selecting the hexagram using the method of tossing coins I accessed an online random number generator and "flipped" three pennies six times, with each flip representing one line. By convention, heads equals 2 and tails equals 3; thus, each toss of three pennies equals either 6,7,8 or 9. If the total of six tosses equals 6 or 8 then it signifies yin or broken line, and if the six tosses equal 7 or 9 then a yang or unbroken line is signified. The sequence of six tosses that I performed using the random number generator produced the sequence of 6-8-7-8-7-6 and, thus, by building the hexagram from the bottom line up we derive hexagram #39 (§I.8, see Appendix, fig. 2) which is, according to our scheme, a "major other-regarding" hexagram. If I were contemplating a particular ethical conundrum by using the selected hexagram or a series of hexagrams also derived by random number generation, the course of my deliberations would be influenced by randomly selected hexagram configurations representing the basic ethical dualisms. While there are many means for spurring multi-perspectival inquiry, this exercise suggests how the causal chain can be interrupted. Arguably, and certainly from a pragmatic standpoint, the more rational choices that we have before us, the freer we may be of deterministic influences. Carl Jung persuasively argues for a non-causal, i.e. non-deterministic interpretation of choices that the *I Ching* helps to generate:

> …in nature one finds no two [quartz] crystals exactly alike…The jumble of natural laws constituting empirical reality holds more significance for [the Chinese sage] than a causal explanation of events that, moreover, must usually be separated from one another in order to be properly dealt with. The manner in which the *I Ching* tends to look upon reality seems to disfavor our causalistic procedures. The moment under actual observation appears…more of a chance hit than a clearly defined result of concurring causal chain processes…While the Western mind carefully sifts, weighs, selects, classifies, isolates, the Chinese picture of the moment encompasses

everything down to the minutest nonsensical detail, because
all of the ingredients make up the observed moment.[36]

The shape and form of crystals might metaphorically be compared to
destiny. Perhaps the crystal is fated to be what it is, but destiny is an
indeterminate fate made possible by the creation of freedom. Human destiny
is conditioned and structured by a vast array of forces that are not exclusively
bio-evolutionary or causal, but those "chance hits" and what to do about
them are the freedom gaps that interrupt the causal chain and, along with
deterministic forces, are what shape destiny.

The notion of an initial exposure to randomness as the mind's birthing
area of freedom has roots in a philosophical tension in David Hume's work.
While Hume proposed that the knowledge of the physical world is based
upon the probabilities of repeated observations, at the same time, he argued
that there is no necessary connection between a cause and its effect because
they are not logically bound together or in any sense accountable to reason
and, therefore, confidence concerning causes and effects can never exceed
their probability. Thus, even while Hume is generally thought of as a
behaviorist in his holding that human behavior is sequence of cause and
effect, and from his statement that the self is a "bundle of perceptions," his
principle of unnecessary connections (as I shall refer to it) is a theoretical
opening for the possibility of freedom and anticipates popular ideas about
quantum physics, e.g. the uncertainty principle, that suggest the possibility
or even the explanation of free will. According to Hume, the sun will not
by necessity rise tomorrow even though vast probability allows us to have
virtual certainty that it will. Knowledge of necessary connections between
cause and effect is outside the ken of human knowledge, but if freedom is
itself a choice it may initially emerge as a spontaneously generated quality
that jumps the causal chain. Gaps in the causal chain, seemingly made
possible by the *principle of unnecessary connections*, may well be the fields
of random exposure in which freedom is created.

Do artists exemplify the confluence of free will and deterministic
necessity? Artists, Nietzsche observes, know

precisely when they no longer do anything 'voluntarily'
but do everything of necessity, their feeling of freedom,

subtlety, full of power, of creative placing, disposing, and
forming reaches its peak—in short, that necessity and
'freedom of the will' then become one in them.[37]

The non-causality of free will emerges from the world of causality. We
might perhaps speak of a 'series' of causal chains rather than 'the' causal
chain, but if 'chain' is shorthand for 'determined' and if the chain or chains
are intermittently getting broken and reattached by acts of free will then we
may very well dispense altogether with the metaphor of "the chain" and
with the term 'predetermined' as well. Interrupted, short chains of causality
are themselves made indeterminate by the interventions of freedom. We
might loosely speak of many disconnected "causal chains" because, surely,
chains of cause and effect govern vast regions of our individual and
collective existence. But amid the vastness of experience and from the
emergence of random possibility free will is capable of interrupting the
predictability of individual lives and the course of human history. But the
theater of freedom is itself part of a larger theater of convergence that
suggests a spectrum of uncertain inevitability or increasing probability that
lie outside the strict confines of causality.

I.10

Convergence, Power and Correction

The treatment of the indigenous Amerindian peoples by the European settlers and later by the United States was in many instances horrific and reprehensible. And yet, the argument that the New World territories that were settled during the European colonial expansion should have been left under the control of the native tribes is unrealistic, absurd and ethically unjustifiable. The notion that the European powers had no right to settle the New World and that, essentially, the vast territory should have been left to the Amerindians because "they were there first" is a delusional fantasy and nothing more. To make this contention would involve a serious failure to come to grips with the moral actuality that the "dispossession" of the Amerindians of their territories was *not* in and of itself wrong. The displacement of the indigenous peoples was inevitable and ethical by almost any wide-ranging evaluation even if the means employed were often wrong and in some cases profoundly wrong. The ends may have been justifiable, but the means to the ends often were not.

The European settlement of the New World was going to occur one way or the other and is illustrative of the process of convergence. The advancement of European civilization made the "discovery" of the western hemisphere almost inevitable, but the manner in which Europeans would settle the vast new territories was an open question. The interrelationship between causality, dialectic and free will drives the course of human history, but it is better conceived of as an unfolding of possibilities rather than as the appearance of the inevitable. Eventualities can indeed be inevitable after tipping points are passed and a critical mass has been reached, but while absorption of the New World territories by the European nations became a virtual inevitability the destiny, which is to say the quality of what was to be the new order in the Americas was very much indeterminate and open to a range of possibilities. The discovery and settlement of the New World was a result of the *causality* that was an advancing European civilization, but a long dialectical interplay ensued concerning the manner in which power was to be asserted and the Amerindians were to be treated. Finally, decisions were focused and narrowed by causal and dialectical processes, and actions of free will in turn became part of causal influences that helped determine the course of history because each act of free will also becomes part of a causal chain. Decisions freely made may ignore causal forces but only at great cost, and they can also choose to resist the progressive force of the moral dialectic. Some historical developments may well become inevitable, but when history points out moral failures and illuminates how moral incoherencies could have been made more coherent, it helps to reshape the future and light the path of human destiny by lessons learned from the past.

Were the Amerindians 'dispossessed' of their lands?[38] For a people to be dispossessed of land would require that they first possess the land. But does occupation of land alone determine 'possession' or 'ownership'? If so, then the very first occupiers would be the possessors. But were the tribes that occupied the lands when the Europeans arrived the first occupiers? The question can never be answered with certainty and whatever answers are given could only be obtained by anthropological research which, while significant from a scientific standpoint would have little political or moral force because in actuality the issues are more complex than who got there first. Rules and principles that guided the Amerindian tribes in the use of land was of a fundamentally different nature than that of European law and tradition. The native peoples used the land and when it was no longer inhabited or cultivated it was open to settlement by other tribes. In any case, the Amerindian use of land was much more informal than that of the Europeans. For the Europeans, 'property' or 'ownership' suggests something that 'belongs' to an individual or a group and remains such until it is sold or given away. But there are qualifications to land ownership. In modern-day America, for example, land and buildings are subject to wide-ranging restrictions. Liens ordered by the courts can be issued for the purpose of collecting taxes or debts. Property taxes are themselves a condition that must be met or, ultimately, the property might be subject to foreclosure, and therefore property whose ownership is conditioned by the payment of taxes is not unconditionally under the control of the owner or proprietor. Zoning restrictions control how land and buildings are to be used and constructed. And property can be expropriated by eminent domain if the government determines that it is in the public interest to do so. Property is far from absolute, but the European/American and Amerindian conceptions of landed property greatly diverged.

Since the Europeans and the Amerindians did not share the same legal conventions, the dispute over land was less a matter of law than of the ethical use of power. As the dominant power, the Europeans and, later, the Americans held all the cards. This is not to argue that the law was always used unethically because such is not the case, but the law that was employed was the intellectual property of Britain and subsequently the United States. The occupation and assumption of authority over the territories of the New World was going to happen, but the fate of the Amerindians is a matter that was very much indeterminate. It is clear that many actions taken were a ruse that disguised a continuing power grab to wrest away control of the lands from the Amerindian nations. Deceit on the part of individual land speculators was widespread and the principal intentionality of the new government of the United States was to protect and defend the interests of its white skinned citizens. But the U.S. government and the British colonial government that preceded it attempted to clothe policy and the law in a moral framework. Much of the effort was in the form of purchasing land from the indigenous tribes because the selling and buying of property is a traditional and foundational feature of Western law and ethics. But the living conditions of the Amerindians grew progressively worse as they were forced to relocate from one territory to another, both as a result of legitimate land transactions as well as trickery, fraud, deceit, extortion and governmental corruption. In time, all pretenses were virtually discarded as the forced relocations to reservations resulted in horrific suffering and destitute poverty.

The road that should have been taken was not the one-sided application of a body of law that the Amerindians did not abide by or sufficiently understand but, rather, the assumption of high morality that could have transcended the intrinsic inequality of the power relations between the two sides. The problem at hand was not a matter of law but of morality and it might well have been vastly better for both the Amerindian peoples and the Americans if the pretense of equality was dispensed with, and supremacy of the Americans was accepted not with the arrogance of power but with a deep understanding of responsibility. Upon assuming this responsibility, the Americans would have created the opportunity for inspired stewardship and noblesse oblige. The noble use of power could have curtailed the greed of the American settlers while, at the same time, the welfare of the indigenous population would have been protected. Progress and the integration of the Amerindians into the new society would have been furthered. The Americans owed the Amerindians protection from the collateral damage of destiny realized, and if properly administered the integration of Amerindian peoples into society would have more resembled the future integration of other ethnic groups more than—which was sadly and tragically the case, the repression and enslavement of African Americans.

We must look at history critically if we are to hope to correct past errors in order that similar mistakes are not repeated. The United States in the throws of its transcontinental expansion was perhaps an unstoppable engine that could not be denied, but the misery and the magnitude of suffering inflicted upon those who inhabited the land for thousands of years before the European colonization was unnecessary and tragic. Laws relating to the sale and acquisition of property simply suckered the Amerindians into a lose-lose situation of misery and destruction. Sometimes the land was taken outright by force or intimidation. The legal system functioned as a disingenuous scheme to take control of the land under the guise of morality. Was pretense the only way to proceed? The United States of America, at least symbolically, represented the advancement of individual freedom and the evolution of free society, and the Amerindian peoples had as much prerogative as any other to be a part of that advancement. A noble use of American power would have acknowledged the moral prerogatives of the Amerindians and jealously protected them, but as it stands America's failure to protect them and the greed in its rush to expansion was a moral failing of enormous magnitude. A system that provided an adequate expanse of territories that simultaneously and proactively encouraged, without coercion, the education and integration of the Amerindians into the new society would have been a vastly superior alternative for both sides. Eventually, the territories would have been largely ceded into the public domain but only after a lengthy process of both reconciliation and the mutual empowerment of both sides. In this methodical process, the preservation of the proud cultural heritage of the Amerindian nations and the integration of their people with the greater society would have been better realized. But what has shamefully occurred, in actuality, is the decimation of the Amerindian cultures and the needless infliction of profound suffering.

There is something tragic and even profane about the proliferation of the casino in what is, in effect, compensation by the United States to Amerindian nations. Weariness of the past is a worthy occupation; the past cannot be undone and may yet haunt the future.

~ *Convergence* ~

The relationship of freedom to convergence is like that of a sailing ship to the currents of the air and sea. The ship will likely get to its destination but it can only ignore the force of the currents at great peril. The ship's captain can navigate but he cannot fight the currents; he must use the sails and rudder to work with the currents and while wind and water currents or weather conditions may force the journey far off its preferred course the ship will most likely reach its destination safely. History carries us ahead and we can no more escape its power than sailing vessels can escape the power of the sea. Convergence = causality + dialectic + free will; the sailing vessel's journey is a metaphor for convergence. The wind and sea currents represent causality, the art of sailing employed by the captain in order to make navigational decisions represents dialectic, and navigational decisions themselves represent free will exercised by the captain or the individual who has the final say. This is not a picture of un-freedom, but there is no absolute freedom. We are free even if freedom is a selection of narrowed choices that have been forced by the circumstances of history. Both the Americans and the Amerindians were swept up in the course of history, but in the case of the Amerindians their choices were largely a matter of how they were to encounter the forces of an overwhelming foe. The Americans, for their part, needed to decide how they were to use the power that history had foisted upon them; for the Americans, there were many choices.

Moral issues were in the minds of many of the Christian settlers and, for them, wresting away control of the land from the Amerindians was a matter of substantial consternation. Dialectically forced issues created a set of divergent choices between fair and just treatment of the indigenous peoples on the one hand and the need or desire to expand Western civilization on the other. The dialectical play of the basic ethical dualisms can be seen: a) *Beneficent* behavior made manifest in duties, obligations or, at least, responsibilities towards the Amerindians, a mission to convert them to Christianity, and making best use of the newly discovered lands; b) *Compassion* for both the struggles of the settlers who were blazing the trail of a new nation as well as for the indigenous peoples; c) *Fairness* with respect to Amerindian nations who only wanted to maintain a way of life that had existed from time immemorial. The confused entanglement of ethics and law combined with greed resulted in unnecessary tragedy. Better decisions could have been made, and it was a tragedy of enormous proportions that the Amerindians were in large part deprived of the opportunity to fully participate in the unfolding of history. The treatment of the Amerindians was a moral failure. Viewed from the perspective of moral coherency and of how far from moral equipoise was the calamitous treatment of the indigenous peoples, a far more coherent outcome may well have been possible—as remarked previously, that would have cultivated peaceful co-existence, mutually beneficial relationships, and a non-violent or at least less violent path to peaceful integration.

The indigenous cultures were owed the opportunity to thrive much as immigrant cultures have thrived while also assimilating, in varying degrees, with the greater society and culture. As much as pluralism and the encouragement of cultural diversity is a fundamental principle for a free society, the opportunity to freely assimilate is equally fundamental. The U.S Supreme Court decision in *Wisconsin v. Yoder* (1972), in very different circumstances, is another example of the obstruction of just opportunities for the assimilation of subgroup members. The Court ruled in favor of Amish parents who chose to keep their teenage children out of public high school. The survival of subgroups in a democratic society is important, but are children little more than rubber stamped articles that come off the assembly line with their destinies sealed? It was argued in expert testimony that universal compulsory high school attendance for the Amish would "ultimately result in the destruction of the Old Order Amish church community as it exists in the United States today."[39] While religious orders and other cultural subgroups lose members to assimilation, should they on that account be immune from challenges that affect all groups in the greater society? Is the United States comparable to a museum curator or a protector of endangered species in its preservation of the viability of cultural subgroups? The interest of a free society is not the protection of cultural subgroups *per se,* but rather in protecting the rights of individuals to determine the course of their own lives so that they may freely choose to remain within a subgroup or leave. This point is all the more clear in Justice William O. Douglas' dissenting opinion in which he voiced the view that, at the very least, the teenage children involved should have had the right to express their views. Rights for social subgroups derive from the individuals who comprise them, and the spectacle of the state sacrificing an individual's well-being to the interests of a subgroup of which he is a member is incoherent. The moral standing of a group is grounded on the collective will of its individual members and, in the long run, it is from individual citizens that groups derive ethical standing, not the reverse. There is no sense protecting a group if by so doing it endangers the rights of its individual members. Vibrant cultural diversity is, surely, a source of great social empowerment, but *artificially* maintaining group divisions can subject group members to a personal destiny underserved.

The United States fought in Vietnam to save Southeast Asia from Communism but today Vietnam has a growing capitalistic economy that, as in China, is mixed with a Communist political system with its Big Brotherism perhaps slightly moderated. If the increasing convergence of modern Vietnam were to have been foreseen by the architects of the Vietnam War and the sheep herd that followed them, would there have been sufficient support in the electorate for the prolonged prosecution of the war? The elements of morality cannot be buried by a dictatorship forever and the moral sense can be blurred for only so long. Free markets give way to freer spirits, people desire wealth and they desire to be happy, and pressure against economic repression inevitably builds after the people have tasted political freedom. Freedom can be thwarted and stalled for many generations, but misdirections by opiates of religious and political dogmatism that brainwash the miserable into believing that they are truly happy is eventually overcome. While the eventual destruction of humanity by a despot is a possibility, such a scenario would spell defeat for the despot as much as for the foes of despotism. A world made smaller by communication and technology makes the erasure of despotism increasingly imaginable; unfortunately, this happy image is offset by the equally imaginable destruction of civilization by weapons of mass destruction falling into the hands of ideologically or religiously addicted extremists, or by sloppy and morally incoherent actions of a "civilized" power.

The convergence in moral behaviors and political systems suggests certain similarities with biological evolution. Morality tolerates much diversity within the streams of convergence. There is an enormous diversity of life on earth but, by virtue of evolution, there are underlying principles and similarities. Even Spencer's "survival of the fittest" may be interpreted humanely on the grounds that ethical convergence much like biological evolution values competition and functional adaptation. However, a Social Darwinism that smiles at human suffering is an incoherent ethics that, in its rejection of the fundamental equality of position between Self and Other, is a condoning of brute force and might makes right and, as with Rand's "virtue of selfishness" it is an amoral ethics and hence, not really ethics. The success of the moral project would be the crowning achievement of evolution: the overcoming of the principle of intrinsic conflict and its replacement with the principle of intrinsic cooperation and love. This idealized evolutionary outcome is, of course, consistent with the claimed goal of many of the world's religions as symbolized by the biblical fantasy of the lion lying down with the lamb.

Convergence in certain respects is not inconsistent with the great themes of philosophy that view the purpose of human life as that of living in harmony with the universe. The problem with doctrines like Stoicism, however, is that the harmony that is preached is a stipulation to conform to a code of ethics that posits a questionable harmonics, i.e. the harmony may be with the code of ethics but not with nature. Stoicism's conservative bent tending towards maintaining the status quo and the acceptance of one's lot in life is clear. If you are a slave, then accept your lot! If you are a noble or man of great wealth, then accept that "burden" as well. Perhaps this is an oversimplification; the high moral calling of Stoicism was not despotic, but most of the classical philosophies of harmony view the social system as the objective basis or standard to which one must accommodate oneself. Hegel's harmony principally entails the acknowledgement of the State as the Absolute expression of World Spirit, and Marx converted Hegel's conservatism into radical Communism that would overthrow the existing order that would eventually lead to peace after the "dictatorship of the proletariat" had its way. In the end, while there is much talk about conforming to higher principles or living in harmony with nature, these aforementioned philosophies are programs to compel individuals to live in accordance with a specific set of doctrines dictated not by nature or by God but by philosophers.

The ancient Chinese philosophy of Taoism provides a different perspective. It contains no rigid doctrine and is, essentially, a *description* of the humility and power lived within the forces of nature called the *Tao* (or "The Way"); in this respect it is consistent with the view espoused herein, that ethics is concerned with realizing overall harmony between the "yin and yang" of moral intentionality and action. Arguably, Taoism is a philosophy of convergence because all things enter into the convergent flow of the Tao. An ethics foundationally based upon ethical rules or preconceptions rather than on descriptions of the elements of morality can be manipulated for inapplicable non-moral reasons for the very basic reason that they *prescribe* rather than *describe*. The meaning of words that are abstracted and carried over from inapplicable situations and contexts parallel the forced application of abstract ethical principles, and Wittgenstein's later work is a model of how understanding is best achieved through description rather than prescription. The moral actuality that is shaped by convergence can only be described. The conundrums of convergence, as exemplified by the historic encounter between the European and Amerindian nations, can only be described in terms of the ethical elements upon which prescriptions may follow but are not preconceived. Harmonic forces, tempered by convergence, retain the non-relativism of the ethical by virtue of the creative genius of loving intention that binds its essence to the moral contour of the situation itself.

The "Serenity Prayer," authored by the theologian Reinhold Niebuhr beautifully captures the ethics and spirit of convergence.

> [God] grant me the serenity to accept the things that I cannot change, the courage to change the things that I can

change, and the wisdom to know the difference.

Causality, expressed as unshakeable physical reality. *Dialectic*, expressed as the possibility of change. And *Free Will*, expressed as decision to act or let be. It is not rational to attempt changes when none is possible, but it is equally irrational to close one's mind to positive change when change is possible: thus resides the delicate balance between "traditional" and "progressive" inclinations. Moral actuality is always convergent but the future is always indeterminate. Serenity can be found in the dialectic of change when actions (or inactions) are weighed in the fullness of one's personal wisdom and faith in oneself. Change can be proactive. The serenity of courage can result in convergent developments being anticipated, and actions proactively mandated by means of a pre-convergent ethics that generates greater freedom. Actions influence the causal chain and sometimes a post-convergent ethics of waiting may unnecessarily eliminate preferable choices leaving the serenity of acceptance as the only "choice" that has become forced by inaction.

~ *Power* ~

It is reasonable to believe that the ethical use of power, because it is used in harmony with human nature, is more powerful than the unethical use of power. The ethical or morally coherent use of power resonates in harmony with man's place in the universe. Unethical uses of power possess degrees of incoherence that by the same ratio reflect broader dissonance and dysfunction.

Dictatorial tyrants repress their populations by capturing control over the political, military and socio-economic machinery of their countries, but the demise of their regimes is inevitable over the long term. True, the long term might last for many generations but over the sweep of history the moral forces are indefatigable while morally incoherent forces are in a perpetual state of dissolution requiring the continuous reinforcement of brute force. Moral coherence tends to strengthen because resonance is generally self-perpetuating, whereas moral incoherence continually weakens from within, ultimately dissolving and disassembling. The wrongful use of power harms those wielding it as much as it does their intended victims. When we consider the ever-increasing power of the ability to destroy, it would seem that our fate is in the balance. It may be cliché to say, but the greatest power in the world is the power of love. Love is the very glue that binds humanity, if not all rational beings together. If loving intention as the guiding force of ethical reasoning were to be rejected and expunged it would be as if gravity slowly began to dissipate until total chaos is restored to its primordial origins. Moral evolution is very different than biological evolution. Biological evolution naturally works in favor of the most physically fit. Human beings, however, are not the most physically fit of animal species. Ants and cockroaches have long preexisted us and will likely outlive us. The key to human survival, however, is not our physical state but our moral state. Human survival is dependent on its moral evolution.

Convergence shapes the massive confluence of causal and dialectical forces that, like an electoral winnowing process, delivers options needing ethical deliberation. An individual deliberating an ethical question will carefully evaluate the basic ethical elements, expose himself to a diversity of perspectives, and will seek consensus while equally exercising courage of conviction. But like a person who has gained significant weight but chooses to avoid the scale, power and freedom are lost if the *power* to decide rightly is evaded. Positive action or inaction is participation in the process of moral convergence. Unlike willow reeds that bend with the wind, formalities, ego and preconditioned thinking can become rigid and inflexible and prevent free thought. Convergence demands both courage to stay the course of tradition and convention, as well the courage to change, rectify and correct incoherencies. Far too frequently, we bow down to the false idols of infallible belief and intractable ideology, and have presumptuously worshiped our particular conceptions of God or bloated egoistic conceptions of ourselves. The greatest power in the world is love, but it is equally vital that we be prepared to accept and use it with both humility and power.

~ *Correction* ~

Are moral corrections merely punishments like those meted out by a judge or jury? Punitive justice may derive some of its merit from an emotional need for retribution to hurt the one who has done the hurting, but from our purely non-legal ethical perspective the only concern is greater moral coherency. Affirmative action programs, established by both legislation and decree, may be ranked among the noblest of laws ever enacted. Minority groups denied equal opportunity for employment, admissions to colleges and universities and denied other civil rights justly deserve compensation.

Affirmative action programs seem to some to be unfair because individuals passed over in favor of minorities were not party to the original injustice. And without viewing affirmative action in terms of convergence, it could well be argued that the affirmative action policies favor abstract group identities more than they do individuals, but such is not the case. Unlike the *Wisconsin v. Yoder* decision, the intent of affirmative action is all about empowerment of individuals. The U.S. Supreme Court did not allow the Amish teenagers a voice in determining their own destiny by failing to avail them of the opportunities of the greater society. *Wisconsin v. Yoder* favored the group over the individual. Affirmative action, in contrast, represents an intervention on behalf of individuals. Justice William O. Douglas precisely states the essence of *Wisconsin v. Yoder* in his dissenting opinion specifically addressing the failure of the Court to solicit the opinions of the children who were kept out of high school:

> The Court's analysis assumes that the only interests at stake
> in the case are those of the Amish parents on the one hand,
> and those of the State on the other. The difficulty with this
> approach is that, despite the Court's claim, the parents
> are seeking to vindicate not only their own free exercise
> claims, but also those of their high-school-age children....
> On this important and vital matter of education, I think
> the children should be entitled to be heard....If a parent
> keeps his child out of school beyond the grade school,
> then the child will be forever barred from entry into the
> new and amazing world of diversity that we have today.
> The child may decide that that is the preferred course, or
> he may rebel. It is the student's judgment, not his parents',
> that is essential if we are to give full meaning to what we
> have said about the Bill of Rights and of the right of
> students to be masters of their own destiny.[40]

In *Wisconsin v. Yoder* the Court dealt with the convergent issues that the case brought to light by favoring an abstraction of group rights over a concern for the concrete rights of individuals. In contrast, despite the rancor that pits whites against blacks and this group against that group, affirmative action policies are designed to protect the rights of individuals who continue to suffer debilitating discrimination based upon racial, ethnic and other group identifications. The Court majority in *Wisconsin v. Yoder* chose to ignore causality and favor instead a particular dialectical line that prioritized a particular group's interests over that of individuals. Causality in the form of dramatic material changes in knowledge and technology was overlooked in order to endorse the idea that group identity supervenes upon individual rights. Affirmative action acknowledges wrongs committed carte blanche against a cultural, ethnic or religious subgroup and seeks to compensate for the wrongdoing; in a sea of convergent forces, it can plant seeds of individual destiny for multitudes that would otherwise be denied. In contrast, the *Yoder* decision demonstrates how acts of social empowerment, e.g. the insistence that every child has the *opportunity to have opportunity* afforded him or her in adulthood, can be effectively stifled by the prioritization of group identity over individual dignity. The only possibility for resisting the overwhelming convergence in favor of individual rights in democratic societies would be something on the order of the curatorship of the Court and a disregard of compassion.

It should not have taken one hundred years following the American Civil War for an affirmative action policy to have been put into effect to help compensate for the wrongs committed against generations of African Americans during slavery and its aftermath. Was a century of dialectical movement and political consensus necessary to create the imperative for political action? The dialectic of emancipation was underway well before the formal abolition of slavery in the United States in 1865, which was then followed by a hundred more years of shameful discrimination. Causal forces in the form of political pressures paralleled dialectical forces culminating in the historic Civil Rights movement in the decades following World War II, the turbulent 60s, and continuing in the present day. Basic progress in human rights would not have been so torturously slow in a genuinely empowered society. A civil rights movement for all must now be ongoing and never-ending. It is a foundation and hope for future peace.

PART II

Reflections

Ruminations

II.1

Clarity

Ethical rules have been devised to create a sort of pseudo verifiability, but ethical reasoning much like factual reasoning ultimately relies on observation, description, consensus and the wisdom of experience. A courtroom jury, for example, assigned the responsibility of deciding guilt or innocence will presumably decide its verdict based upon an examination of the facts aided by the shared wisdom of the panel. Since reliance on fallible rules often fails, many ethical decisions dispense with rules and rely on the moral sense in order to comprehend something deeper and more essential. The essence of ethical decision consists of implicit principles, conceptualized here in the form of the basic ethical dualisms in §I.7. It is necessary to untangle and dissolve the confusions that obscure and distort the implicit principles that are basic to morality. Wittgenstein wrote about how confusions can occur in everyday language when they are applied to very different contexts of philosophical argumentation and reflection, and similarly the basic ethical principles or dualisms are clarified by clearing away the debris of preconceived ethical conception.

Pre-conceptualization can obscure the understanding of moral actuality. Mental clarity requires the clearing of knee-jerk beliefs, fallacious or myopic ideologies and dogmatisms, and other forms of preconditioned hypnotic thinking that are vestiges, shards or debris of other beliefs that are irrelevant or inapplicable to the matter at hand. In the spirit of Nietzsche and of Foucault, there is a genealogy and an archeology of belief and of institutions. And while history has many lessons to teach, lessons can also be questioned, and blind acceptance is not wisdom. Are we mere ideologues incapable of distinguishing intellectualisms when they become divorced from the essence of morality? Social, cultural, religious and political affiliations are of enormous importance because they bind us together and help form the collective consciousness that is the gift of a shared history. But they are, ultimately, secondary ethical considerations. The great diversity of tradition, ways of life and ways of thinking are subordinate to love in terms of both their moral intentionality and effectuality. Our traditions, concepts, institutions and customs are formalities that stand in need of either modification or eradication when they no longer serve our purposes or when it is understood, perhaps, that our purposes were never served.

Attachments to customary ways of thinking and behaving become, in the minds of those so accustomed, ends in themselves. But the only end of morality is that rational action conform itself to the expression of loving intention in myriad and dialogical forms. Much as in the case of freedom, love can be rejected and rejected freely. Ethical expressions are not the only form of rationality, but unethical thinking may be not so much a choice as a product of ethical confusion. It is probably both; love can be rejected and replaced by pure selfishness but it is often the case that moral incoherence may lack bad intent. In the end, dedication to fairness, beneficence and compassion in the dualistic expressiveness of the fundamental Self-Other relationship is the path to ethical empowerment. The basic dualistic elements of fairness, beneficence and compassion are implicit in any ethical deliberation even if they remain unrecognized by the obscurantism of rules and the fog of preconceived notions. A process of dualistic questioning concerning oppositional self-regarding and other-regarding forces checks excessive imbalances that permit the emergence of a greater clarity freed from the blockages of arbitrary preconception and division. Fairness demands the questions, "Am I being fair to the other? Am I being fair to myself?" and if the answers are seriously probed and considered surprising implications and ramifications emerge. The same may be said of the other basic ethical dualisms, "Am I being beneficent to the other? Am I being beneficent to myself? Am I being compassionate to the other? Am I being compassionate to myself?" Clarity precedes empowerment, and empowerment sows seeds of virtue.

A willingness to forgo reliance on preconceived ethical rules and preconceptions does not, as some might suppose, make ethical deliberation easier or simpler, on the contrary, greater complexity may surface absent the artificiality of faux clarity. After all, do not ethical rules exist so that we might not need to think so deeply? There is nothing like pretended clarity to stir great confusion. Clearly, ethical rules and preconceptions are important in the pursuit of ethical clarity, but it is vital that ethical validation be ultimately made in the light of basic ethical principles that express the essence of morality. Morality is not at the beck and call of tradition and pet concepts that have lost their moral coherency. Inevitably, societies and cultures make necessary changes or suffer the consequences of inaction. Over the long term, humanity does not have the option of acquiescing to moral incoherence because doing so would be tantamount to rejecting the basis of its own existence. Most animals cannot choose freedom, but humankind and rational beings can and do. Fulfilling the moral project is love's desire and is, as such, an existential imperative. But the success of the moral project is not possible if the essence of morality is confused by the misdirection and clutter of preconceived thinking.

II.2

Interiority

There are two landscapes of the human mind, its interiority and its exteriority, and while their features are distinct they are also in large measure, respectively, each a product of the other. No clear boundary exists between the interiority and the exteriority, and they are historically intertwined as the interior and exterior minds project shadow images upon each other. Even the natural environment that is part of the landscape of the exteriority has the fears and desires of the interiority projected upon it. And cultural traditions, institutions, conventional behaviors and practices, the law and ethical restrictions, technology, and money also reveal the projection of the interiority upon the exteriority. But the exteriority also reflects itself back onto the interiority. Ethical and social empowerment start with self-motivation, but where does self-motivation begin?

Self-motivation is an essential aspect of the ethical interiority, of individualism, and of free society. Free society is not conceivable without self-motivated individuals living productively and peacefully together. But motivation may be viewed from the different perspectives of the interiority and the exteriority. While internal self-motivation is distinguishable from external sources of motivation the line between them blurs in the framework of the Self-Other duality. Self-motivation has its origins in external forms such as culture or religion or society, but as moral development ensues the external impulses become internalized and increasingly autonomous as it becomes less dependent on external reinforcement. The development of moral desire, i.e. of self-motivated moral behavior, becomes a bulwark of resistance against societal or other external forces that may challenge it. And the tension between the individual self-motivational forces of the interiority and the elaborately formed social motivations of the exteriority is the essence of societal change.

The proposals of radical libertarians and radical socialists are crippled by moral incoherence pertaining to the relationship between the interiority and the exteriority. If an advocate of free markets is blind to fairness and to the need for encouraging individual *and* collective greatness he is morally blinded by dogma. A morally blind economics is worse than absurd. The production of wealth, creativity and productivity are primary goals of any economic system, but if its performance discourages the maximal flourishing of both individuals and society then it ought not be described as successful by the measure of its productivity alone. Ethical deliberations can cut through the formalities of economic dogma. Human flourishing in all its respects is the very aspiration of moral life and should also be the goal of any economic system. Economics ought never be divorced from ethics. The best economy is one that, in addition to being a great producer of wealth and economic security, is also driven by highly self-motivated individuals whose output resonates with good will and purpose.

A system that bases financial decision on financial criteria alone irrespective of ethical criteria also reflects a system that can be as morally incoherent as one that is communistic. A morally coherent economic system encourages, through financial incentive, each individual to strive for his or her individual best along with caring for others. The relationship between the *interiority of the self* and the *exteriority of the self* is an evolving relationship that mirrors the relationship between Self and Other. The interiority is largely dependent at the beginning of life by the nurture and the inspiration stemming from the exteriority, e.g. by familial, social, cultural, educational, political, economic, and other environmental influences. With maturity greater autonomy of the interiority develops, but the inextricability of the Self-Other relationship persists throughout ethical life as each individual develops deep concern for others. Indeed, each good citizen will ask herself what she can do for country and for humanity, but an expectation that your country and the greater world community will offer a helping hand is a vision of a an ethics that proudly empowers both the individual and society. The human spirit needs tending regardless of whether the tending is by the Self to the Self, the Self to the Other, or the Other to the Self.

II.3

Exteriority

Basic needs comprise a central part of the human exteriority. Are basic needs things that ought to be earned? To be sure, there is a risk that the universal provision of basic needs could be disempowering by encouraging a culture to be content with a life of mere subsistence and mediocrity. But is fear of starvation a stimulus to success or greatness? The question entertained here is: Would expanding and broadening the concept of basic needs encourage or discourage accomplishment and greatness?

A perspective of basic needs as objects of achievement may not be the best strategy. Some individuals oppose the societal provision of basic needs because they have themselves worked hard to provide food, shelter and security for their families, and they expect others to do the same. This point of view reduces to a "survival of the fittest" principle that is premised on the belief that basic needs for survival should be earned. However, when basic needs are provided the energy expended on pure survival could theoretically be used for higher forms of achievement. Which is more ethically empowering, a) A dog eat dog or survival of the fittest mentality that compares human survival to animal survival in the jungle? or b) a mentality built upon the premise that human creativity, inventiveness and productivity can be jumpstarted at a higher level of consciousness than that of the lowest common denominator of survival?

It is incontrovertible that the burden of basic subsistence has often been a critical barrier that has prevented great achievement by creative and original talents who never manage to "get over the hump" of basic financial security. The burden of attaining basic needs in these cases can be ethically disempowering by its thwarting of advancement in broad areas of personal development. How many great writers, artists, and industrial geniuses have failed to reach their potential because of society's regressive insistence that you must prove that you can earn a loaf of bread? And is it fair or just that the fortunate offspring of the affluent have never had to face the same challenges? Oh! How the world has suffered from lost opportunities of individual greatness! The principle behind Spencerian survival of the fittest arguments is that they allow the cream to rise to the top so that, ultimately, human societies and the human species as a whole advance. However, if a society can overcome barriers preventing individuals from reaching their full potential so that their energy is redirected towards achievement rather than mere survival, then the struggle will be transformed from one of survival to one of flourishing. If basic needs were to serve the function of both survival and accomplishment, then a foundation of basic needs will be laid in the exteriority that is consistent with an empowerment ethics of Self and Other.

From the moment of a human being's birth there begins a structuring of the relationship between Self and Other. The relationship is closely connected to the development of the interiority and the exteriority. The interiority of the Self consists of habits, beliefs, thought patterns, expectations, fears and more. The exteriority of the Self—which includes the relationship with others—consists of culture, society, religion, markets, politics and institutions. The interchange and the relationship between the interiority and the exteriority is one of partnership and equality. Quibbling over which of the two is more significant or critical for human development is a senseless argument that misses the essential point that the interior and exterior features of the Self are an inseparable interrelationship in which each decisively impacts the other.

II.4

Dogmatic Slumberings

Hypnotic trances don't last a lifetime, but belief systems and dogma can. The continuous reinforcement of formality and traditional beliefs function as posthypnotic suggestions that misdirect and obstruct critical examination, while blinder-like focus and absorption exclude or block challenges to doctrine.

Immanuel Kant was one of the greatest philosophers, but even geniuses can be entranced by their own beliefs. Brilliant thinkers may be even more susceptible than others because the vividness of their ideas can powerfully engross their minds with hypnotic-like absorption. Kant wrote that his rationalist oriented philosophical positions were "awakened from his dogmatic slumber" after reading some of the work of David Hume. For Hume, human consciousness is "nothing but a bundle or collection of different perceptions," and human understanding of cause and effect in nature permits no "necessary connections" but only the laws of non-binding probability and their intrinsic element of uncertainty and un-necessity. The rationalist school of Kant's "pre-awakening" period is nearly diametrically opposed to Hume's radical empiricism. Kant was humbled by his realization of the essential truth of much of Hume's argumentation.

Awakening from the slumberings of belief, however, can lead to a sober period of synthesis. Chuang Tzu said, "Only after we are awake do we know we have dreamed."[41] But then what? The great Taoist philosopher suggested that life is itself a dream, and Kant's metaphorical awakening from his dogmatic slumber does not dismiss the possibility that he was merely awakening into a new slumber and a new a dream. How can we be certain that we will not awaken again and again to an unending string of new actualities? Awakenings are opportunities that can provide rare insight into new actualities that can lead to further questioning. They, in turn, can become the first step toward the creation of other actualities and paradigms that, eventually, may themselves become the next prolonged period of slumber. Philosophically, however, the question may not be of practical importance because whether slumbering or dreaming, philosophers need always to keep asking questions!

Kant's awakening led him to glimpse dual realities of the mind and of the physical world that helped to create new paradigms for philosophy in epistemology, ethics and metaphysics and the philosophy of science. His conception of a structured mind that provides form to all perception and experience broadly foreshadowed Freud, Jung and even neuroscience while providing for science the conception of a firm foundation in natural law that, for some, Hume appeared to threaten. Kant's awakening was an awakening for philosophy that influenced a multitude of philosophical movements and philosophies up to the present day. German Idealism, Hegel, Schopenhauer, Nietzsche, existentialism, essentially all of Continental philosophy and, indeed, all subsequent western philosophy could be viewed as both commentaries as well as reactions to Kant's work. His work exhibits a strong tension between formal certainties and the purity of uncertainty, between pure freedom and rigid conformance to moral law. Philosophical positions as disparate as Hegel's absolutism and the rejection of all absolute categories by Nietzsche, and some existentialists, may all be viewed as part of Kant's legacy.

It is good to dream, but philosophy should accustom itself to short naps rather than long slumbers. A book that is principally a work of philosophy possesses the liberty of making audacious and even preposterous proposals. After all, it is only philosophy, some would like to say. But audacious proposals can be taken seriously and you, dear reader, have the liberty to dream or awaken or do both if, indeed, they are not the same. Allow your dreams or awakenings to see beyond the paradigms and the existing actualities. Are not dreamers also the awakened ones?

II.5

Madness and Wisdom

Michel Foucault associates some thinkers and artists with "madness" or "unreason." The connection with the broader history of the institutionalization of the insane with works of great and sometimes troubled artists seems unclear; perhaps it is forced but by so doing Foucault finds meaning in "unreason" particularly when it later emerges as a worthy challenge to convention. Is the mad genius truly mad, and at what point may the conventional wisdom itself become a collective madness?

> The simplest and most general definition we can give
> of classical madness is indeed *delirium*: "This word
> is derived from *lira*, a furrow; so that *deliro* actually
> means to move out of the furrow, away from the proper
> path of reason."[42]

But it not infrequently occurs that "the proper path of reason," i.e. the conventional wisdom, is closed to truths discovered by delirious thinkers who have broken ranks with the old order. Is not the path of reason more like a fluctuating maze than a neatly dug out furrow? Foucault suggests that brilliant thinkers and artists such as Nietzsche need to slip into the world of insanity in order that the world at large might come around to embrace new perspectives. But he concludes that, "nothing in itself, especially not what it can know of madness, assures the world that it is justified by such works of madness."[43]

Perhaps intellectual madness is suggestive of a messiah complex in which one's own sanity is sacrificed for the sake of wisdom. However, before we get too carried away with the connection of madness and wisdom we should keep in mind the reality that a belief that you are the Messiah is not its own justification. It would seem that psychiatric madness or insanity is rarely if ever the necessary prelude for an authentic awakening or, at least, the fact that some thinkers may have lived in a state of severe "madness" does not necessarily mean that it was the necessary ingredient for their creative productivity.

The roots of madness may not always reside in strange or novel fantasies and delusions that seem to spring from the unconscious. Obsessions with misguided but conventional beliefs that are closed to review and reexamination are also forms of madness. Ideological and extremist views that wallow in the morass of moral incoherence are certainly mad and certainly insane even if they don't appear as such to an immoralist. What does someone who rejects morality, rejects love and rejects all things other than self-aggrandizement know about reason? Is there any greater exemplification of profound unreason than the rejection of that very quality—moral intentionality, which drives higher reason? Without moral intention reason is driverless, and the non-rational passions then fill the vacuum and take over control of the ship. It is the moral dialectic combined with the play of reason that instills the courage to make dreams possible, and sometimes those dreams are the dreams of "madmen."

Following the path for ethical and social empowerment requires that one be as adept in breaking free of convention as in conforming to it. An ethical conclusion may require staying true to convention, but on other occasions some "madness" may help to break old molds when circumstances have made them indefensible. A "madman" can be as completely absorbed by fantasies of changelessness as by fantasies of change. We ought not fear morality's adaptations, accommodations and convergent expressions but we also ought not fear conformity when the coherent expression of moral actuality may in some cases require nothing more than staying the familiar course. But while ethics certainly requires staying on the path of reason, the path is not always a furrow but can, at times, be a wildly winding and unpredictable path that requires 'deliro,' i.e. a movement out of the path in a necessary quantum leap that preserves both moral coherency and sanity.

The conventionality or unconventionality of wisdom requires a comprehension of many perspectives of change and resistance to change. A commonality of conventional and unconventional wisdom is the need for adaptation within the moral context. Change or the maintenance of convention requires continuous reframing! But insidious ulterior and incoherent motivations—of both conscious and subconscious origin, seek to compromise and challenge the underlying moral unity and are marks of an angry and uninspired madness.

II.6

Reframing of All Values

William James wrote that we are all "extreme conservatives" resistant to change and loyal to our preexisting beliefs. The resolution of the intellectual standstill comes when a new idea or perspective can be "graft upon the ancient stock with minimum disturbance."

> The most violent revolutions in an individual's beliefs leave most of his old order standing...I...urge you to observe particularly...the part played by the older truths...Loyalty to them is the first principle—in most cases it is the only principle; for by far the most usual way of handling phenomena so novel that they would make for a serious rearrangement of our preconceptions is to ignore them altogether, or abuse those who bear witness for them.[44]

When an idea becomes *preferable* change is sure to follow. The pragmatic principle is that ideas or beliefs or values don't matter much when a superior alternative comes along, and James' observation that intellectual courtesy for old beliefs facilitates modest change anticipates the "life reframing" technique pioneered by the great psychiatrist and hypnotherapist, Milton Erickson. The technique facilitates behavioral change by enabling *both* acceptance of the existing behavior at the same time that it is reinterpreted or *reframed* into a different perspective. Erickson's concept contains the insight that patients in psychotherapy want some form of validation for their behavior but also have a need to see their situation from a new perspective. Reframing the issue accomplishes a transformation by preserving something of the past thereby facilitating preferable outcomes and positive change.[45]

Reframing can play a significant role in bridging the ubiquitous schism between abstract and concrete values by means of detachment and reunification. Initially, the schism broadens and deepens because the contradiction between values in the abstract and values in the concrete is shown by myriad applied and misapplied abstractions that may reflect varying degrees of incoherence. We cannot trans-value these abstractions because doing so would be like attempting to redefine the color red. However, we *can* reframe them. And the reframing of values is possible by detaching from egoistic abstractions that create artificial conflict, and reunification with the deeper essence of the moral actuality as it applies to the uniqueness of the situation. Thus, in the reframing of values, old abstractions are retained but find a home in new and better applications and solutions.

Nietzsche, in his argument for a "revaluation of all values," recognizes the severe limitations of abstract values and their impotency in establishing a workable basis or complete framework for ethical reasoning. However, his answer was not in finding the concrete forms of abstract concepts but, rather, in the concrete or base instincts of egoistic self-interest.

> ...what is unegoistic is everywhere assigned absolute
> value while what is egoistic is met with hostility. [46]

> To choose what is harmful to *oneself*, to be *attracted*
> by 'disinterested' motives, almost constitutes the formula
> for *decadence*...Disgregation of the instincts!
> —Man is finished when he becomes altruistic. [47]

But even Nietzsche seems to have been aware of the extreme incoherence of these views. The self-regarding instincts that bring benefit and power to an individual are not incompatible with other-regarding instincts such as kindness or compassion. Rational individuals possess both types of instinct in abundance and, while the process of reconciliation may be a struggle, they nonetheless find ways of balancing them out. The reconciliation need not be that of one instinct driving the other into submission. Self-aggrandizement and self-interestedness are not incompatible with selflessness and altruism. The altruist is not inconsistent when she helps herself or promotes her self-interest. The self-promoter or opportunity seeker is not inconsistent when he gives of himself selflessly. And Nietzsche acknowledges the possibility, even the likelihood, of a deeper essence of morality in this passage from *Beyond Good and Evil*:

> For all the value that the true, the truthful, the selfless
> may deserve, it would still be possible that a higher
> and more fundamental value for life might have to
> be ascribed to deception, selfishness, and lust. It might
> even be possible that what constitutes the value of these
> good and revered things is precisely that they are
> insidiously related, tied to, and involved with these
> wicked, seemingly opposite things—maybe even one
> with them in essence.[48]

Selfishly motivated actions are intrinsically morally incoherent because they are done with disregard for the welfare of others. But self-interested actions can also reflect a highly ethical path. For example, depending upon the situation, an individual's action can be altruistic to another while also being kind and beneficent to oneself because under the harmonic moral umbrella what is rightly beneficent and fair is beneficent and fair for all.

It is understandable how Nietzsche and more myopic thinkers such as Rand would blast altruism because it is a fact that "love thy neighbor" has been far more the center of focus in most ethical theories than has "love thyself." The connotation of the word 'morality' is loaded far more in favor of the other-regarding aspects of the Self-Other duality. The great attraction of works such as Rand's *Atlas Shrugged*, and to some extent in Nietzsche's work as well, is their audacious celebration of individual strength. Ethics needs to be *reframed* so that self-flourishing is placed side-by-side with collective flourishing and together form the core of ethical reasoning. The strongest society is one that is comprised of strong individuals, and is one that recognizes that there are many paths to greatness that include the College of Hard Knocks along with esteemed institutions of higher learning; this is the attitude of a culture that nurtures strong individuals without prejudice! And the great individual who benefits from the smart and shrewd policies of a beneficent society will in turn benefit that society equally as much as another great achiever who is a "self-made" man or woman, or who has benefited from support by family or other private parties. A strong society is not a "nanny state" any more than parents are guilty of coddling when they do everything they can to help their children. But parents are neglectful when they do not provide what is within their means to encourage and facilitate the development of their children. The reframing of all values does not idealize the individual or the state but sees their mutual flourishing as an organic unity of the whole.

How many wars have been fought between enemies who espouse principles of freedom while each side accuses the other of being freedom's greatest threat? Justice, honor, privacy, to name a few, are examples of abstract values that are endorsed by virtually everyone but, in their concrete expressions, are often greeted with great discord. If priority were to be given to the expression of concrete value over *merely* abstract value the eradication of much conflict becomes possible! The reframing of abstract, idealized values would leapfrog over unnecessary dogmatisms and ideologies that are distortions of the concrete continuum that is the relationship between Self and Other.

The reframing of values is the culmination of deep moral processing. Our values are precious not because they are autonomous constructions that derive their meaning and beauty from nothing but themselves. Do such things even exist? If that were the case, there would be no schism between abstract and concrete values because their coherency would never waver. Each abstract value would fit together like pieces in a jigsaw puzzle. But values are far from being cookie cutouts. Rather, values are changing formations that like beautiful crystals are a diverse expression of transcendent beauty.

II.7

Ethicalities

The promise is the foundation of civilization! It is the basis of friendship, marriage, business dealings and documented promises otherwise known as legal contracts. Extenuating circumstances may legitimately circumvent a promise but, these conditions aside, human relationships depend upon assurances that promises will be honored. Breaking promises are not infrequently quite cavalier, such as the case in which a promise that a good word on behalf of a job applicant would be passed along to a potential employer or a person of significance, but then the promise isn't kept because it was said lightly or not very seriously and became all too forgettable. But to the person to whom the promise was made it may have been a promise of hope that was denied. Are these broken promises small ethicalities? Perhaps so, but small ethicalities can become compounded and turn into patterns. A book is borrowed from a friend or acquaintance but is never returned: no big deal. Patients just don't show up at the doctor's office; "no shows" have become a modern plague of inconsideration and, often, reflect the low self-esteem of the frivolous no show or promise-breaker. Apparently, promises are cheap, like the broken promises that are made to oneself that are part of the epidemic of low self-esteem that is spreading like a virus and infecting the collective psyche.

~   ~   ~

A vital organization requires the resilience and the spirit of high self-esteem in which individual initiative ensures that policy is not blindly applied. Surely everyone has dealt with the ubiquitous customer service representative who listens to your problem, presumably enters the complaint on a form and then fails to follow thorough; but contrast the other type of employee who is proactive, takes charge and intervenes to make sure that his or her high self-esteem rubs off on the organization. I remember two or three years ago I was parking my car in front of my office and there was much snowplow activity digging out after a big storm and certain areas had temporary "No Parking" signs posted. I spotted a nearby police officer and he assured me in no uncertain terms that I could park in a particular area. And so I did, but sure enough, I was ticketed. There was going to be no point, I felt sure, in fighting city hall, but much to my pleasure an explanation over the phone to a city hall clerk was all that was needed to clear up the matter and get the ticket nullified. The clerk could easily have dismissed my accusation and routinely instructed me to contest the ticket, but by using her good sense she could discern that an error had been made and so she took the initiative and voided the ticket. This city worker has, no doubt, long forgotten this uneventful incident; it is the nature of virtue that rightful conduct is mindful and second nature.

~   ~   ~

The police officer is the most ubiquitous of public servants. The officer is on call, risking his or her life and safety in order to protect the citizenry from criminals who care nothing of others. And the police officer is the most ubiquitous symbol of the power of the state over the individual and, therefore, has a solemn responsibility to dispatch his public duties with dignity and respect. While the confrontation of violent activity does not leave much time for etiquette, the respectful and courteous behavior by police officers during ordinary interactions is an important symbol of civility and humility. Unfortunately, some cops seem to be only interested in letting you know who is boss. I remember once I was pulled over by an officer who noticed that the registration decal on my license plate had expired. I was unaware that the plate had expired! As the officer wrote me a ticket he let me know in a rather harsh tone that he could have me thrown in jail on the spot! Should I have thanked him for not throwing me into the slammer? The officer's warning could have been stated in a manner that would have gotten the point across without brutish behavior backed by the power of the state. An insecure cop's undignified demeanor affronted the dignity of his position. The noble exercise of power is a duty, and a police officer is a microcosm of power.

~ ~ ~

Exam cheating combines characteristics of theft and false representation. It falsely advertises academic performance and maliciously deflates the value of academic currency by counterfeiting grade value. And a counterfeiter of money may feel no ethical concerns with what he does because he cares little if he undermines the financial system and, by extension, the entire foundation of valuation. The destruction of monetary value in the economic sphere spills over into moral value in the ethical sphere: worthlessness propagates and begets more worthlessness. The reverse is also true as an authentic basis for moral valuation builds self-esteem and self-worth in the social and economic spheres. The interiority and the exteriority mutually project self-worth onto each other. But decadent behaviors such as exam cheating create decay in both the exteriority and the interiority; they are reciprocal and compounding.

~ ~ ~

Legally justified actions can be ethically wrong. There are few principles of decision weaker or more inane than "If it is legal it is right." Regulations that allow the use of construction materials that a builder believes to be inferior or unsafe do not ethically justify their use. Doing what the law allows can be a serious wrong. The overuse of certain pharmaceuticals is a prime example of ethically unjustifiable behavior that is legally acceptable. At least since the 1970s when the holistic and natural health movement began to build momentum, the use of vitamins and other supplements, and the role of fruits and vegetables (especially organic) in preventing disease and, in some cases, helping to cure them were disparaged by the medical gurus of the day as a waste of money. Today the aggressive commercial promotion of pharmaceuticals despite recognition of their extreme over-reliance and overuse is literally *sickening*. It's a world turned upside down when it comes to pharmaceuticals. Pharmaceuticals can unquestionably save lives, extend life and cure, but their exclusive use and the failure to use alternative natural remedies as a first resort—rather than, as most typically, ignored completely—is justifiable by principles of profit, but not necessarily by principles of wellness. The health of the economy is the other victim of the raging pharmaceutical madness. Over-reliance on pharmaceuticals kills as many people as do illegal street drugs, but fortunately, alternatives to the Big Pharma monopoly continue to emerge.

~   ~   ~

We would be well advised to examine our intergenerational relations. In the West we sometimes overlook our innate responsibilities and obligations to senior generations. Young people today in the United States are concerned that Social Security benefits will be exhausted by the time that they reach old age, and it is as much a responsibility for each generation to be a good steward for generations that follow them as for generations that precede them. It is a moral imperative that we look after each other. The Social Security system is a system that is broken and must be fixed. Radical solutions will be necessary. However, the solution need not and should not be exclusively governmental. Consider pension programs for professional athletes and entertainers (actors, musicians, and others). In these professions, workers commonly risk poverty while the relative few who are successful attain heights of phenomenal financial success. Many members of past generations who helped to build lucrative professional industries live in or near poverty. Should not professionals who have benefited so greatly from the struggles of the pioneers who preceded them have an ethical obligation to lessen the financial burden of those to whom they are indebted? Do not the pioneers who now suffer *deserve* to be rewarded? The expression of caring and gratitude would be fair and just. There are many vocational groups that could invest in the security of their fellows after they reach retirement age. It is reasonable and fair that the most lucrative professions should reward their predecessors most lucratively. In summation, in addition to resolving the basic problem of universal governmental retirement income for retirees each guild, trade or career association should look after their extended families. The showing of genuine respect may involve more than the utterance of platitudes.

~   ~   ~

Nikola Tesla was a great scientist and inventor who, while largely unknown in the popular pantheon of scientific greats possessed a genius that was probably on a par with that of Einstein. But Tesla also exemplified how being too good, too kind, too generous and too trusting can be self-destructive. In Tesla's case, his good-natured and trusting character did incalculable harm to civilization and social progress, not to mention his own career. Among Tesla's many revolutionary achievements was his invention of the Tesla Polyphase System of alternating current (AC) generation that today provides virtually all of the world's electricity.

George Westinghouse recognized the enormous potential of Tesla's breakthrough. In 1888, Westinghouse and Tesla entered into a contract that was to earn for Tesla $2.50 per horsepower of electricity sold. Tesla positioned himself to be become an extremely wealthy man, however, cutthroat tactics by J.P. Morgan's companies put extreme pressure on Westinghouse that ultimately forced him to ask Tesla to terminate his lucrative contract; with amazing grace or stupendous foolhardiness he agreed. He expressed to Westinghouse his profound loyalty and indebtedness for his past support; and then Tesla tore up the contract! According to the 1897 annual report of the Westinghouse Company, Tesla was paid $216,000 in lieu of the royalties that had been promised him in his contract *and* to cover the purchase of pertinent patents.[49]

Unfortunately, Tesla's kindness and generosity, unlike his penetrating scientific insight and technical ingenuity, were not employed as virtues. His willingness to renegotiate his contract with Westinghouse was understandable given the dire consequences of maintaining the status quo, but surely he could have renegotiated far more favorable terms. Certainly, an agreement could have been reached to reduce the royalty payments or to even temporarily suspend them pending a business turnaround, which would have occurred once Morgan's turpitude was beaten back. Many fair and just alternative arrangements could have been reached. But Tesla was too good, which is to say he was not good at all in taking care of himself. His self-abnegation was a serious unethicality committed against himself. Henceforward and for the remainder of his life a lack of funding would plague Tesla, and some believe that many of his astounding and still mystifying achievements have been suppressed. Tesla's ill-advised and unnecessary generosity towards Westinghouse thwarted enormous scientific and technological progress and, in light of the mysterious disappearance of many of Tesla's papers, it is arguable that the development of powerful alternative technologies continues to be impeded.

Tesla was an incredibly generous man while, on the other hand, it has been reported that Edison cheated Tesla out of $50,000 that was owed him.[50] Tesla had the heart of a saint, while Edison—if allegations are true that, at his behest, dogs and cats were stolen and electrocuted so as to arouse the public's fear of AC—may have had the heart of a dog-fighting promoter. The dualistic nature of morality is crystal clear when comparing these two men. Self-regarding desire and other-regarding desire must balance and check the excesses of the other, and the rejection of either is a cavernous flaw.

~   ~   ~

An institution reflects flaws in human nature because they enforce a necessary corrective. But the goal for any institution, at least theoretically, is that the training wheels be removed, i.e. that the institution should be ultimately dissolved when a wiser, more mature society and culture no longer requires it. Good institutions can outlast their good, and in some cases their ultimate dissolution is the surest marker of their success. This is mostly a dream, but not entirely, because we probably have too many institutions or we may be on the cusp of needing fewer of them.

~   ~   ~

The continued existence of world hunger is proof of how far we have yet to go. The volume of misery on account of the world's unnecessary starvation boggles the mind and challenges the will. The excuses, the rationalizations and disharmonic institutionalizations constitute an ethical disempowerment in the face of grotesque moral incoherence. The continuation and perpetuation of world hunger is a sure path to moral implosion. Nation-states that permit or cannot stop such wanton misery represent a cumulative perpetration of moral crime or crimes of incompetence. World hunger is the paradigm of blindness to the principle of beneficence. When it comes to world hunger, incompetency is the near equivalent of malevolence; they are equally inexcusable, and the urgency seems to make the distinction between intentionality and effectuality vanish. The time has arrived for discarding formalities that pathetically excuse the insufficiency of compassion needed to create political and distributive mechanisms to end world hunger.

II.8

Mindfulness

Mindfulness is the conscious and subconscious awareness of virtue and that which is not virtue. Children are taught to "Always say thank you" when they are shown acts of consideration or kindness, and to do so without pause or hesitation. But adult life is far more complicated, and fusing ethical thought and action do not always come so easily and seamlessly. Virtue is a product of wisdom. The *Tao te Ching* is a treasure trove of wisdom, but I do not fully agree with Lao-tzu's conception of virtue. Lao-tzu suggests that virtue is always a form of non-thinking, and that the self-consciousness of trying to purposefully act in accordance with virtue is in and of itself not virtue. (§I.1) Virtue for Lao-tzu is a stage of wisdom that is akin to a high state of *being* more than of knowing. If only the Taoist Sage were a realizable dream of an achievable state of all-unknowingness—by *not* knowing and by surrendering to the Tao—then simple being would be the highest attainable self-realization. But does not the mentality of ethical deliberation as exemplified by Aristotle and Western philosophy also have a role? For Lao-tzu deliberative paths to virtuous action are intrinsically inferior to Taoist virtue. But is not deliberative and analytical ethics also part of the Tao? Mindfulness and the realization of virtue require deliberation and conscious thought as much as it reflects the spontaneity of action earned by experience or ingrained in one's character.

Mindfulness involves embracing formalities and old beliefs as much as it does rejecting them. A lack of mindfulness can be characterized by bad habits that get in the way of mindful thought and behavior. "I have always done it this way and thought this way and I will always do so" is the motto of tired old minds that no longer care or have never cared much about thinking. But mindfulness is awareness of the moral center that frees the mind from an over-reliance and over-dependency on habits of thought or, at least, provides the confidence for discarding or amending them when necessary. The dilemmas of both individual and collective life largely concern the struggle of determining when to conform to a formality and when to break away and separate. In order to achieve a state of mindfulness, the moral center must always be as ready to accept convention as to embark on an alternative path.

Be mindful of trances; do not confuse awakening from a trance with truth or the awareness of truth. Be satisfied in knowing that you have been given a new perspective. Escaping from unexamined, preconceived beliefs is not so much like awakening from sleep as it is staying awake and realizing that your work is unfinished.

Mindfulness demands the courage and toughness to follow through, but not on preconceived conviction but on deep ethical deliberation that can bolster the ego as well as cut it down to size. But in the end, the self expands in accordance not to its self-aggrandizement but to its moral authenticity. An expansive self does not require a big ego.

It would be a highly dangerous state of mind to lose all sense of self-consciousness and self-interestedness because it can easily morph itself into a sense of grandiosity and infallibility. All of the great mystical traditions pose this risk. The very notion of the direct intuition or understanding of Truth or Divine Will, by its nature, runs the risk of too much certainty, and too much certainty is far more dangerous than too much doubt. The rational mind requires constant checks and balances, and even an oversized ego is better than the total abandonment of ego because, at least, a meal of humble pie is a corrective always waiting to be served. But when the wise man or guru or spiritual sage is so wise that a pretense forms that s/he knows everything because s/he feigns to know nothing, then *nothing* can humble the wise man. In truth, most spiritual teachers are gentle, humble and wise but there is always a concern that students of egoless ego will drift into dogma. The one genuine absolute truth is that there are no absolutes and thus human beings are fallible and imperfect. "If you meet the Buddha kill him"; but this koan is especially practical and starkly true if you meet a guru or Kabbalistic rabbi or other priestly master who wants a piece of your net worth not to mention your soul. Of course, don't kill, but by all means, run for the hills!

Inaction can be as consequential as action, and action can be as inconsequential as inaction. The law of karma, if this metaphysic exists, is as much a record of actions as of inactions. Consider that simple acts of kindness or failures in performing them may be mere products of habit. Certainly, the act of kindness is mindful and its omission is not. However, can a robotic, preconditioned act of kindness be mindful if it is only a facade devoid of feeling and, essentially, performed *mindlessly*. Perhaps what matters is that an act is indeed performed because, after all, the act is all that matters to the recipient of kindness. But what if on subsequent occasions a dearth of compassion stymies rightful action or suffocates the inspiration for ethical inquiry? Accordingly, it would seem that mindfulness concerns everything that enters into ethical decisions of action or inaction, including their intentionality and emotion. But, speaking personally, when I reflect upon my life it seems that I regret most the actions not taken. Actions taken are easier to rationalize.

II.9

Courage

Courage and bravery should always imply *moral* courage. Risking one's life in the performance of a heinous act can hardly be called virtuous, hence it is not an exemplification of courage. The 9/11 hijackers certainly gave their lives in carrying out heinous crimes but it would be wrongheaded for anyone who considers their acts to be villainous to also consider them to be acts of courage. We simply would not describe someone who dies in the process of building a bomb intended to blow up a train as having died courageously. Rather, we would most likely describe the explosion as a product of hatred that ultimately consumed the perpetrator. Acts of hatred are not courageous. There are deranged or misguided or confused acts performed without regard to one's own safety, but those qualities hardly possess the virtue of courage. Courage is a virtue and, as such, it is a harmonic act of ethical intention and action. If 'courage' is a moral predicate, then it is incorrect to *knowingly* use the term to denote an act done with bad intention or without moral purpose. "My dear, this diamond necklace is such a lovely gift!" But if the gift was acquired by means of burglary and at gunpoint there is nothing lovely about it. Discounting intentionality in the use of approbatory language is done at a cost. Accordingly, the use of 'courage' is here presupposed to be an affirmative ethical usage, which like any ethical affirmation may be arguable on ethical grounds.

"Toe the party line!" "Stay true to your own opinions!" "Don't waver!" "Don't rock the boat!" While toeing the party line may require considerable toughness it does not necessarily involve *moral toughness*, and courage always involves moral toughness. By 'moral toughness' I refer to the intellectual courage that often involves discarding formerly held beliefs in favor of new ones, or holding on to old beliefs but in the light of ethical conviction that is more than knee-jerk formality. Moral toughness requires flexibility, openness and receptivity to new ideas as much as possessing the capacity to hold onto old beliefs. Merely standing behind your party or standing up for your beliefs, or coming forward in favor of change are not acts of courage if they are done without self-examination and justification of motive and potential consequences. Each new belief is in the process of becoming old from the moment of its adoption, and so ethical judgments are always subject to reexamination and of weighing in on the opinions of others. True courage reflects wholehearted decision and action that incorporates genuine ethical reflection. Certainly, the virtue of heroism may require spontaneous action when a moment's delay could be catastrophic. But if there is time to reflect about the rightness of an action, would-be heroes are not exempt.

Blind allegiance to group identities or to a herd mentality, while not intrinsically wrong, is fertile ground for individual weakness. Contrary to Nietzsche's view that democracy is "only a form of decay, namely the diminution, of man, making him mediocre and lowering his value,"[51] democracy also has the potential to produce *both* the greatest and most morally tough individuals. Popular culture is not intrinsically shallow, but it often is. Radical and impulsive swings in popular culture can be an influence that retards and stymies the intellectual and moral development of individuals. Democracy can drag society in the direction of the lowest common denominator, but it can also inspire greatness. Nietzsche fails to see the complementarity of democratic pluralism to his own perspectivism. If Nietzschean "overcoming" of obstacles and barriers is essential to the development of greatness, then it would seem that the negative and regressive influences of democratic culture and the challenges that they represent can be the very hurdles that spur individuals to great achievement. The most fertile ground for greatness is the diversity of a pluralistic democratic culture where battles for great ideas are won and not merely bred. We live in a critical period of history because it is feared that scientific and technological knowledge may be outpacing our ethical, intellectual and political development. Our age requires morally tough individuals who not only have the courage of their convictions but who also are willing to break conventions to solve difficult problems. But weakness also creates opportunities for the overcoming of oneself. Did you know that acknowledging error is a high virtue for overcoming weakness, and to which everyone can aspire? Generally, greatness is the child of courage.

II.10

Greatness

The so-called "great man theory" argument of Thomas Carlyle and its counterargument—the most notable proponent of which is Herbert Spencer, frames the discussion of great individuals in terms of their relative replaceability or essentiality respective to the unfolding of history. For Carlyle, great individuals are born with the right talent, intelligence and nature to shape the direction of history. Spencer, on the other hand, connects greatness with the societal conditions and influences that allow and encourage individuals to flourish.

Extreme positions rarely escape at least some form of adulteration. An exceptional individual who greatly impacts the world is, nonetheless, largely a creature of the collective shaping of the world by others. Destiny is the realization of possibilities, and the appearance of a great individual depends upon the development or formation of underlying conditions that potentiate his greatness. References to "standing on the shoulders of giants" by Newton, and others, colorfully convey the indebtedness that greatness has to collective accomplishments and wisdom that help form pathways to greatness. Great individuals emerge in the context of convergent possibilities in the unfolding of history. Once we escape the limitations of pure determinism and introduce the wild card of free will, the notion of the "great man" of history is filled with a magnitude of such indeterminateness that makes theorizing less definitive. Human potential can be created or snuffed out by social mores or political intolerances and, therefore, if society wishes to encourage greatness it should assume that each newborn child possesses the potential for greatness. The only social policy that is consistent with an agenda that supports and inspires greatness is the promotion of individual empowerment that is also a path to greater collective empowerment.

A culture of individual and collective greatness requires an ethical framework that insists on social institutions that are empowered because they empower individuals. Great individuals—perhaps a revamped and more altruistic Nietzschean *Ubermensch*, may become the trailblazers who pave new paths in the concrete expression of a genuine love-based ethics that replaces mere platitude and lip service. It is time to discard ethical "idols" that are empty labels that masquerade as substance and block the destiny of free moral beings. The world's stock of values will become far richer when they are created by virtue that resonates with the goodness of intention coherent with the effectuality of action. Great political, economic and social systems promote greatness in individuals. The resonating coherence of moral actuality requires not a social static but, rather, an oscillating ethical harmonics that is a continuing adaptation to the needs of both Self and Other. Dogmatists have not appreciated that true harmony is unforced and uncoerced but, rather, is a finely tuned unity of diverse parts. And in the harmony and the fine-tuning of an empowered society greatness is encouraged.

II.11

Detachment

Humility does not entail pure detachment or pure attachment. But humility is power. While the arrogant man or woman who is full of ego and self-satisfaction has a mind that is closed to the opinions of others, the humble individual is capable of detachment from self-delusions of autonomy. But humility hardly entails intellectual meagerness or fear of big ideas; quite to the contrary, openness to the ideas of others facilitates the development of big ideas! Attachment to beliefs can be done with great humility when it is coexistent with a facility for detachment, but if the attachment persists without any justification it is likely a reflection of jealousy, selfishness, fear of the truth or love of dogma. Humility, in its openness to new ideas, perspectives and understanding requires the strength to embrace attachment as well as detachment. New beliefs and understanding may be the objects of attachment only to later become objects of detachment that leave a fertile soil for new beginnings.

In Buddhism, attachment is believed to be the source of all suffering. Nirvana ultimately is attained when attachments to all things: material, physical, intellectual and emotional are released and transcended. Some Buddhist sects, however, teach more practical modes of detachment. The Stoics, most notably the philosopher Epictetus, taught that a rational individual should detach herself from things not under her control. According to Epictetus, we can control our thoughts and our responses to events, but nothing else. We cannot control what other people think of us. We cannot control social turmoil and destructive events that may engulf us. We cannot control illness and inevitable death. Accordingly, the Stoics believed that it is essential to extirpate emotion and desire to control things that cannot be controlled and, by so doing, harmony with the world can be realized. To be 'stoic,' means serenity in the face of pain, suffering and all forms of disappointment, as well as our individual role and place in society and the universe.

The Taoist interpretation of detachment is one of letting go of thoughts and behaviors that are inconsistent or are in disharmony with the Tao (the way of the universe). The universe is a constant flux between Self and Other and of the enumerable dualisms or polarities that are expressed in the behavior of the universe. Thought and behavior that is consistent with the Tao cannot be preconceived or preplanned. We cannot afford to build our beliefs like castles in the sky, and it is essential that our thinking about worldly matters be practical and flexible enough to adapt to changing and unexpected circumstances. The arguments presented in this book are not, in my view, uncomplementary with Taoist philosophy, which is also complementary with the Noble Eightfold Path of Buddhism. This book is also much in agreement with other non-legalistic and non-rule-based ethical systems. And it agrees as well with a pure Christian ethics that is ultimately based on love. And it is in harmony with Kabbalistic mysticism that recognizes divine love as the essence of morality but also warns of the danger of too cavalierly ignoring rules or their significance.

Attachment and detachment are the warp and woof of an ethically engaged life. Attachment is the conscious energy that shapes the world. Think of an artist who throws her mind, emotions and the fullness of her being into her work. She is totally and completely attached and at one with her work. But then her project is completed and her work is done! What must she do next? She will detach and let go of her engagement with the completed work, and will then attach herself to the next project. Rational intelligence is a process of engagement with experience, and the more engaging the experience the more you will have lived! But then we must detach. The work ends. Life moves on. We form new attachments only to ultimately release ourselves from the contrived unity once again. We grow older. We die. And when we die, will we be able to detach from this life with the welcoming consciousness of detachment? The stronger the attachment the more energy and power will have been invested, but its eventual detachment may yet occur with calmness, serenity and grace. Detachment may be the truest hallmark of heroism and of greatness.

Qualitative change does not occur through theoretical contrivance. Change emerges from the oscillation between attachment and detachment, each reacting to the other as egoistically held positions recede and new actualities are ushered in. The unity of opposites is purely and simply the history of past attachments which have been let go and in turn become an integral and genealogical part of the new actuality. Is the quest to realize Nirvana actually a paradoxical attachment to detachment? And, equally paradoxically, can it not be argued that the only true detachment is a pure attachment to doing good and acting rightly in the spirit of love? Attachment to good is, I submit, the only means for achieving detachment from desires that may distract an individual away from the path of living a good life, i.e. one that is inspired by love. The attachment to promoting and inspiring good is the truest form of detachment.

Social

Empowerment

II.12

Social Harmonics

Social harmonics may be compared to the clearing of physical, emotional and mental blocks in an individual as practiced, for example, by various holistic health modalities in order to empower greater health and well-being. Ethical empowerment is both an individual and a social matter; a virtuous individual may exist in an un-virtuous society, but a virtuous society proactively empowers individuals with the potential of virtue. The empowerment of society is exemplified by the clearing of blocks so as to facilitate the mutual flourishing of both the individual and society.

In a perfect world populated by perfect people a pure laissez-faire society would certainly be best. If minimal government *a la* Herbert Spencer or Ayn Rand could indeed contribute to the happiest, most productive, most creative and most just society then there would be no rational reason to oppose it. Spencer's fantasy, characterized as "the perfect man in the perfect society," conforms to what he calls "the law of equal freedom" that states, "Every man has freedom to do all that he wills, provided he infringes not the equal freedom of any other man."[52] Both humanity and society, Spencer argues, will be perfected when individual behavior adapts (i.e. evolves) to a social system that has the bare minimum of governmental interference. For Spencer, government is the primary block to moral perfection but he acknowledges that time would be required for humans to evolve or adapt successfully with minimalist governmental interference or support. Libertarian utopianism aside, however, it is apparent that a combination of external, socially motivating influences and internal, self-motivating forces are key to both individual and collective empowerment. The human animal is social, but it is also individualistic as exemplified by celebrated lone wolfs who are creative geniuses. While man is far too complex a species to be pigeonholed into a socialistic or laissez-fare viewpoint, these political modes can be complementary incommensurables that have roles to play in their purest states as well as in states of adulteration. In the real world, when it is viewed without the hindrance of ideological distortion, there are ample examples of disruptive blocks to social harmony both in terms of excessive governmental interference *and* inadequate or ineffective governmental intervention.

Social evolution is shaped by the convergent forces of causality, dialectic and free will (§I.10), but there is no assurance that the convergence will be morally coherent. Moral coherence cannot prevail without the cooperation of free will no matter how small its influence is relative to broader forces of causality and dialectical persuasion. Free will may not align itself with loving intention and its dialogical unfolding; it can deny its highest calling. Humanity's greatest hope is its "moral sense" that may in a sense be said to comprise a universal and unconscious will, deeply embedded and engaged in dialectical development and making itself more conscious over time. I am suggesting a mood of German Romantic philosophy here by invoking an underlying moral sense motivated by loving intention as humanity's unconscious Will. And this Will—it does not hurt to occasionally frame language in terms of perspectives from bygone eras—empowers by clearing blockages and barriers that, directly and indirectly, obfuscate and frustrate the realization of moral coherence in thought and action. These blocks are largely in the form of formalities, preconceptions and dogma and their institutionalized reflections.

A moral blockage in the social order may not have been consciously created but could be an unwitting consequence of ethical intention, but when the incoherent consequences of good intentions become manifest the failure to correct them may then be viewed as intentional blocks to social harmony. What would an empowered society look like? It would be a society that is dedicated to achieving moral coherence, empowerment and greatness in all spheres of activity. While there are no guarantees for the attainment of virtue, the social harmonics of an empowered society is freer to realize it. It is our best shot. Imagine a society in which libertarians and socialists love each other. I hear loud laughter! But yes! They will love each other because polemical and ideological political labels will all but have disappeared along with the rabid and pointless divisiveness that currently infects political discourse. While meaningful differences of opinion should always thrive and be encouraged, they can also embrace the complementary incommensurables that have remained hidden behind fogs of ideology. When the disharmonic social blockages are cleared, the untapped potential that crisscrosses and transcends laissez-faireism and social caring will become the new social tapestry of a harmonic and empowered society.

II.13

Conservatisms and Progressivisms

> The whole modern world has divided itself into
> Conservatives and Progressives. The business of
> Progressives is to go on making mistakes. The
> business of Conservatives is to prevent mistakes
> from being corrected. Even when the revolutionist
> might himself repent of his revolution, the
> traditionalist is already defending it as part of
> his tradition.[53]
>   G. K. Chesterton

Conservatism, liberalism and progressivism are political labels that, if cleansed from the public discourse, would redound to the great benefit of society and political life. But while self-criticism can be difficult for individuals, it is even more difficult for the collective ego when there is over attachment to traditions or particular visions of change.

Conservation of traditional ways and advocacy of political change are sources of constant political tension. A progressive position may quickly become established as a tradition that is resistant to change, and a conservative position may be the mark of a true visionary who rightly seeks a return to a lost tradition that is in desperate need of rediscovery. But a true visionary can also be a progressive who transcends the world of formalities, accepted actualities and their paradigms. An ethical visionary can be a lover of tradition as much as a lover of change, and foolery is less likely when ideas are cultivated in the moral dialectic of loving intention rather than in worship of the past or in a blind felicity for rejecting it.

Comfort in wearing both conservative and progressive hats is a virtue; however, you need to have good fashion sense to be taken seriously.

~   ~   ~

Complementary incommensurables can be a tough pill to swallow for both lovers and haters of ideology. But an appreciator of the complementary incommensurable neither loves nor hates ideology: he merely takes what is resonant and leaves the rest.

~   ~   ~

The acceptance of gross financial and social inequalities set from the moment of birth is indeed a long and revered tradition! Sadly, this is not satire. Some parents may even boast that their children have advantages over others by no other reason other than their own social or financial status. However, if basic needs of children e.g. for health maintenance and education become a commitment assumed by society and made completely separate from the financial capacity of their parents, then conservatives and progressives should both be happy. Human progress and the conservation of the familial institution will both be advanced. The basic needs of children are social needs just as much as they are needs of individual families. No cost for providing basic needs is too high because, if the costs are really too high, then they are not basic needs.

~   ~   ~

It would seem that pederasty was a firmly entrenched tradition amongst the aristocratic class of ancient Greece. It is incomprehensible for the modern moral sentiment to fathom that perverse pedophilic behavior was common at the highest circles in the much revered culture of ancient Greece. As with any tradition, the beginnings of this perversion likely got its start in hypnotic-like fashion that subsequently took root over a period of conditioning and acculturation. There is probably nothing more reprehensible and vile to the modern sensibility than pedophilia, however, witness how aberrant and vile behaviors such as extortion or murder by criminal gangs and organized syndicates can take hold of the young or the weak-minded as they descend into a life of crime. Sometimes, those who have fallen into lives profoundly decadent and immoral finally wake up from their slumber; while it is too late to undo the wrongs it is never too late for the deep cleansing of authentic remorse.

~   ~   ~

In the United States, religiously inspired "blue laws" prohibited retail activity on Sundays but, with some exceptions, have largely faded away. The material needs of commerce and competition created economic *causal* pressures to rescind the blue laws, and *dialectal* forces seemed to press religion towards the conclusion that abolishing or weakening the blue laws was not contrary to its ethical perspectives. Causal and dialectical pressures were converging that created opportunities for a new consensus. The prevalence of blue laws was based on a prevailing moral actuality, i.e. a social consensus that economic and religious interests coincided. The imposition of limitations placed on commercial activity on Sundays was deemed beneficial or acceptable, but when the causal and dialectical factors shifted the blue laws were modified or abolished.

~   ~   ~

From the point of view of gay marriage supporters, the same-sex marriage controversy is a matter of equality and justice, but for conservative opponents marriage symbolizes a tradition that they believe reflects a harmonic state of affairs. Is the legal equivalency between traditional heterosexual marriages and same-sex civil unions progressive? If all financial and political benefits and rights are equal, it would seem that the only need remaining to be satisfied is the appropriation or forced legal acceptance of a term. The gay rights movement has made a good deal of progress in advancing equality and justice for homosexuals, and alongside other great advances in civil rights and universal justice these advances must be recognized to the point that their acceptance is second nature as a matter of basic justice. Societies are becoming more homogeneous but a diversity of traditions has enormous value. And values are precious commodities precisely because they are heterogeneous, and acceptance of their heterogeneity is part and parcel of a harmonic society. The diversity of traditions is important because they reflect the diversity of humanity that makes its unity deeper and stronger. "The whole is greater than the sum of its parts." The adoption of a term other than 'marriage' to designate same-sex civil unions could, arguably, be a useful and perhaps even a desirable bow to tradition, but the controversy over semantics does not impact progress one way or the other. The organized opposition to same-sex marriage has created a semantic war as a distraction to cover its true agenda, which is the repression of social equality. As it happens, the dialectical change in favor of same-sex marriage is making the controversy increasingly irrelevant, as a transformation of dialectical change into causal change occurs when votes cast in voting booths or the legislative bodies take effect. Convergent justice will ultimately trump the mores of cultural convention.

~   ~   ~

The gold standard is an example of an old conservatism that needs to be rediscovered and re-instituted in one form or another. Since 1971, when President Richard M. Nixon took America off the gold standard and adopted valuation via market bidding, the U.S. dollar has lost its value more than tenfold in relation to the cost of an ounce of gold. A return to the previous model may well be unnecessary and there may be better adaptations that could be instituted, but the "progressive" abolition of the gold standard and its replacement with a biddable financial instrument is not progress but, rather, a descent into madness. Values are not absolute, including the natural fluctuations of monetary currency, but it is foolish to abolish much revered traditional values without a rational replacement. Currency is the necessary foundation of many ethical values: cheapen the value of a national currency and the values of most everything else in this physical life will be—and are, devalued as well.

~   ~   ~

George Washington, in consideration of his recommendation that the American people stay clear of political parties, should be considered to be one of the greatest progressives of all time. If the American people were to finally take his advice and de-institutionalize the political party, one of the first unsavory elements to fall would be none other than the egoistic and delusional labels of conservative, liberal and progressive. Hardened conservative and progressive mindsets stick to political parties; politics used to be *about* issues but now it seems to be more about ideological attempts to *define* all issues. Ideological skunks are stinking up our politics. I have a dream in which statesmanship and ethically inspired leadership will dominate politics once it is freed from the broadly disempowering influences of the political party.

~   ~   ~

The "war on drugs" is more than metaphorical. And perhaps the dream of ending all wars is as applicable to the war on drugs as it is to wars between nations. War is an evil word unless you are a lover of war, but is not a war lover essentially the idea of evil? And if war is intrinsically evil it must only be waged as a last resort that is necessary for the survival or freedom of a people. War is probably the largest of institutions, but it seems to appeal equally to conservatives and progressives, thus exposing their facade. In the case of the "war on drugs" there seems to be little effort in the United States to seriously consider alternatives. Peace is clearly more effective than war when it comes to personal addictions. For example, waging peace between the conscious and subconscious minds is more successful than warlike dieting to lose weight. Similarly, overcoming drug addiction is best achieved by a sustained program of education, various forms of addiction counseling and treatment, and the controlled legalization of addictive substances that would wean addicts away from their dependencies. And the controlled legalization of street drugs will cut off the profits of the criminals who wage their war of greed and personal destruction. The war on drugs can be won by waging peace, and it may well be instructive for the prevention of other wars.

~   ~   ~

A unified Europe is desperately necessary, but a unified currency and overbearing market regulation may be another matter entirely. Singular currencies that attempt to represent diverse disparities between diverse economies are as much wishful thinking as they are false thinking. Stable and supportive monetary value requires a diversity of currency mix with a rational mechanism or system to adjust currency value so that it functions as a rational basis for fair inter-currency trade. By so doing, depressed and underdeveloped economies will have a basis for growth, and expanding economies will have a manageable fiscal roadway to the future. Stable currency values also have a critical influence on the foundations of ethical valuation and, hence, rational change in the institution of monetary values is as profoundly conservative as it is profoundly progressive.

~   ~   ~

The labels progressivism and conservatism are generally thought of in terms of the political arena, however, they easily wind their way into any area of intellectual controversy. Certainly, one such area is science and technology. As in the social arena, scientific conservatism has many redeeming characteristics. Caution with respect to radical change is generally prudent. One can argue that it is morally coherent for scientific work to stay within existing paradigms, but some of the greatest advances in sciences have been the paradigm shifts that redefine "good" science. As in politics or social controversy, the labels of conservatism and progressivism are worthless because the question is not whether to change or keep things as they are but, rather, what is supportive of "the good" and of "the truth." Well, "the truth" may on some occasions clash with "the good" but a prejudice in favor of truth is always in order. Repression or suppression of the truth without convincing ethical justification is a deep moral incoherency that is a sore slow to heal.

II.14

"The Conventional Wisdom"

William James' observed rightly that we are all "extreme conservatives" when it comes to our favored conventions. There is an enormous amount of power, ego and money invested in the ship of conventionality to keep it steady on whatever course it is heading. While the conventional wisdom may be generally correct most of the time, it is often wrong. Where is the line to be drawn between reasonable theories or assertions of fact and those that, without additional evidence to support them, do not warrant serious consideration? Knee-jerk stupefaction stupefies regardless of whether they are products of progressive or conservative thinking or non-thinking. Promoters of unconventional wisdom are not infrequently dismissed as crackpots, frauds or pseudo-scientists, but when the defenders of convention are proved wrong they are most generally let off the hook by the amnesic effects created by the prevailing winds of the new convention.

~ *The quest for truth is democratic* ~

There is adequate reason to question why it is that JFK's body has never been exhumed. The Warren Report states that Kennedy was shot in the back of the head while conspiracy theorists have generally argued that he was shot from the front as well as from the back. If there is a reasonable possibility that an exhumation of the body could decide potentially critical facts, is there not sufficient justification to proceed? Numerous doubts have been raised concerning the autopsy; what is the justification for not proceeding? What reason could supercede the exhumation of Kennedy's body in order to learn the truth about his assassination? If public opinion polls are accurate, the "conventional wisdom" of the Warren Report is no longer the conventional wisdom of the American people, however, the conclusions of the Warren Report do represent the conventional wisdom of those in position to force an exhumation of the body. The willful prevention of factual disclosure constitutes significant persuasive force for believing that whatever it is that is being protected is certainly not the protection of the people's right to know the truth. And the willful repression of knowledge is the repression of wisdom and the suppression of democracy.

Some may believe that the exhumation of the body would be wrong or disrespectful to the family of the deceased. But who should decide what is respectful here? Putting aside the legitimate argument that the good of the nation trumps other considerations, why not simply ask the spirit of John Kennedy? No, I am not suggesting that the Congress of the United States conduct a séance. But the rational use of imagination is appropriate. Use the power of your imagination and ask the spirit and the soul of John Kennedy if he would wish that the people of the United States employ all reasonable means to discover the facts of his murder. Now, what in your wildest imagination do you think his answer might be? I hereby do just that: I am now addressing John Kennedy's spirit, if the exhumation of your body has a reasonable chance of uncovering the truth of your murder for the sake of America and for the integrity of history, do you assent? Can anyone doubt that Kennedy would want the nation to learn the facts relating to his murder? Would any victim of murder want any less? Lincoln's body was exhumed multiple times in the relocations of his burial site and provides a precedent for the exhumation of a president's body. In unblocking, as much as possible, facts relating to the JFK assassination deep psychic wounds buried in America's collective unconscious could at long last be given an opportunity to heal. The conventional wisdom of the minority that has prevented the exhumation of Kennedy's body is a stranglehold on history and recalls the wisdom of George Orwell, who in *1984* wrote, "He who controls the past controls the future, and he who controls the present controls the past."

~   *Scientific method is but one method of reason*   ~

There is a fundamental confusion concerning the distinction between scientific knowledge and rational thinking. Scientific method and controlled experimentation constitute an exacting basis for the acquisition of knowledge about the physical world, but it is only one form of rational thinking. It is worthwhile noting that while science is the offspring of rational thinking it is not the sole form of reasoning relevant to factual truth, falsity or the probability of phenomena. Juries and judges decide guilt or innocence and, in some cases, life or death by means that are largely not amenable to scientific method. Circumstantial evidence, criteria for assessing motive, eyewitness reports, consistency, etc. do not have the exactitude of experimentation in a laboratory, but no one of sane mind is suggesting that the suspension of all criminal court proceedings would be thereby justified! Which is not to say that Reason should not have enormous pride in the accomplishments of Science, but it can surely be said that Science is an impudent child if it should not grant other forms of reason their due respect.

The confusion regarding valid forms of reasoning is evident in the argument between evolutionists and creationists. While the creationist argument that the universe is the result of intelligent design is not an irrational argument, it is not a scientific argument. And the scientific-evolutionist argument in support of the theory of evolution is also a rational argument, but it too is not completely scientific. The theory of evolution is a theory and not a body of facts even if in general terms the evidence for evolution is broadly supported by many facts. The theory does not exclude the possibility that evolution is an intelligent design; it is not excluded because science does not and cannot explain *a priori* conditions that may have been in force before the universe began or before life and, in particular, human life began. Science describes behavior and the processes of life as well as other physical phenomena, but the question of the intention or purpose of life or of the universe is not in its purview. While science may have the potential to detect human intention, the theory of evolution can neither support nor refute the creationist argument because it cannot address hypothetical intentions of preexisting divine beings without, like religion, presumptuously assuming an understanding of the mind of God or gods.

The conventional wisdom finds a home in both camps. The creationists would like the biblical story of creation taught in science classes because they pretend that religion is science; perhaps scientists should demand that science be taught in religious classes? Quite absurd, but teaching science in

Sunday school would underscore how absurd the whole argument has become. However, evolution turned into a scientific theology is perhaps as foolish as is an extreme fundamentalism that worships a scripture's every literal word. The conventional wisdom of science condescendingly rejects as primitive the thinking of those who deign to think that an immaterial realm might exist. And the conventional wisdom of creationism has the audacity to insist that it is science. Neither science or religion are The Truth yet, at times, they each pretend that they are its sole protector. Pretensions such as these make a mockery of truth.

~ *Can the conventional wisdom be open-minded?* ~

Power institutionalizes itself as knowledge. Or perhaps conventional belief institutionalizes itself. The dynamic relationship between power and knowledge is probed in Michel Foucault's voluminous work. The lunacy of knowledge as nothing other than institutionalized belief was made embarrassingly clear by the dis-invitation of British physicist and Nobel Laureate Brian Josephson and distinguished physicist Dave Peat from a workshop entitled the Foundations of Physics. The letter retracting Josephson's invitation said,

> It has come to my attention that one of your principal research interests is the paranormal...in my view, it would not be appropriate for someone with such research interests to attend a scientific conference.

The dis-invitation also went out to physicist, David Peat:

> It has come to my attention that you are the author of books on Jungian synchronicity and quantum physics, and on connections between Native American Indian thought and modern physics...in my view, it is not appropriate for an author of such books to attend a scientific conference.[54]

The politicization of truth is certainly one of the most insidious forms of corruption. Briberies and kickbacks can be found and expunged, but the soiling of truth by political power complexes is a stain that can take generations to remove. The politicization of truth *should* be considered an oxymoronic idea, but the truth is that the political infestation of the truth is so common that it is generally taken for granted. Any yet, if there is a legitimate quest for the truth it will need to move beyond all barriers that hinder and obstruct it. In courts of law the obstruction of justice is a criminal offense, and seekers of truth outside the courtroom should be equally intolerant of practices and behaviors that thwart the advancement of knowledge. The only legitimate and acceptable path of truth-seeking is one that escapes the multi-layered obscurantism of ego, greed, power and their institutionalization that corrupt and stain knowledge so badly that what is called "wisdom" is merely the farcical repetition of lies. Certainly, virtues of wisdom and truth-seeking entail in their essence an avoidance of the perverse distortions that in Orwellian-like fashion seek to turn ignorance into strength.

Science is no less influenced by ego, greed and power than any other field of inquiry. Thomas Kuhn and Michael Polanyi (who significantly influenced Kuhn) acknowledge that the nature of established scientific theory and practice tends to exclude theories and anomalous phenomena that fall outside of what Kuhn refers to as scientific paradigms. A "paradigm shift" requires a sea change in the weight of evidence, or a long, ongoing chipping away at the foundations of old paradigms. Kuhn writes that paradigms of the conventionally accepted belief systems of science appear to be an

> ...attempt to force nature into the preformed and relatively inflexible box that the paradigm supplies. No part of the aim of normal science is to call forth new sorts of phenomena; indeed those that will not fit the box are often not seen at all. Nor do scientists normally aim to invent new theories, and they are often intolerant of those invented by others. Instead, normal-scientific research is directed to the articulation of those phenomena and theories that the paradigm already supplies.[55]

However, both Kuhn and Polanyi seem to argue that this narrowing is necessary, and the dramatic advances achieved by science would not have been possible without paradigmatic focus and its exclusion of distracting anomalous phenomena and theoretical lines of thought that fall outside the paradigms. Kuhn describes science as a sort of evolutionary process and Polanyi similarly describes science as a step-by-step advance of knowledge. The intricate political web that is integrated in this quasi-evolution is succinctly described by Polanyi:

> The rejection of implausible claims has often proved mistaken, but safety against this danger could be assured only at the cost of permitting journals to be swamped by nonsense.[56]

> All institutions serving the advancement and dissemination of science rely on the supposition that a field of potential systematic progress exists…scientists are appointed for life to the pursuit of research and permanent subsidies are granted to them for this purpose. Many expensive buildings, pieces of equipment, journals, etc. are founded and maintained in this belief. It is the most general traditional belief which a novice joining the scientific community accepts in becoming a scientist.[57]

Both philosophers acknowledge the ambiguous line between description and prescription in the process of science but, ultimately, it would seem that what is being described is a de facto prescription in the sense that "this is how science is done." Polanyi's statement (similarly echoed by Kuhn) that scientific journals would be "swamped by nonsense" is the central claim that needs to be addressed. While paradigmatic focus on scientific research, development and theory is the primary activity of science, could not standard scientific methodology be logically expanded so that the institution of science is not a monopoly exclusion of non-paradigmatic pursuits?

The subject of scientific paradigms presents a model for both the positive and the negative sides of the conventional wisdom. As with the conventional wisdom of science, paradigms have facilitated an unprecedented growth of scientific knowledge, much of which has come after paradigm shifts have occurred. But there are other methods of reason besides scientific method, and the first inklings of a paradigm shift can come from outside the paradigm. Even if scientific revolutions are an evolutionary process, how could a potential cure, for example, not be seriously evaluated and objectively investigated. As if research money is never needlessly expended on questionable projects! What is truly laughable is the laughter and scoffery staged by protectors of the paradigms who put on blindfolds to make sure nothing upsets the paradigm just in case there may actually be something that might jeopardize job security or dogmatic bliss. There is great wisdom in convention, but there is also great folly in thinking the conventional ways account for the only wisdom.

~ *The conventional wisdom and the new plebeian class* ~

Along with genuine loyalty to longstanding belief and the psychology behind it, the conventional wisdom can often also have the ulterior and more insidious motivations of ego, money and power. And while the conventional wisdom can be more ulterior than genuine, its promulgation is often accepted in large measure because of the esteemed status of those who promote it. An inner conflict can then ensue between the purity of a desire for the truth and the faith that has been invested in the trusted conveyors of the conventional wisdom.

The complexity and vastness of modern knowledge, and the fragmented specialization that has formed around it has produced many fiefdoms and foci of knowledge. A new power complex has developed that in large measure depends upon a culture of unquestioned trust in the experts. Without the blessing of experts, novel claims, theories and principles are not taken seriously. The power complex is informal and relatively disorganized but outside the loop of intersecting interests are the rest of us, who might well be called the new plebeian class. This new class of plebes is outmaneuvered by mass media owned by power interests, a university culture that protects the existing paradigms and their income stream, government regulators that are interlocked with revolving doors of past and future employers who sometimes—because of conflicts of interests—guard the public interest as well as the fox guards the hen house, and other instruments of power such as a patent system that permits patents to be bought and then buried. It would be incorrect to describe the power complex as an elite class because members of the complex may themselves be outside the power loop respective to specific specialized areas of power; a plebe is a disempowered individual respective to specific foci of power, therefore, most members of the power complex are also plebes.

Conspiracy theories, alternative health remedies, food safety such as the preponderance of foods that now contain GMOs, technologies that challenge existing paradigms, UFOs and other theories that affront the conventional wisdom are marginalized. The marginalization may occur *not* because of a dearth of plausible evidence worth serious consideration but because power centers from the media to government to academia to big business have vested interests in maintaining the status quo, or because of ideophobic fears before which the powerful meekly cower. While the interests of this power complex are propagated by means of the conventional wisdom it may encounter significant popular doubt, but the doubts are neutralized by the experts who assure the public that alternative views are groundless and should not be taken seriously. The JFK assassination is a case in point; a large majority of Americans believe that the president was the victim of a conspiracy but the political machinery remains unmoved. The expert mouthpieces of the power complex tell us to ignore contrary evidence, essentially, because they say so and are the only voice of reason qualified and worth listening to. Of course, we believe the experts. And the ruse generally works! The opinion of the experts is, virtually, the only opinion that matters or has any weight. We, the new plebeian class, are the herd who follows because there seems to be no other choice. However, we can empower ourselves with knowledge and truth. How? By developing a credible plural perspectivism that succeeds in establishing esteemed and authenticated multiple rails of truth.

II.15

On "Pseudoscience":
Tales of the Pot and the Kettle

"You espouse falsehoods and deception," says the Pot to the Kettle. "I am the keeper, the shiny container of pristine truths. I am the light. Look at you! You spew nothing but falsehood and the ignorance of your darkness must be stopped at all cost so that my light may illuminate the world." The conceited Pot only sees the Kettle as worn-out with use, but does not also see that its arrogance makes it equally flawed and prone to error. Are not all we humans imperfect and all too prone to error? We must always be weary of the destructive sin of hypocrisy.

The shouting matches between practitioners of so-called mainstream science and practitioners of so-called pseudoscience constitute a real life drama of the Pot and the Kettle. The unnecessary schism between mainstream and alternative science is reinforced by the likes of Wikipedia.com, which loves to pin the tag of 'pseudoscience' in many of its articles that touch on alternative science and technology in order to carefully demarcate mainstream science from science outside the mainstream. Mainstream science and, more broadly, skeptics of alternative science who play the part of the Pot derisively argue, "What you are calling science outside the mainstream is not science! You are fraudulent science and I'm not even going to look at you!" And when alternative science (a.k.a. "pseudoscience") assumes the role of the Pot it tells the Kettle of scientists and skeptics that, "Your mind is frozen to old concepts that are incomplete and flawed; both your mind and your eyes are closed to any evidence that challenges your precious paradigms!" The term pseudoscience is inherently arrogant and derogatory in the same breath, but it is humbling to recognize that new paradigms in science may well have been considered pseudoscience before they became the norm. The truth is that the line of demarcation between mainstream science and alleged pseudoscience can at times be quite blurry, but the latter is routinely beaten back by tactics of suppression to make sure it never sees the light of day. Sometimes the suppression is subconsciously perpetrated and at other times has been quite intentional. If mainstream science signifies theories and technologies that have undergone rigorous empirical investigation and experimentation, what does one say about inventions that are rejected not on the basis of experimentation but simply on the grounds that they cannot or should not work? If it is claimed that an invention cannot work because it appears to conflict with a prevailing scientific paradigm, "law" or principle and on that basis fails to experiment and investigate, then at that point science becomes mere dogma or ideology. Mainstream science feels entitled in the name of science to define what science is, and force conformance and compliance with what Thomas Kuhn refers to as "normal science." Inventors and alternative practitioners can be subjected to libelous campaigns waged against them, restraint of trade and worse. However, there is very good reason to believe that, in some cases, inventions of "pseudoscience" have been tagged as such not because they could not be validated but because validation was not in the interest of the power complex of business, political and academic interests or, more simply, money, ego and power. While there is little question that there are plenty of fraudulent "pseudo-scientific" claims afloat, there are also ample cases of pseudo-claims made against alternative science and technology that are perpetrated by institutions and other power interests. While it is not always the case, frequently the Pot that is calling the Kettle black happens to be none other than institutions and the nexus of power.

~ *Cures, treatments and profit* ~

There has been a revolution in the American diet and in the natural health field over the past thirty to forty years. I remember when someone I knew used to argue that there is little or no relationship between health and the foods that people eat. A bit later this person happened to hear a physician on the radio talk about the importance of diet for the prevention of many diseases and he promptly changed his opinion because now he had it on *expert* authority that there is a relationship between diet and disease. This person's opinion was not at all uncommon a generation ago. I also recall during the early days of the natural health revolution in the late 1970s or early 80s watching on television a well-known and respected physician and TV health analyst being somewhat dismissive of health foods such as oat bran stocked on the shelves of little heath food stores that had begun sprouting up, by more or less saying that we shouldn't get too carried away with this health food thing. We have come a long way from the days when the importance of fiber in the diet was a revelation and words like 'antioxidant,' 'phytochemical' and 'phytonutrient' were little known to the public (or not yet in use). Today, there is little doubt that the foods we eat can both help to cause as well as help prevent disease. It is also becoming increasingly accepted that herbal and dietary supplements can have significant medicinal value.

The holistic health and natural dietary supplement industries and the mainstream medical and pharmaceutical industries each play the role of the self-righteous Pot accusing the Kettle. The modern bias of technology over nature is strange: Is processed "American cheese" a culinary or dietary advance? Perhaps nowhere is the bias more prevalent than in the over-reliance on synthetically developed pharmaceuticals even as the danger of their overuse it is becoming increasingly clear. As has been widely reported, prescription drugs use now kill far more Americans than illegal street drugs do. While it is foolery to deny that there have been many advances in the pharmaceutical treatment and cure of disease, the foolery works both ways. There is no doubt that some holistic health companies have been guilty of exaggerating health claims of their products, but it is unfortunately also true that the medical establishment has been prone to arrogantly dismiss natural and alternative methods that do not fit the prevailing medical paradigm that equates medicine with pharmaceuticals. So who is calling the Kettle black? Surely, the correct answer is both of them! The focus here, however, is on the role of the Pot that is played by Big Pharma and the power complex that dominates the conventional wisdom of mainstream healthcare. There are two very compelling reasons why we should be interested in objectively determining when herbs and dietary supplementations are effective alternatives to synthetic pharmaceutical preparations: 1) Herbal and dietary supplements have far fewer and less serious side-effect than do pharmaceuticals and, 2) Reducing unnecessary dependencies on pharmaceuticals would significantly reduce the cost of healthcare.

A 'medicine' is today generally thought of in terms of prescription drugs and over-the-counter preparations as contradistinguished from natural supplements that consist of herbs and food extracts. However, the ancient practice of using medicinal foods and herbs has been empowered by modern science. The active phytochemicals in foods and herbs are now scientifically studied, and their biological effects and dosing requirements are becoming better understood. Nature is a vast biochemical laboratory that has over a period of millions of years evolved botanical compounds that have the potential to treat and cure disease. Nature's wisdom may at times be a preferable alternative to powerful and expensive pharmaceuticals whose side effects are not infrequently unpredictable and extremely serious. But despite their growing popularity, there is a strong bias against the medicinal potential of natural supplements, led by the self-proclaimed "quack watchers" who are the most self-righteous of the Pots who name-call the Kettle. Bias against natural medicinals is maintained despite the fact that many formal scientific studies have indicated that a wide variety of herbal and other forms of natural dietary supplementation possess antiviral, antibacterial, anti-inflammatory, anti-carcinogenic, and anti-aging properties relating both to the prevention and the treatment of disease. Could money have anything to do with the lethargic research on the potential use of natural supplements in the curing of specific diseases? The medical establishment or complex of revolving doors between Big Pharma, university and medical research institutions and the FDA continues to enforce the ongoing bias.

The Dietary Supplement Health and Education Act (DSHEA), which was passed by the U.S. Congress in 1994, stipulates that health claims made on the packaging of herbal and dietary supplementation products be accompanied with the disclaimer that "This statement has not been evaluated by the Food and Drug Administration. This product is not intended to diagnose, treat, cure, or prevent any disease." The DSHEA is a landmark legislative achievement that gives to Americans freedoms and rights for deciding how to manage their health, and is far more preferable than the increasing regulatory repression of the European Union. However, the law has unfortunately also helped to segregate dietary supplements from the mainstream of healthcare. The DSHEA has, essentially, institutionalized the notion that dietary supplements are not serious medicine for the treatment of disease. What is now needed for the empowerment of both physicians and individual consumers is a systematic, ongoing and scientifically rigorous evaluation of the usefulness of dietary supplementation respective to the prevention and *treatment* of disease, including the development of dosage guidelines and findings respective to effectiveness and safety.

While there is prejudice against dietary supplementation because it violates the prevailing pharmaceutical paradigm, far more prejudicial is the equation of treatment with profitability. Natural ingredients are not patentable and, therefore, manufacturers do not stand to make the enormous profits earned on patentable synthetic pharmaceutical drugs. Isn't there something terribly and horribly wrong with this picture? Diminished profit levels for natural dietary supplements combined with a de facto prohibition against determining their efficacy in the treatment of disease is a grotesque disempowerment of society by special interests and their cronies in the FDA, whose ultimate goal appears to be that of making all dietary supplements classifiable as prescription drugs. Indeed, in this period of obscenely rising healthcare costs the U.S. Food and Drug Administration, which was created to protect the health and well-being of the American people, is evidently more interested in protecting the interests and the profit margins of the big pharmaceutical companies. There is no reason other than either ignorance or meekness on the part of the new plebeian class of medical consumers to allow this pattern to continue. But times are changing. Increasingly, dietary supplements are showing promise in the prevention and treatment of a wide variety of diseases. For example, there are ongoing laboratory studies that indicate that the herb milk thistle and its silymarin extracts may have great potential to treat a variety of cancers and other diseases including liver disease. For example, the National Cancer Institute reports that,

> Milk thistle is a plant whose fruit and seeds have been
> used for more than 2,000 years as a treatment for liver
> and biliary disorders...Laboratory studies demonstrate
> that silymarin functions as an antioxidant, stabilizes
> cellular membranes, stimulates detoxification pathways,
> stimulates regeneration of liver tissue, inhibits the growth
> of certain cancer cell lines, exerts direct cytotoxic activity

toward certain cancer cell lines, and may increase the
efficacy of certain chemotherapy agents.[58]

Will there be sufficient financial incentive to develop milk thistle extracts
based upon accepted scientific and medical protocols? And, if not, it is
incumbent upon government on the basis of universal ethical principles to
fill the gap. If there is a public need that the private market cannot fulfill
then it is unethical for the government or public sector not to fill it.

The intentional stunting of aggressive research on natural cures is a
snapshot of fundamental problems with the American healthcare system.
And as we shall now see, the lackadaisical attitude by the mainstream healthcare industry of ignoring and dismissing dietary supplementation is
symptomatic of even more blatant frustrations of progress.

~ *The promise, dubiousness and suppression of Royal R. Rife* ~

The suppression of evidence in support of a revolutionary invention
does not necessarily prove that the invention was "for real" or that it could
have withstood rigorous and objective testing. The suppression of evidence
is almost always a symptom of fear. If there is no fear that the invention
would turn out to be valid, then why suppress it? The primary questions are
these, "Why the fear?" and "Is the fear justified?"

It is easy to deride a technology as fraudulent when fair and honest
testing and evaluation of the device has been blatantly and arbitrarily
suppressed. But it is the tried and true method of debunkers to do what is
possible to create an atmosphere that discourages and prevents an objective
evaluation of alternative technologies. Debunkers and critics of inventions
can only be consistent if they demand a fair and objective evaluation in
accordance with the scientific method that they preach and claim to abide
by, otherwise, they should simply be quiet since they clearly have nothing
to add to the conversation. While truth itself is a matter of perspective, the
first ethic of truth requires that obstructions that prevent the examination of
evidence be removed. Unfortunately, there have been instances of blatant
suppression by the power complex of government, media, business,
academia, and the military that orchestrate evidentiary suppression.
Consider the FDA's enforced confiscation and burning of Wilhelm Reich's

books on August 23rd 1956. There seems little about what Reich was doing that should have caused fear, and less reason to believe that his writings and "orgone accumulators" posed a threat to anyone. But his work did challenge the paradigms of the conventional wisdom and that concern (i.e. fear) was sufficient enough for the FDA to call in the dogs. Perhaps there is indeed some truth in Reich's theories of e.g. "orgone," "bions" and "t-bacilli." A contemporary of Reich whose inventions more substantively challenged accepted ideas about microorganisms experienced similar ruffian tactics. Could Royal R. Rife have invented two machines that would have revolutionized medicine?

The Rife story is reported in compelling detail by Barry Lynes in *The Cancer Cure that Worked!* [59] To summarize, Rife claimed to have invented a highly complex microscope ("Universal Microscope" 1933 model) that could achieve a resolution of 31,000x and a magnification of 60,000x that, unlike modern electron microscopes, does not destroy viruses or bacteria that are under observation. An equally significant claim was that the microscope had the capacity to dye viruses and bacteria with fine-tuned light frequencies thereby setting them up for eradication. Rife would later develop a device that beams radio frequencies (RF) calibrated and coordinated with the "mortal oscillatory rate" (M.O.R.) of the organism set in relation to the color dye refractions.[60] The RF device apparently worked in accordance to the principles of destructive resonance by which an object can disassemble or be destroyed when sufficient energy is absorbed that is resonant with the frequency of its oscillations. Unlike highly dangerous and toxic modern radiation therapy, little if any side effects were apparent. Only structures with complementary resonance were destroyed while the healthy, untargeted elements of the body were left undisturbed. Could resonance be the "magic bullet" that cancer researchers have sought? Today, the viral oncogenesis of a significant number of cancer types is an accepted fact. Rife believed that by eliminating a pleomorphic "BX" microorganism, which he claimed to have isolated through the use of his microscope, many or perhaps most cancers would be cured. Rife claimed to have identified a microorganism or a class of microorganisms that not only cause cancer but are factors in its uncontrolled and abnormal proliferation, and his claims were supported by a number of credible practitioners and researchers of his day. Putting aside consideration of ulterior motives, it is very strange that the revolutionary results claimed by Rife and his group of associates were arbitrarily dismissed, and then beaten back by the power of both professional and governmental authorities without any semblance of scientific testing.

Was Rife a hoax, or a delusional egomaniac not worthy of serious investigation? Many skeptics claim that such is exactly the case. The full truth about the Rife story is unclear, and summarizing it here is not part of an argument for the scientific validity and technical efficacy of his inventions. However, whatever the truth with respect to Rife's inventions, the verdict of history up to this point has unequivocally *not* been the product of scientific method but, rather, of *unscientific* suppression. Therefore, before Rife is dismissed as a charlatan it is imperative in the name of fairness and scientific objectivity that claims made regarding Rife's instruments and their alleged suppression be seriously reviewed and examined.

A) **Destructive resonance**. Galileo discovered the basic principle of resonance while experimenting with pendulums. A little push that is "in tune" with the tempo of a pendulum can increase the level of its motion because energy is absorbed by the swing. Nikola Tesla conducted a famous experiment in which he attached a mechanical oscillator to a steel pillar in a building that housed his New York City laboratory, resulting in the shaking of buildings in surrounding neighborhoods as if an earthquake had struck.[61] Regardless of whether or not this well-known story has been exaggerated, the destructive power of the absorption of sufficient resonant energy is a scientific fact. And resonance is the basic principle behind Rife's principle of M.O.R. Destroying microorganisms in a test tube or a Petri dish is one matter, and destroying them *in vivo* in order to cure disease is quite another. If the resonant energy is a radio wave frequency, could it harmlessly penetrate the body and destroy the offending pathogens and thereby cure disease?

There is good reason the think that Rife's frequency devices could destroy pathogens outside the body. I invite the reader to watch a remarkable demonstration uploaded to YouTube by Anthony G. Holland that demonstrates the resonant destruction of harmless Blepharisma and Paramecium microorganisms.[62] And a relatively recent report out of Arizona State University reports that researchers are using laser frequencies to vibrationally destroy viruses. An online article in *Live Science* reports that according to a January 14, 2008 article in the journal *Physical Review Letters* an Arizona research team explored destructive resonance as means to replace other antiviral therapies that have severe side-effects. The research is remarkably consistent, in principle, with Rife's basic objective of using electromagnetic resonance to destroy infection by microorganisms.

> Scientists may one day be able to destroy viruses in the same way that opera singers presumably shatter wine glasses…Recent experimental evidence has shown that laser pulses tuned to the right frequency can kill certain viruses…Normal cells should not be affected…because they have resonant frequencies much lower than those of viruses.[63]

There are those who are sure to say that lasers are fundamentally different than what Rife was doing. Actually, the article also quotes an Arizona State University physicist as speculating that delivering the frequencies in the form of ultrasound may also be a possible avenue of research. The time may well be nearing when the systematic development and clinical trial of frequency resonance therapies to destroy pathogens and cure disease are taken seriously.

B) **Of mice and men**. A long list of reputable physicians in the 1930s and 40s associated themselves with Rife's inventions, and a number of them were convinced by the clinical results that they witnessed, oversaw and conducted. While worthy of note, this documented and anecdotal evidence is not proof that the inventions worked as claimed. Certainly, as with any therapy, standardized trials would be necessary. However, when intimidation of doctors threatened with loss of their medical licenses, confiscation of records and instrumentation, forced closure of clinics, a mysterious burning of a laboratory, and a concocted lawsuit having little purpose other than suppression are all together taken into account, suspicion of malicious intent is in order. It is difficult not to suspect that the hyper-reactive behavior and organized intimidation by the AMA and federal and state medical authorities were motivated by something other than concern for the public's health. This is especially true when no significant risk to public health had been established. In fact, the lawsuit against Rife and his associates failed, and the motivations for bringing the lawsuit were roundly criticized by the presiding judge. Nonetheless, despite the defeat of this lawsuit, the American Medical Association continued to intimidate physicians with threats of license revocation if they failed to cease and desist in their therapeutic use of Rife's resonant energy devices.[64]

C) **Clinical evidence**. In the summer of 1934 The Scripps Institute, under the oversight of the University of Southern California Medical Research Committee directed by Dr. Milbank Johnson, treated 16 terminally ill patients with resonant frequencies and within three months 14 were considered fully cured. It is also reported that Dr. Johnson opened two additional clinics in 1935 and 1937 with similar results.[65] Multiple examples, many of them largely anecdotal, attest to the great success of the frequency instruments and microscopes developed by Rife and his associates. Dramatic testimony began to appear, e.g. a report that Dr. Richard Hamer of National City, California treated an average of forty cases a day including the remarkable success in curing an 82-year-old man from Chicago who had a severe malignancy on the face and neck. This report caught the attention of American Medical Association (AMA) leader Morris Fishbein.[66]

D) **Suppression**. It is claimed that Fishbein expressed interest in investing in the Beam Ray Corporation but was rebuffed and that, subsequently, it is also alleged that he enticed a disgruntled partner of the Beam Ray Corporation to litigate—as noted above—against the company presumably in an effort to gain a financial foothold in the business. From this point forward Rife and his associates faced increasing pressures from regulatory authorities. As mentioned above, the 1939 lawsuit failed but the AMA and their suppression against Rife and his associates intensified. Physicians using the Beam Ray frequency instrument were threatened with license revocation. At the conclusion of the trial, presiding Judge Edward Kelley rebuked the character of the plaintiff (Mr. Hoyland), and would later express interest in representing Beam Ray in a prospective lawsuit against the AMA, but by that time the company was broke.[67]

After teaming with John Crane in 1950, new interest in the techniques was generated. The suppression resumed. The Palo Alto Detection Lab, the

Kalbfeld Lab, the UCLA Medical Lab, and the San Diego Testing Lab all declared the RF device to be safe but, nonetheless, the instrument was barred from professional use in the United States. In 1960, Crane's office was raided as equipment, documentation and data were confiscated. The confiscated records were not made available to Crane during his 1961 trial. The trial did not allow the admission of evidence that was supportive of claims that the Frequency Instrument was effective, and the State of California undertook little if any effort to evaluate Crane's version of the RF device. *The foreman of the jury was an AMA physician.* Crane continued to promote the Frequency Instrument after his release from prison in 1965, but practitioners were ordered to stop using it and their equipment was confiscated or destroyed.[68]

It is relatively easy to take a dubious attitude towards Rife's work, but the behavior of the medical authorities fails the smell test. There were enough credible reports to warrant not a legal investigation but a bona fide scientific investigation of the efficacy of both Rife's microscope and frequency devices. There seems to have been far more concern in stymieing any possible foothold that Rife might achieve in developing alternatives to conventional drug and radiation treatment for cancer than there was for an open pursuit of the truth. Fishbein's concern appears to have been solely one of profit and monopoly, and the AMA finally removed him in 1949. The later suppression in the early 1960s was a repetition of the thuggery that occurred a few years earlier against Wilhelm Reich. In the end, the primary motive was most certainly money. The tenor of the lengthy and reprehensible harassment against Rife and his supporters was accompanied by violence that appears highly suspicious. Federal investigators looked at Dr. Milbank Johnson's hospital records years after his death and concluded that he was likely poisoned, and Dr. Raymond Seidel's car was shot at after the publication of his article in the Smithsonian annual report describing the Rife microscope.[69]

In addition to banning the use of frequency devices, contemporary suppression takes the form of denial and rejection embedded in expert opinion. For example, an American Cancer Society online article states that, "available scientific evidence" does not support the effectiveness of electrical devices" such as Rife's:

> Some types of electromagnetic energy are approved for
> use in standard cancer treatment. These methods include
> X-rays and radiation therapy as well as radiofrequency
> ablation and microwave ablation, which help destroy
> tumors…However, low level radio waves or tiny
> electrical impulses are not strong enough to produce a
> significant effect on the body. There is no evidence
> that the electromagnetic energy produced by these
> devices can destroy bacteria or any living cells.[70]

But what is the available evidence? Have there been any scientifically organized clinical trials conducted by any officially recognized laboratory to recreate the microscope and RF devices? If resonant radio frequency tests were conducted in the past respective to the particular resonance of specific pathogenic organisms, then perhaps the author of the Society's article might provide the data? But, of course, there have been no clinical trials or scientific efforts to recreate Rife's devices. In fact, the whole point of destructive resonance is simply ignored in the article. The paradigm of nuclear medicine is to nuke cancer cells. The article mentions radiofrequency ablation that cooks them. But the idea of using destructive resonance as therapy, by which low levels of energy become enormously amplified when absorbed by resonant vibrating objects is not addressed or discussed. To summarize, there is no available scientific evidence to support Rife because there have been no scientific attempts to conduct fair and objective scientific testing of his devices. And there have been no clinical trials because in the aftermath of the suppression and the intimidation and the threats preventing further development and clinical inquiry the storyline has been set: "No available scientific evidence." Research and development are either suppressed or simply not carried out, and then the legacy of "no evidence" is passed down as fact to subsequent generations. And in this fashion dogmatisms and dogmatic slumberings are initiated.

In *Wilk v. American Medical Association* (1987) U.S. District Court Judge Susan Getzendanner ruled that the AMA had a history of engaging in violations of the Sherman Anti-Trust Act in a systematic and orchestrated attempt to eliminate the chiropractic profession through boycott and restraint of trade. Getzendanner concluded that "an injunction is necessary…There are lingering effects of the conspiracy; the AMA has never acknowledged the lawlessness of its past conduct."[71]

E) **Back to the future**. On March 1, 2011 University of Manchester (UK) scientists announced the development of a "microsphere nanoscope"[72] that, in effect, may provide evidence for the plausibility of the Rife microscope. A news release states that by "combining an optical microscope with a transparent microsphere [objects can be viewed that are] as small as 50 nanometres (5 x 10-8m)—under normal lights."[73] The news release states further that the new microscope has the potential to allow the inspection of the interior of cells and, unlike electron microscopes, it might be possible to inspect living viruses.[74] Modern light microscopy may have achieved, or is on the verge of achieving, what Rife and his associates claimed for the Universal Microscope eighty years earlier. High-powered light microscopes such as the microsphere nanoscope may yet discover tiny organisms that are undetectable by electron microscopes. And since the organisms will be viewed in their live states the means for their eradication—provided that their discovery will not be suppressed as was allegedly done by Sloan-Kettering Cancer Institute as recently as 1985[75]—may follow and, perhaps, rather swiftly. The task of ascertaining the M.O.R. frequency specific to pathogenic forms, and the willingness to seriously test the claims of Rife and his associates seems to be inching towards a resolution, even if the name of Royal Rife has been forgotten or dare not be spoken by most present-day scientists. The microsphere nanoscope further demonstrates how modern technology, as also exemplified by the Arizona State University research (that uses resonant laser frequencies to destroy viruses) may yet follow a path similar in principle to Rife's.

Healing the body is one matter and healing the human spirit is another. Much could be accomplished by acknowledging profound wrongdoings perpetrated by governments, professional organizations and others in the persecution and hardship inflicted on dedicated innovators who were far ahead of their time and who did not waver in their dedication to the furtherance of their goals. Individuals like Royal R. Rife—and even those whose ideas are later proved wrong—should be commended and celebrated for the strength of their conviction while enduring tremendous hardship in the process. And when these visionaries of science are vindicated they should be given credit. When "new" ideas and technologies reemerge, the failure to acknowledge the debt owed to others especially when they have been scorned and forgotten is a wrong and a damnable one at that. Failure to acknowledge the truth of the past only insures a future plagued with self-imposed limitations that inhibit and retard moral, spiritual and intellectual development. A veil of ignorance will merely hide still other truths that exist beyond the paradigms.

*   *   *   *

Suppression of technology can have consequences that are comparable—in terms of resultant misery, economic woe and loss of life—to the most heinous of crimes. Judgments about the scale of criminality, of course, require proof that the suppressions occurred, and proof that the technologies would indeed have worked as claimed. Even if suppressed technologies are not validated, it is quite plausible that the acts of suppression could have stymied important advances in research and development that would have developed absent the interference and obstruction. The history of suppressed inventions should become a mainstream field. History can be more than a retelling of that which has occurred from the point of view of the historian, it can also change the future. Latter-day corrections of past faults may yet empower the future. But the wrongs of the past, if left uncorrected, are projected into the future. And continued suppression of technologies in fields such as medicine and energy can result in future losses of life and of wealth that are of such magnitude that, like compounding interest, profoundly deepen by the day.

~ Fears of "free energy" ~

The reports of Rife's successes may have not been accurate and they may even have been fraudulent, but the ruthless suppression by government and medical authorities strongly suggests otherwise. While the writer is not a scientist, I do know the difference between a fair and objective assessment of the facts and behaviors associated with it, and the behavior of obstruction and suppression. When assessing the possibility of a fraudulent invention, the motives and tactics of those who would prevent the objective evaluation of an invention or a scientific claim are likely to be as a important as is the fair and objective evaluation of the invention itself.

The suppression of Rife's work came to be scoffed at as "pseudoscience" by skeptics and other obstructionists who felt no need to actually test the inventions, and employed the "logic" of "it can't work, therefore, an opportunity should never be afforded to prove otherwise." And yet, as has been discussed, scientists today are seriously considering light powered microscopes that may challenge or surpass the power and usefulness of electron microscopes, as well as resonance theories for destroying viruses. Obviously, the technological advances over the past seventy years have a look and a capacity that were not possible for Rife. But the high-tech use of microspheres and software seem to be doing something that is essentially similar to Rife's unique use and configuration of prisms to restrict light to compensate for its dispersion during magnification. While the use of resonance induced by lasers is certainly different than the use of radio waves, the notion of using resonance to destroy microorganisms is essentially the same. And so we are back to the future, and the opportunity to undo possible suppression of the past by wedding it to modern technology may have finally arrived. But the convergence with the past will likely require some shifting of the paradigms.

Hyper-paradigmatic thinking hypnotically rejects even the possibility that certain "laws of physics" may be wrong or incomplete. Foremost among these "laws" is probably the "law of the conservation of energy" which states that a closed system (e.g. an energy generator) cannot produce more energy than is put into it. A coal-powered electric generator, for example, cannot produce more energy transformed into electricity than is produced by the burning coal that fuels the generator. However, alternative theories of "zero-point energy" argue that there is energy stored in "the fabric of space" that is not measurable because it is outside the closed system of what is conventionally considered to be the known universe. If beings lived in an air bubble and the only the gases known were the gases inside the bubble, the denizens of this closed system would be unaware of the immense sources of gas and other forms of potential energy that exist outside the bubble. The universe is said to be spherical and space is said by Einstein to be curved. But the curvature of space suggests that it is a quasi-substance and, hence, perhaps a source of quasi-energy. If wormholes can theoretically be bored into space with the expenditure of enormous energy, it seems strange that something requiring such vast amounts of energy to penetrate, curve or warp would not be itself in one fashion or another a reservoir of more energy. And this does not even touch upon the question of what if anything exists outside the bubble of space or spacetime.

Solar energy is "free." Wind power and hydroelectric power are "free." So, what is the basis of the claim that "free energy" is a scientific impossibility? The notion of energy embedded in space is outside the conventional paradigm even though the Big Bang theory posits a simultaneous creation of matter and space, and as matter moves further into space from the point of origin space continually expands. It is unclear which is the better metaphor: Is matter the mother of space or is space the mother of matter? Is it a stretch to conceptualize the possibility that space, like matter, is part of the continuum between matter and energy, a space-matter-energy continuum that is an integral expression of the universal energy. Should the embedding of energy in space someday be verified, the notion of limitless energy could just as easily be considered to be "free energy" as today sunlight, wind, and water may be a considered to be free because they are ubiquitous, in some cases virtually unlimited and are available to anyone who has the technology to tap it. "Free energy," though, is a bad term. Arguably, petroleum is free energy if we look at all of the earth's resources as free, but this point of view is certainly not helpful because sunlight and wind cannot be monopolized while oil clearly can be and continues to be monopolized. And water is to a certain extent prone to disruption as, for e.g. during military conflicts and, of course, it is also subject to natural shortages. Solar energy is hardly free today because the ratio of the cost of investment to the production of energy is *not* cheap; it is a matter of scale as, for example, solar energy for heating a home or operating a business is not free but solar power is virtually free when it comes to powering a small calculator. The hypothetical development and investment involved in making a "zero-point" or "overunity" power generator could be quite expensive but, on the other hand, if the energy output is vast and ongoing any associated costs could make it very cheap as compared to the existing energy technology and, for all practical intents and purposes, virtually free over time. The real question, then, does not concern "free" energy but, rather, the possibility of very inexpensive or cheap energy that is available readily to all with minimal expense, and ceases to be a principal motivation for war. The world's economic potential and the empowerment that would result from free energy would be unprecedented.

The basic view espoused here is that without proper scientific review, testing and openness of mind, an invention should not be arbitrarily dismissed. Roughly paralleling the years in which Royal R. Rife was developing his microscope and resonant frequency devices and confronting obstructionist greed and suppression, another man by the name of T. Henry Moray was astounding spectators with a machine that appeared capable of powering 5000 watt light bulb banks with no apparent incoming source of energy other than an antenna that seemed to draw the energy out of thin air. By 1925 the device was generating a few hundred watts,[76] and by 1939 its output had improved to 50,000 watts and was being demonstrated to many witnesses that included a number of highly credible observers.[77] Moray B. King (no familial relation to the inventor) writes that in his view Moray's radiant energy device is founded on the hypothesis that "abrupt, synchronous, ion surges in plasma appear to coherently activate the zero-point energy (ital.)"[78] King reviews some of Moray's patents for clues that may help explain how the radiant energy device may have worked. King's book also discusses the work of many other inventors and scientists whose work in zero-point energy relate to Moray's.

The suppression of inventions, many of which are of potentially enormous significance, is in and of itself a powerful argument, indeed, the most powerful argument for demanding that fair and objective inquiry be carried out in order to determine the truth or falsity of claims made. The issue goes well beyond science—and the demand for good science surely should be enough, because it concerns the moral imperative of evaluating potential alternative technologies in light of the basic principles of ethics; suppression decidedly falls short of open-minded, multiple perspectives of the dualistic principles of fairness, beneficence and compassion. These suppressions, if true, are utterly incoherent both in terms of the intention to do harm and the incalculable harm potentially or actually done to humanity. Moray's demonstrations are less documented than Rife's but there are sufficient reasons to be concerned. Both cases pass the smell test; neither Moray nor Rife come across as con men or frauds, they devoted their lives and virtually all their money only to see their dreams ruthlessly taken away. In Moray's case, reminiscent of Rife's treatment by the FDA and Fishbein's

AMA, he claimed harassment by the Rural Electrification Administration of the U.S. Department of Agriculture, a mysterious disappearance of over a dozen patents from the U.S. Patent Office, death threats and a violent gunshot attack in his lab that left him wounded.[79]

The most compelling evidence supporting the need to seriously investigate the truth regarding Moray's energy technology—at least for anyone whose mind has not become closed to the enduring need for examining and reexamining the assumptions and presumptions of truth, is an affidavit that was written and signed by the esteemed physicist Harvey Fletcher about two years before his death. The Wikipedia article on Fletcher states that he "was an American physicist. Known as the 'father of stereophonic sound' he is credited with the invention of the audiometer and hearing aid. He is remembered as a trail-blazing investigator into the nature of speech and hearing, and for his numerous contributions in acoustics, electrical engineering, speech, medicine, music, atomic physics, sound pictures, and education."[80] The notarized affidavit, signed on May 25, 1979, states that in 1928 he was invited by officials of the Mormon Church to one of T. Henry Moray's demonstrations. Fletcher writes that the output of the device powered twelve 75-watt 110-volt light bulbs plus a 500-watt 110-volt electric iron. Dr. Fletcher concluded his affidavit by stating, "I did not know how the device functioned and do not know today, but I do know that it did function for the several hours of the time that I observed it. I could discern no batteries, and could observe no other known methods of inducing electric power into the box or its loads."[81] (See Fig. 3 in the Appendix to view and read the original document in its entirety.) What is the appropriate response to this document? It appears, at least in part, to be the product of a man who had something on his mind that he wanted to clear up and get off his chest before he died. It certainly does not appear to be an irrational statement of an old man who was no longer of sound mind. What could have been Fletcher's motive? Does it confirm that Moray's device did what was claimed? Clearly it does not. But it is not only disrespectful to the integrity of a man like Fletcher to not at least take his words seriously, it is also patently foolish. Should Moray's invention—and perhaps other inventions with similar functionality—eventually get validated it will certainly rank among the most momentous inventions (or class of inventions) in history and would, almost overnight, bestow economic and personal freedom undreamed of by "realists" everywhere. Fletcher's intention in leaving his affidavit to posterity can be reasonably interpreted as an effort to spur the scientific and engineering communities to open doorways to the possible that, for his own reasons, he was unable or unwilling to do himself when he was at the height of his influence. Fletcher is asking scientists to avoid repeating his mistake and failure to act, and to take off their blinders so that they might actually take a serious look. And if there is nothing to see, so be it. But some courageous scientists, for e.g. physicist, Steven E. Jones, are willing to seriously explore the possibility of the significant potential of alternative energies. "Until we learn its fundamental origin," Jones calls the subject of inquiry "Freedom Energy."[82]

~ *Quantum Convergence* ~

Physicists theorize that there are an unlimited number of potential futures. For example, theories concerning the possibility of time travel run into the problem of the "grandfather paradox" that conjures a man who travels into the past to a time before his father was born and then kills his paternal grandfather. Ordinary logic would seem to indicate that the time traveler would cease to exist because his father's father would have been killed before he was conceived. However, quantum theorists theorize that at the moment of the killing the timeline would be split into two separate parallel timelines: one in which the homicidal time traveler exists and another in which he doesn't. Quantum time splitting comes to mind when we consider "what-might-have-been" scenarios with respect to inventions that were suppressed or unrealized for other reasons. Let's say, for the purpose of speculation, that Rife's inventions are valid or would have become so with some further development if the AMA and the FDA did not shut him down, and we could also consider the same sort of scenario with respect to Moray's radiant energy device. If we were to be able to time travel into parallel timelines we might observe the world that might have been had the suppressions not occurred. However, there is a more practical possibility! What if suppressed inventions, some long forgotten, were to be revisited, scientifically investigated and finally validated?

The excavation of inventions or lines of thinking lost to history and brought back to life with renewed vigor is entirely plausible when one considers the tunnel vision of scientific paradigms. In fact, tunnel-like focus is the very purpose of scientific paradigms in order that anomalous material can be dismissed so that scientists can stay on track and, well, continue to put most of their efforts into proving existing paradigms. If a dedicated institutional body with adequate financial and political resources could follow thorough on the research and development of suppressed technologies, then there might well occur what may be called a quantum convergence. Is it possible that the vacuum tube is an area of experimentation that still possesses gems of discovery yet to be realized? Those tubes in their various forms are little testing grounds of quantum events that an individual inventor—such as T. Henry Moray—could explore in his lab. The digital age would not have occurred without the transistor and solid-state circuitry, but inventors like Moray perhaps provide a glimpse into technologies that were bypassed by the inevitable tunnel vision of the new technology. This little reverie on the vacuum tube is just that and nothing more, only a speculation concerning how paradigms and prevailing trends have almost certainly left behind discoveries and leads for further inquiry that await rediscovery or discovery for the first time.

My focus in this section has been the inventions of Rife and Moray, however there are many forgotten or suppressed inventions that warrant close examination. Another energy device worthy of serious investigation is the "fuelless generator" developed by the inventor Lester Hendershot, first demonstrated in 1928. A number of devices invented by more recent and contemporary inventors have also been ignored by mainstream science. Clearly, the merits of inventions are critical, but evidence of suppression in the form of intimidation, bribery, heavy-handedness by government, violence and restraint of trade in all its guises are, in and of themselves, justification to aggressively *seek* justice in the form of serious examinations of suppressed inventions. Or has justice lost its appeal? The excavation and revisitation of suppressed technologies would likely stimulate inter-paradigmatic cross-fertilizations that can marry missed opportunities with a grateful future. By means of a quantum convergence of the past and the present, we may find that by saving the past we will have also saved the future.

~ *Paradigms and Plural Perspectivism* ~

There is a fundamental epistemic, scientific and societal need for the creation of official institutions or centers of contra-paradigmatic research. Restricting competing perspectives that challenge existing paradigms and actualities in particular fields only compromises the integrity of the state of knowledge. But while technologies and theories that challenge existing paradigms should be encouraged they are, in fact, discouraged. And inventions and ideas that do not fit into the conventional paradigms are not only discouraged but the pursuit of them is done at great risk to professional reputation, funding of research and even loss of career. The suppression of technology that contradicts accepted beliefs are largely motivated by ego, money and institutional pressures to conform, but they have little to do with the advancement of knowledge. Fear of shifting paradigms is nothing other than the fear of knowledge and of progress by those who do not care much about either.

Consider the enormous investment in research and development that has been expended on programs that are only marginally justifiable at best. And what would it cost to explore the potential of missed opportunities in the form of suppressed inventions of bygone years? There is very little to lose but incalculably much to gain. The argument that all alternative technologies are fraudulent because they are "scientifically impossible" is itself the supreme height of pretense, arrogance and is a true pseudo-scientific attitude. Every paradigm shift that has ever occurred is an irrefutable argument against the arrogance that suppresses inventions and ideas that contradict currently accepted beliefs. Plural perspectivism (§I.8) encourages and seeks perspectives that challenge beliefs, theories and opinions that currently hold sway; in contrast, the scientific paradigm— while enormously important, can degrade itself into "paradigmism" or scientific religion that worships existing paradigms and excommunicates any wanderer who dares to challenge the orthodoxy. Just consider the precious funding wasted on frivolous projects that do not advance knowledge a whit and never had a chance of doing so. And consider the high probability that there are at least some jewels of progress that have been buried by ignorance or fear. If inventions such as Rife's microscope and resonant frequency healing device, and Moray's radiant energy device have any chance of validation or have been needlessly repressed then they are well worth pursuing. While scientific paradigms are clearly necessary, and they do indeed advance the progress of science, a *close-minded* science that arbitrarily rejects and suppresses opposing viewpoints is the worst sort of epistemic fraudulency. But if paradigms can co-exist within a broader philosophy of plural perspectivism opportunities could be boundless, and a quantum convergence of the past and the present is possible.

Centers of contra-paradigmatic research need to be embedded into official academic, governmental and industrial research institutions so that a spirit and a mission of paradigmatic challenge becomes an intrinsic part of the culture of science and innovation. "Never look back" is a maxim that does not apply to any field of endeavor that seeks to shape the future. We must look back not only so that we do not forget the lessons of history but also so that we might recover lessons that have been lost or may have never been learned. Centers of contra-paradigmatic research would be assigned the task of looking backward as well as forward. Scientific research and development should welcome the challenge and will be far the better for it. The clinical testing of natural dietary supplements as treatments that are declined by Big Pharma because of insufficient profit potential or because of paradigmism, or both, is a worthy area of contra-paradigmatic research. Institutionalizing paradigmatic challenge would not weaken or distract from "normal science" but it will open the door to a quickening of change. And by institutionalizing paradigmatic challenge we may degrade the rather ridiculous spectacle of advocates of mainstream and alternative science taking turns in playing the role of the Pot calling the Kettle black. Or, we can simply continue to ignore basic ethical principles that demand the betterment of the human condition. We can also close our eyes to the possibility that our "progress" has actually been a potpourri of missed opportunities and, like an ancient sailing vessel, merely a prisoner of the prevailing winds.

II.16

Ethics of Invention

Patent law and its effects on technological creativity and progress should empower. An ethical patent system is, or ought to be concerned with both social progress and protecting the commercial interests of inventors. The current patent system, however, can allow a patent to serve as a counterproductive vehicle that serves greed and obstructs progress.

Laws reflecting a morally coherent ethics of invention would protect inventors' rights while simultaneously protecting society's interest by encouraging and facilitating technological progress. The rights of the inventor and the interest of the society naturally coincide. The most empowered patent system would be one that facilitates both technological invention *and* commercial and practical applications of new inventions. Intellectual property laws relating to patent and invention should have three concerns: a) To best motivate and stimulate invention, b) To most effectively and safely introduce new inventions into the marketplace, and c) To protect both the financial interests of inventors and the interest of society in realizing the benefits of invention.

Empowerment requires a climate of both external motivation and internal self-motivation. It would be most advantageous to have a system in which the inventor is motivated by potential financial reward for his work, but which is also paralleled by motivation coming from society and culture that deeply reflects and supports these interests. Can anyone doubt that important inventions have been delayed for lengthy periods of time, if not completely thwarted, because financial hurdles were too great a burden for inventors of modest means to overcome? At the present time, a patent typically has a fixed term of twenty years. However, is a monopoly on the development of the patented invention in the best interests of the inventor or of society? It is hereby proposed that, in place of the current patent system that assigns exclusive market rights of an invention to the patent holder (and its licensees), there should be instituted a universally accessible, fee-based *open patent system* in which any party may commercially utilize inventions after payment of license and royalty fees to the inventor or patent holder. The fees would be determined by standardized *pro forma* schedules or by an impartial patent board in order to facilitate expeditious development and marketing of the invention and provide fair compensation for the inventor (individual or corporate). In the proposed system, a newly patented product will rapidly begin to benefit both the inventor and society by enabling other parties to bring the invention to market upon payment of the initial licensing fee. The inventor or patent holder will continue to benefit throughout the term of the patent from royalty payments or commissions based on sales. Since patents would be universally licensable, inventors could benefit enormously from the development of their inventions by a diverse source of developers. Industry, meanwhile, will flourish as companies compete to market products that utilize the inventions that they are licensed to develop and market. Product development of inventions will improve far more rapidly under this proposed system than in the traditional system of exclusive control over development by patent holders. It could prove desirable to extend the patent term period beyond twenty years to provide even further financial incentive for inventors.

The existing patent system encourages corruption by facilitating the suppression of invention. In the current system, a patent can be purchased and then left in cold storage. If the inventor is an individual or small business it may feel trapped by financial pressures and other circumstances and have no choice other than that of selling the patent to parties whose only interest is in protecting their market share by suppressing the new invention in favor of an existing and, perhaps, less desirable product or technology. The present proposal will circumvent the suppression of inventions because patents would be available for development by others almost from the moment that the patent is approved. The development of new inventions could not be thwarted by the purchase of patents solely for the purposes of suppression because, under the proposed system, there would be no limitation on the ability of others to purchase licenses to develop the invention that might otherwise be the target of suppression. There would no longer be any point of buying patents only to keep them in the freezer. All that the would-be suppressor could accomplish by paying a licensing fee to use a patent would be to become a legitimate participant in the advancement of progress: but the patent would no longer be an instrument of suppression.

The inventions of Royal Rife or T. Henry Moray, if their inventions have validity, would have been more difficult to suppress if the opportunity to participate in the development of paradigm shifting technologies had been made open and accessible by a patent system such as the one proposed. Of course, government regulatory suppression could remain an issue, but the introduction of multiple developers would create political pressures to block any effort to suppress the active development of transformational or paradigm shifting technologies. There is an enormous array of inventions that have allegedly been suppressed, and an open patent system encouraging universal opportunities for licensing and development will be a very large step in the direction of reclaiming the peoples' collective right to technological progress, and towards a government that protects rather than, as has been alleged, conspires against them. Suppressions would be effectively discouraged and progress would be effectively encouraged, not by dreams of monopoly but, rather, by a truly democratic marketplace that rewards both creativity and invention and ensures the advancement of knowledge and technology. A system that encourages the development of invention by guaranteeing inventors fair compensation for the development of their work by others will lift unnecessary secrecy that deeply threatens progress. The inventor or patent holder will want its invention to quickly enter into the public arena, and the clouds of secrecy that in the past dampened progress because of the fear of theft would evolve into a culture of information sharing; patents will become seeds for progress that assures profit for the inventor that under the current system may never be realized. The proposed open patent system would rapidly stimulate multiple lines of technological advancement.

Should the vindication of those who have suffered unjust suppression of their inventions be cause for compensation? Should it be mandated that a patent that has been unjustly rejected, or an invention unjustly suppressed on grounds of "pseudoscience" or arbitrary paradigmism later be awarded compensation retroactively, either to the inventor, the inventor's estate or the corporate patent holder? Should a government or its agency that sanctioned the suppression pay compensation? Should the corporate or financial interests that initiated or orchestrated the suppression be forced to pay? What would justice require? Doing nothing would seem unjust.

II.17

The Market Dogma

D ogmas are intellectualisms that may be compared to old moats designed to protect castles. But against what does dogma defend? The truth needs no protection and repels attack more effectively and with greater agility than the most clever of propagandists. But, of course, dogma defends not the truth but only itself, much as a moat protects the castle even when its monarch has shown disregard for the welfare and safety of the people. The dogma that in all cases the "free market" is both a good ethical and a good economic concept is, like all dogma, a Trojan horse. In the case of the market dogma, selfishness may be disguised as freedom, justice or prosperity. And like many dogmas it attempts to generalize limited relevancy into absolute adherence.

~   ~   ~

When we think of dogma, the first area that generally comes to mind concerns the philosophies of politics and economics that are today marked by the opposite poles of libertarianism (or laissez-faireism) and socialism (or governmental interventionism and activism in the market). The principle of complementary incommensurables makes it possible for each of them to have dominance in there their respective spheres of applicability. However, many Americans grow up indoctrinated by libertarian gospels of free market dogma in which any government interference is at best a necessary evil that should be applied in extremely limited circumstances. The indoctrination can also occur later in life, and there is no truer devotee than the converted. Clearly, indoctrination and conversions occur on the socialist and progressive sides as well. Dogmatic tunnel vision makes compromise nearly impossible.

To *partially* echo Thoreau, the best roles for private enterprise and for government are that each do what it does best. In a universe of complementary incommensurables libertarian and socialist philosophies each thrive in their appropriate domains and the best social systems have aspects of both. In America, *everything* seems to be viewed in terms of "the market." Should there be no clear edge to either market orientation, the edge should always go the private sector: this is a legitimate libertarian principle. Commonsense also dictates that financial responsibility can sometimes be shared between the private and public sectors. But capitalistic dogma should be deeply questioned with respect to the relevancy of the profit motive in the spheres of education, the practice of law, and caring for the sick and infirm.

~   ~   ~

Loving intention is neither capitalistic nor socialistic. There is nothing morally incoherent about the profit motive, in fact, it is the stimulus for the creation of products and services that enormously improve lives and advance civilization. But let us examine what we want to get out of the profit motive. A good shoe manufacturer wants to produce a superior shoe but it also wants to make a profit, and profit motivates the production of superior footwear or inexpensive footwear, but whichever direction the manufacturer takes profit is the reward of successful competition in the marketplace. We would not want to see profit motive removed as the primary motivator for most consumer products. However, the market dogma seems to suggest that the economics of education and healthcare is no different in-kind than the selling of footwear or fast food. Certainly, *cost* is a critical factor in providing any service and there is a limit to how much an individual or society can spend, but the role of profit in the provision of healthcare is a fair question for any fair-minded person. The very utterance of "capitalistic medicine" sounds oxymoronic. Straightforward market forces do not apply when profitability takes precedence over the basic moral imperative to adequately care for the sick. The mission of society and the only morally coherent path respective to the provision of healthcare is that it be effective without breaking the bank. Whether healthcare is libertarian or socialist, profit in and of itself has little urgency in the moral dialectic of healthcare. The health of private insurance companies does not have priority over the health of people.

Does a rich man have more right to live than a poor man? If you answer 'Yes,' then at least you have honestly acknowledged your support for the essence of opposition to universal healthcare. But if you answer 'No' then you agree that while a wealthy man should have every prerogative to buy more expensive shoes than someone else, his right to live and to receive medical treatment should not favor him or be decided by his income. Every person by virtue of birth deserves healthcare that is limited only by the ability of society to provide the same service for everyone.

~   ~   ~

These are perverse times in the United States in which the costs of higher education and of healthcare have grown to astronomic absurdity. In the case of healthcare, if the government assumed an active if not the major role in the research and development of pharmaceuticals, and then entered them into the public domain for manufacture by private drug companies, the cost of pharmaceuticals would significantly or dramatically become less costly. Additionally, the open patent system proposal (§II.16) would lower the cost of the private development of pharmaceuticals. And further cost reductions would be achieved by the subsidization of research concerning effective usage of natural dietary supplementation for the treatment and prevention of disease. (§II.15)

The moral incoherence of high profits also applies to the education industry. And as is the case with healthcare, significant costs can be saved if paradigms relating to the profit motive are shifted. The essence of academic learning is the relationship between a reader and her books, not a massive infrastructure. But if the culture were to cultivate a renewed passion for reading, then learning would advance rapidly throughout society. How could the world's great art and literature, discoveries, inventions and entrepreneurship have occurred when the cost of education was only a fraction, in relative terms, of what it is today? The world has fallen in love with the exteriority of achievement and out of love with the quiet humility of pure learning. The seductive quality of profit that continually seeks more demand and more profit can be dispiriting and *devaluing* for industries such as education and healthcare. When do excessive demands for profit in endeavors such as these finally turn their professed value into a disingenuous sarcasm?

Higher education—especially in the age of the internet—can do with less infrastructure and administrative overhead, and benefit from a renewed focus on the teacher-student relationship. Furthermore, the amalgamation of research and teaching only serves to increase the cost of education. There is no good reason for scientific research to depend on funding by institutions of higher learning. Research should be publicly and privately funded and should no longer be used as a rationalization for high-tuition costs that few can afford. Education simply does not need to cost as much as it currently does. Clearly, it is necessary for there to be relationships between universities, research laboratories and industry but entanglements that unnecessarily increase the costs of higher education need to be undone. There can be a return to the basics of education that are separated out from other commercial interests. In other words, the balance sheet of an educational institution should reflect investments in education, education and then some more education. Financial and business arrangements outside that which is directly involved with the education of students should be completely independent and self-sustaining. Funding for higher education should be in the form of tuition, public subsidization and other subsidies that may *flow from* affiliated interests. However, if funding by institutions of higher learning that *flows to* any entity or activity not strictly concerned with education and teaching is eliminated, then education would once again become affordable. Buildings on the college campus may be smaller, fewer and more modest but higher education would be richer, and graduates will start life without a daunting debt or their parents unfairly burdened. The improving status of online higher education buttresses this argument.

~   ~   ~

There is a legal market for attorney services, but would we be comfortable in characterizing that marketplace as the "justice market?" But the actuality is that if the best and most talented defense attorneys are unaffordable by some if not most, then those who can afford better legal representation have an unequal share of justice. But unequal justice is not justice. Justice in America, at least when it comes to hiring defense attorneys, *is* a market. But if justice is something that can be bought then there is no denying that the scales of justice are a farce. In America, it seems that no activity is too sacrosanct for the profit motive to take center stage.

~   ~   ~

The market is holy in America, but as a result the sense of value can become lost. The price of oil swings wildly. And better and more efficient forms of ethanol or biofuel that are derived from sources other than corn would be much more cost-effective and would not drive up the cost of food. But there is very lucrative market in the instability of oil prices that have produced unprecedented profits for the petroleum industry. The silly fiction that the price at the pump has any connection to real value is not taken seriously by anyone, especially the oil company executives who play us. But all this is quite proper when the only definer of value is the market.

~   ~   ~

The Great Recession of the past several years that resulted in the famous bank bailout was truly a sight to behold. And then, after the bailout, credit card rates were universally and dramatically jacked up while lending became scarce if not nonexistent. The behavior of the banks tells you what you need to know about unrestrained markets. Self-interest is a legitimate motive that drives profit, but there is a greed threshold. It is like a controlled explosion in an internal combustion engine; when the force becomes too extreme the machine will explode or simply stop working. Likewise, there are points at which greed can exceed the economy's tolerance and, if left unregulated, its implosion becomes inevitable. Rather than the spectacle of The Great Bank Bailout, here is a case in which the free market and antitrust actions should have been allowed to reshape the banking industry.

~   ~   ~

Profit is a good thing and is, in fact, the principal external motivator for good deeds both mundane and monumentally great. However, as in all things, moderation is the universal delimiter. There are innumerable examples of the incoherence of excessive profiteering or greed, some of which will be addressed in sections that follow. A glaring example of conventional wisdom that almost everyone recognizes as unethical and morally incoherent, most probably including the culprits themselves, is the age-old matter of excessive profits in lending money. The excess is often, strictly speaking, not in usurious interest rates but in total profit (although excessive interest rates, of course, are also culpable) accrued by means of compound interest in an ever-expanding cycle that begins to unfold when the original terms cannot be met. The conventional wisdom is locked into the formality that justifies lending practices that expand the obligations of debtors by compounding interest virtually without limit. The U.S. government is currently paying well over $1 billion in interest payments per day! And this ridiculous scenario is only one of the most blatant pictures of a morally bankrupt financial system that today permeates every corner of the globe. And moral bankruptcy often ends in financial bankruptcy.

The exponentially increasing U.S. debt is mirrored by the personal debt of millions of individuals, families and businesses everywhere and is systemically encouraged. The *unlimited* expansion of debt through compound interest is an economic vampirism that parallels the practice of the fictional vampires who suck the blood out of the living. Currency is the lifeblood of economic activity and excess interest charges in lending are the deeds of vampires created by a system inspired by greed, already dead in spirit, that drains the economic life of others. The World Bank and the International Monetary Fund conspire to help poor developing nations descend into a syndrome of increasing debt that is impossible to repay. Bankrupting the poor and bankrupting the most powerful of nations is an embarrassing display of how far otherwise intelligent human beings will descend to dismiss the injunction to love thy neighbor as thyself, done with a stiff arm and arrogant disdain for the everyman. The bankers that comprise the pseudo-private Federal Reserve and other banking agencies are getting richer and destroying currencies not necessarily by charging unreasonable interest rates but by reaping shameful profits. How much profit is enough? The answer, of course, is that where greed is concerned nothing is ever enough because greed is insatiable. When the practice of exorbitant profiteering via the limitless expansion of compounding debt is replaced with a financial practice that places *reasonable limits on reasonable profitability*, then profitability and affluence will revitalize both the world's economy as well as its spirit.

~   ~   ~

It is a common credo that has become dogma that says, "We can never go back to the gold standard!" The momentous change in discarding the old gold standard in favor of market bidding has contributed greatly to the unprecedented loss in the value of the U.S. dollar in relation to an ounce of gold, as well as to the general instability of currency values worldwide. The various forms of the gold standard in the past were not perfect, but they had clearly produced far greater market stability than the current system of bidding on what is essentially the value of monetary value. However, the old versions of the gold standard were also flawed; a new proposal is made in a subsequent section.

~   ~   ~

The *Selling of the President 1968* by Joe McGinnis, the bestseller with the unforgettable cover showing a pack of cigarettes with Richard Nixon's face on it revealed the ever-deepening and transforming relationship between American electoral politics and money. The notion that elections are for sale has deepened enormously ever since as campaign spending in America has soared. There is more to getting elected than the amount of money a candidate spends, but it is undeniable that the candidate and the party with the most money has a significant advantage. Questions may be asked, "How much campaign spending is too much? "How can what is spent be more fairly distributed amongst the candidates?" But if the concern is framed in terms of requisites and basic needs, the intent of these questions can be posed this way: "What level and what form of spending can most fairly and effectively give the electorate the best opportunity to make impartial and informed choices?" While the level of spending on election campaigns must be addressed, the primary concern ought to be the quality of the election process. In the skyrocketing of campaign spending in America we, again, see an activity fundamental to democracy conducted in terms of market principles when philosophical principles of fairness and societal empowerment would more correctly address the essence of the matter. If spending vast sums and clever fundraising tactics are the best way to conduct election campaigns, then we might as well condone a system that encourages political candidates to spend like drunken sailors. But an alternative approach would be far preferable. If the electoral process shifts from a focus on fundraising and its inevitable association with special interests, to one that is dedicated to informing the public about the issues and the candidates the electorate will elevate itself *and* the candidates that they elect.

~   ~   ~

If substandard construction materials that are "within code" are knowingly used it can only be construed as a hypnotic-like adoption of the view that the greatest profit equals the greatest good. It could also be a symbol of the dogma that one should "exploit selfish interests to the fullest extent of the law!" And while it is certainly true that the law is not and cannot be a substitute for ethical decision, the law should inspire achievement beyond the lowest common denominator.

II.18

A Corruption of Justice

Money and justice mix about as well as oil and water, which is to say, they don't. The obvious truth that a purchase of "justice" is intrinsically corrupt is obscured by the philosophical dogma that makes profit a nearly exclusive motivation for the provision of goods and services. But profitability does not always apply. The dogmatic embrace of profit and the "justice market" was touched upon in the preceding section (§II.17) and we will delve a bit further here. Justice is as basic a requisite for civilized society as are usable roads and running water. But while there are ample opportunities to use money to make our lives easier, more enjoyable and more luxurious the purchase of justice ought not to be one of them. Of course, paying for a high priced attorney can get someone out of legal difficulties, but this reality makes the point that justice bought is not justice. The purchase of justice is best described as a form of legalized corruption.

Profit is not the only distraction that is embedded in the justice system. Disreputable prosecutors may be more motivated by ego or by misplaced pressures to get a conviction rather than in keeping an open mind to all the facts. And with the advent of DNA testing we have seen the fallibility of the justice system verified too frequently. A lawyer who cares less about justice than about winning a case produces a contravention of justice, and the contravention occurs regardless of whether he is a prosecutor or a defense attorney. Of course, a lawyer's job is to win the case, but regardless of whether a judicial system is adversarial or inquisitorial there is something perverse about a justice system whose primary motive is not justice. And there are too many motives, with the profit motive leading the list, which distract from justice. In a justice system, nothing should matter other than an interest in seeing that justice is served. The principle at work here is a general one that is applicable for commercial activities in which the profit motive, when functioning as the central principle, is intrinsically corrupt. The reality that justice can be bought is no less nauseating and reprehensible than making the cost of higher education or a cure unaffordable to many—or only at the cost of financial ruin.

Another issue that is corollary to profit and that distracts from the pursuit of justice is press and media coverage of courtroom trials in the United States. Press coverage of trials as well as coverage leading up to them can seriously bias a jury and threaten a just outcome. Whereas the justice market and its system of profiteering lawyers is an intrinsic corruption of justice because greater purchasing power may get better legal representation, press coverage can also interfere with the procurement of justice by creating an unnecessary risk of biasing the jury. Constitutional issues concerning freedom of the press and the impartiality of the jury are not the issues here: hail the privilege of philosophy in discussing ideas without the nasty practicalities of existing legal and constitutional constraints! Dismissive remarks such as, "Well, this is the way our judicial system works" is a valid point, but is also beside the point because a legal system should always be philosophically open to self-examination and change. Press coverage and the broadcasting of trials flies in the face of the solemn social responsibility to do everything possible to ensure that the parties concerned are handed a decision that is as objective and as impartial as possible. Frankly, the First Amendment of the U.S. Constitution does not pertain to the fairness of a trial and if its application interferes with the process of achieving a just verdict, then it is a moral incoherency that should be addressed. Dear reader, the matter is transparent once you put yourself in the position of a person innocently accused of a crime. Would you give a damn about the "rights" of others to follow your case in the media if there were any chance that applying the First Amendment could bias your trial's outcome or its subsequent appeal? Of course not! Louis Brandeis' statement that free speech rights do not support "yelling fire in a crowded theatre" is an exemplification of the sacred priority of justice over First Amendment concerns. In truth, justice ultimately overrides any countervailing consideration simply because if it isn't just it isn't right. The freedoms of speech and press do not trump justice, and the profits of press and media companies are not, need we be reminded, protected by the Constitution.

Some defense attorneys may rationalize their agreement to defend those whom they believe to be guilty because they may value their fees more highly than they value justice. The legal defense of those believed by the lawyer to be guilty is itself unsettling even if sometimes necessary, but its encouragement by means of unfair profiteering badly compounds the issue. It can be said with accuracy that the current "justice market" can finance the victory of injustice. The defense of wealthy criminals, from Ponzi schemers to mobsters to celebrities-turned-criminals makes the potential corruption of the justice system much too clear to be ignored.

> *It must be a tug of duty too powerful to deny that*
> *inspires the impassioned cry, "Every accused*
> *deserves a defender!" And so the profiteering lawyer*
> *nobly defends the wealthy criminal whose plea of*
> *innocence he knows to be a lie. Touching! Justice is*
> *the last thing on* that *lawyer's mind.*

The vomit-inducing thought of hardened criminals getting a superior legal defense is made possible only because justice has been made a marketable commodity. Profit is no more applicable to a system of justice than it is to educational or healthcare systems. If profit is removed as a barrier to justice, and justice is no longer viewed as something that can be bought, and if the quality of legal defense is not based upon how much a defendant can pay, then the criminal will finally lose the capacity to *outspend* his way to an unjust defense.

II.19

Eclipsing the Political Party

A democracy flourishes and thrives when it expects and encourages its elected representatives to possess moral toughness. What type of individual is weaker and softer than the party man? By referring to the "party man" my intent is not to broad-brush anyone affiliated with a political party, but I do refer to those who abrogate their intelligence to the party. A party man's mentality is a form of the herd mentality; new ideas and creative solutions are discouraged in deference to party loyalty and party ideology. Party loyalties are instinctively defensive or aggressive, whichever is better suited for service or submission to the party line. Moral toughness, on the other hand, requires an instinctive openness and self-reflectivity or, to echo Socrates, a ready willingness to self-examine one's positions. While our quest to understand what is good, right and true is never more than pragmatic and conditional, we must nonetheless pledge ourselves to that quest which, while antithetical to the party, is much in agreement with principles of any high-minded democracy. Moral toughness in politics is an unshakeable commitment to help guide national conduct, its laws and its policies without untoward bias, dogma or ideology as best as leaders and citizens are capable of comprehending what is right. The morally tough must follow an independent path, which may also be a popular path provided that it is embodied with the courage of rational conviction.

George Washington's "Farewell Address" (1796) to the American people warning them against the formation of political parties (as James Madison had done earlier in "The Violence of Faction" in the *Federalist Papers*) was largely ignored by the politicians and the citizens of his day, but it has perhaps never been more powerful and more needed than it is today:

> ...the common and continual mischiefs of the spirit of

> party are sufficient to make it the interest and duty of
> a wise people to discourage and restrain it. It serves
> always to distract the public councils and enfeeble the
> public administration. It agitates the community with
> ill-founded jealousies and false alarms, kindles the
> animosity of one part against another, foments
> occasionally riot and insurrection.

It is not surprising that Washington's vision has been conveniently ignored by generations hypnotized into believing in the necessity of the political party. The basis of moral weakness is the abdication of reflectivity, self-examination and moral probing in favor of lazy, anti-intellectual reliance on groupthink. Artificially hardened liberal and conservative formalities drone on endlessly over the radio waves like a monotonous drumbeat. Conservative radio talk show host Michael Savage says, "Liberalism is a mental disorder" but in actuality many sorts of preconditioned and oversimplified thinking—as exemplified by the herd of conservative knee jerks on the radio, exhibit preoccupations and obsessions that resemble mental disorders. Dogma, be it close-mined liberalism or close-minded conservatism is unhealthy for both individualism and for society. The only long-term cure is the eventual de-hypnotization of the patient from his dogma and the rediscovery of the healing power of intellectual and political freedom. And a good place to start is to excise and eclipse the social cancer that is the political party.

In *Democracy and the Organization of Political Parties* (1902), Moisei Ostrogorski wrote that the institutionalized political party developed as a replacement to the old social classes that were being transformed by democracies:

> The advent of democracy shattered the old framework
> of political society. The hierarchy of classes and their
> internal cohesion were destroyed, and the time-honoured
> social ties which bound the individual to the community
> were severed. As the old fabric had to be replaced by
> a new one, the problem was to find out how the
> individual could be reunited to society...some modern

democracies have endeavored to solve it…in the form
of disciplined and permanent parties.[83]

Ostrogorski recommended a de-institutionalization of the political party. The question becomes whether in the twenty-first century there is any useful role for the political party, other than obstructionism and the dumbing down of electorates which, without parties, would have to actually study individual candidates before casting their votes. A presidential democratic system such as that of the United States votes for the person who will preside as president or political leader, compared to parliamentary systems that are based on party rule or party coalitions that comprise the majority in the government. In either system, the political party institutionalizes political divisiveness and acrimony whereas a no-party or independent political system would encourage an environment in which individual lawmakers can agree or disagree issue-by-issue absent institutional pressure to toe the party line. Without political parties, whose only interest is winning elections, legislators—who are already under great pressure to balance personal conviction against casting votes that are representative of the collective will of their constituencies, would be unconcerned with party allegiances that interfere with the best interests of democratic governance. Following along the lines of Ostrogorski's thinking, we can see a social evolution that has been progressively minimizing class divisions as it places more value on the integrity of the individual. Ironically, some individualism has morphed into an ideological groupthink along libertarian or Randian lines that is a faux individualism, which is really only another herd mentality of party or dogma that acts to inhibit expressions of the Self-Other duality that pervade *both* social and individual life. Intrinsically, a political party, whether it is on the left, the right, or anywhere in-between is an insidious impediment to individual expression by its interference with coalition building and coalition un-building that naturally galvanizes or un-galvanizes around the diverse issues of the day.

An independent political system, combined with radical campaign finance reforms, would empower the American polity. Local, state and congressional officeholders would be obligated to constituency and conscience only. *An independent non-party and publicly funded political system would replace corruptive funding processes that are tied to the political party and political lobbies.* The influence of lobbying groups would no longer be financial but would instead be exclusively derived from the legitimate voices of their respective memberships. Legislative activity and the political coalitions that form around it would be organized eclectically through naturally intersecting interests that are free of artificial party division. Let open nonpartisan primaries have ballots that are free of party labels or identification other than that of the candidates' names, and if there is no clear majority let the top two finishers compete in a runoff election. In U.S. presidential elections a series of winnowing elections would lead to a final runoff election, unless the winner has a clear majority, in which case, a runoff would be unneeded. Let all political advertising appearing on broadcast media be financed publicly or donated by broadcast stations. Let society encourage a return to straightforward political discourse by discouraging to the extent possible all political commercials and advertising save for unembellished talk, i.e. conversations or speeches by the candidates and their respective supporters. For the sake of encouraging intelligent discourse in the electoral process—and intelligence is indeed the bedrock of freedom—the basic conservatism of straight talk in politics needs to be embraced! Or we can continue to enjoy a political system that discourages moral toughness and encourages a political discourse dominated by pabulum and the party line.

An extremely hopeful development is afoot in American politics, as nonpartisan primaries seem to gaining some momentum in California, Washington and several other states. I have long advocated nonpartisan qualifying primaries in which candidates run without any party affiliation; if one candidate receives over 50 percent of the vote s/he wins, but if no candidate receives over 50 percent a final runoff election will decide the winner. This type of electoral system has been used in U.S. city governments for many years and is an outgrowth of the Progressive Movement to help fight party corruption, and has also been used in various forms in democracies around the world. However, political parties generally continue to play important roles in politics. In addition to guaranteeing that the winner of a democratic election earns over 50 percent of the vote, the system advocated here would clear away social blockages to political empowerment by prohibiting outright the institutional slating of candidates, and by instituting public financing as the primary, if not exclusive source of funding political elections. While organizations of all variety would certainly support political candidates and act as donation-free lobbyists that endorse individual candidates, there would be no slating of candidates and no labeling of party or other group identification on the ballot: the only names on the ballot should be the names of the candidates. *An empowered nonpartisan and independent political system would, as such, require a political culture that inspires confidence in the art of informed political discourse freed of party biases, and made freer by a broad diversity of opinion.*

II.20

Day of Greatness

A depoliticized society might be inspired enough to have a holiday that celebrates great achievers besides war heroes and political leaders. What an original idea! Yes, I am being facetious; I am certainly not opposed to celebrating national independence and great political leaders. But there is something troubling about the nearly exclusive emphasis of national holidays on the celebration of political leaders and war heroes. A nation is more than its political and military apparatus, and it is high time that the notion of a great national leader be inclusive of all walks of life, from the arts and sciences and literature, to invention, to business and entrepreneurship, to medicine and healing, to spirituality, to athletics and entertainment and any realm of beneficent achievement. A Day of Greatness much like World Peace Day should be a holiday celebration in every nation! Every nation has holidays to celebrate its great political leaders, but how many nations celebrate great historical leaders of other nations? Most nations are myopically preoccupied with their own national leaders, but the greatness of some historical leaders transcend national borders; Gandhi is as worthy of celebration in America as much as Washington or Lincoln is in India.

Great achievers would be periodically nominated, annually, as the foci for the different Day of Greatness celebrations in the various nations. Each year the various nominating committees of the various nations would nominate, respectively, a historical figure to be the focus of its national celebration. The day would be a celebration and an opportunity for learning about inspiring and thought provoking stories of struggle and great achievement. Is not the genius and courage of Galileo a timeless story worthy of celebration in any nation? Great scientists and inventors who had to endure the scorn of their contemporaries would certainly be fitting subjects for a Day of Greatness celebration. The remarkable qualities of true heroes who have often been forgotten will finally and justly be told to millions. Surely, a man like Nikola Tesla is worthy of this posthumous honor and much knowledge would be transmitted in the process. A Day of Greatness can be an opportunity to rediscover jewels of wisdom that hitherto have been buried by history and lost to humanity *up to a point in time*. These rediscovered jewels could be hope yet to be realized.

A Day of Greatness would help to build a peaceful world by the embrace of national celebrations of great heroes and achievements that may be *outside* the host nation's historical narrative, or which have not traditionally been the subject of national holidays. The common humanity of great men and women would be celebrated and embraced by the diversity of peoples and nations as their own; indeed, true heroism is the heritage of all humanity. There is no greater example of progress than enduring peace, but it is true that winning the peace has not infrequently meant fighting wars. Honoring those who died or fought for their countrymen is certainly worthy of solemn commemoration, but where are the holidays that celebrate the heroes of peace and nonviolence? The United Nations has declared September 21st as an annual World Peace Day. Temporary ceasefires are encouraged and public events are held around the world to celebrate the day. But we must go much further. Much like the proposed Day of Greatness, World Peace Day should be a *national* holiday in every nation and a day of thoughtful reflection on serious strategies of peace. More than pomp and parades, imagine a media day overflowing with documentaries on the quest for peace, lectures abounding in big cities and small towns, workshops for peace held at universities and between governments, and contests on creative solutions for peace. True heroes who with creativity, genius, wit and courage had fought off violent conflict should be celebrated. Martin Luther King Day is an American holiday that honors a great hero of nonviolent action who tragically died a violent death, and an energized World Peace Day celebrated throughout the nations of the world would also further peace. A World Peace Day and a Day of Greatness would go hand in hand. World Peace Day, if taken seriously, could orchestrate cooperative and creative worldwide efforts on behalf of peace. And a Day of Greatness would honor great men and women who in their splendored diversity of achievement have created opportunities for peace and human flourishing.

II.21

Instituting Monetary Value

Monetary value and moral value both require a rational basis. However, the contemporary currency market may be described as a non-rational means of assigning value to money. Its radical fluctuations weaken currencies and create a palpable sense of devalued money. A rational basis at its best is both flexible and meaningful. For example, when ethical values are understood as expressions of basic ethical principles they transcend any particular abstract value, but in the concrete succeed in deepening the sense of moral value. But like moral relativism, today's currency values are without any real rational foundation because the basis of money is inordinately influenced by financial speculation. Currencies are valued through market bidding, much in the same manner as a barrel of oil or securities on the stock market.

The value of the U.S. dollar in relation to the value of an ounce of gold has fallen about tenfold since President Richard M. Nixon took America off the gold standard in 1971. The dollar no longer possesses a workable basis for valuation, and it is apparent that the current system has been a significant contributor to the steadily worsening condition of the worldwide economy. Currency needs a standard as much as the building trade needs a standard of measurement. Imagine the effect on the quality (i.e. value) of building construction if units of measurement such as a foot or a meter were to change day by day. It's an exaggerated comparison but correct in principle. Or how about allowing competing sports teams to change the rules or standards, by fiat, before each game! However, while pegging currency values to the gold standard is much preferable to the current bidding system, the gold standards of the past had their own issues, among them the false notion that currencies need to be "backed" by a national storehouse of gold locked in a vault somewhere. Gold has great historical value as an exceptionally stable commodity, but its importance as a monetary standard is not that it can somehow "back" currency like property collateralizes a loan, but that it can provide stability to currencies when their values are pegged as ratios to an ounce of gold. While it is true that the price of gold has increased dramatically in recent years, the cause of the increase is panic-stricken investors who fear that currency values will continue to fall through the floor, and so they buy gold because it is a much more secure and stable investment. If currency values are stabilized the price of gold will also stabilize because investors won't need to buy gold of offset their valueless currencies. How can currency value be stabilized?

A world currency board could effectively replace the currency market with a judicious application of the gold standard. The world board would be made up of a broad and balanced international cross-section of economic experts who would function as a supreme court for ascertaining and adjusting currency values. Rational valuation would then become the solid foundation of the world's currencies. But what would be the basis upon which the world board makes it determinations? While it would peg currency values in a ratio to an ounce of gold, it would also adjust currency values by periodically fine tuning the peg. In the past, governments or central banks would deflate or inflate the value of its currency by decree or *fiat* by a setting a new ratio of currency value to the value of gold. But in the proposal made here, the world currency board would keep the world currencies honest as rational adjustments will apply to currency value far more coherently than by market bidding, or by allowing governments to fiddle with the world's economic security. What does stability for currency mean? Stable currency value should reflect the actual strength of the economy that it represents, and this rational determination is not accomplished when currencies are traded like commodities or valued by government fiat. The result of the market-based trading of currency has been the destabilization of the entire financial system. A far more rational means for setting the value of a currency is a fair, consensual and objective determination by a broadly respected and impartial "supreme court" for currency valuation, i.e. a world currency board. Not everything is reducible to a market, and while markets drive capitalism, capitalism would benefit most if the determination of currency valuation would be removed from the financial markets and placed in the hands of an internationally balanced and highly qualified and esteemed expert board.

Is market bidding really a rational basis for establishing the value of the world's currencies? The rise and fall of currency values in the currency market reflect, as does any financial market, the perceptions of the self-interest of investors, by investors and for investors. Unfortunately, the calculations of investors may have little to do with the real worth of a particular currency, which is a reflection of the relative strength of the economy it represents and the political authority that backs it. The valuation of currencies by the currency market is influenced by current events, rumors, and speculation about events that might or might not occur that in any event ramp up the market's herd mentality. Speculations are the self-fulfilling prophecies of all financial markets. Wars and terrorism also affect the bidding in the currency market. National elections affect the values of currencies before the newly elected leaders even have the opportunity to demonstrate their competency, and speculations concerning governmental actions are made before the new government even takes office. Or, the market will bid on governmental policies based upon its collective biases, rather than a patient withholding of judgment until policies have been implemented and evaluated. Is this really a rational means for determining monetary value? The spectacle of setting currency exchange rates by market bidding is surely one of the greatest absurdities in the modern world. We should return to a system of "pegging" the value of currencies as a ratio to the price of gold determined, not by governmental self-interest, but by allowing their relative values to be periodically evaluated and adjusted by a world currency board. The value of currencies would then be rationally determined not by speculators but by an impartial court of economic experts and judges. The world currency board will periodically adjust currency pegs based upon ongoing reviews of meaningful and relevant economic indicators contradistinguished from faux indicators such as rumor and speculation that only feed the herd mentality of profiteering investors.

In gold standards of the past, nations would manipulate their currencies by arbitrarily modifying their valuation in relation to gold in order to achieve a more favorable position in international trade or to moderate inflation, but in the system proposed herein the only authority to modify the peg would be the world currency board. The charge has been made by many gold standard proponents that today's U.S. dollar is a fiat currency, but so too was the practice in which governments pegged the value of their currencies *by fiat*; in fact, this is where the term originated. A "fiat currency" is simply a currency whose value is arbitrarily set or assigned, be it by a central bank or the "full faith and credit" of a government that seeks to assure its value or good worth. The proposed world currency board would create the first true non-fiat currency, because the value of currencies would be established in as rational and as objective a manner as possible. If monetary value does not have an objective basis it becomes arbitrary. The old governmental pegging of currencies to gold standards was not only arbitrary, it could also be regressive. When he was still an unequivocal Randian advocate of laissez-faire economics, Alan Greenspan wrote:

> The financial policy of the welfare state requires that
> there be no way for the owners of wealth to protect
> themselves. This is the shabby secret of the welfare
> statists' tirades against gold. Deficit spending is simply
> a scheme for the 'hidden' confiscation of wealth. Gold
> stands in the way of this insidious process. It stands as
> a protector of property rights. If one grasps this, one
> has no difficulty in understanding the statists'
> antagonism toward the gold standard.[84]

Greenspan advocated the gold standard as the last best defense against deficit spending, which he viewed as enabling the state to rob from the wealthy. The *old* gold standard that Greenspan had advocated was regressive because, as he states, it prevents "the welfare statists [from being able] *to use the banking system* as a means to an unlimited expansion of credit."[85] But unduly restricting the expansion of the money supply and credit would place undue limits on economic growth and beneficent social programs. In contrast, the proposal put forward here is that of a *progressive* institution of the gold standard intended only as a means to monetary stability; the only limits on spending would be based on the need for economic viability and financial sensibility. Any resulting impact on currency value caused by imprudent monetary expansion would be assessed and adjusted by the world currency board. The board would be a progressive institution, but also one that protects the conservative principle of stable monetary value.

The value of international transactions should be fixed in terms of their value in gold at the point of transaction, and not by fluctuating currencies. Artificial manipulations of currency can *artificially* upset the balance of trade between nations and their national indebtedness. Fair monetary value will encourage economic justice. If a loan is transacted at the equivalent of 500 million ounces of gold, the principal amount (in terms of gold) will be paid in currency that equals 500 million ounces of gold, not more and not less! The loan balance, including interest, would be expressed in ounces of gold and paid in currency that is carefully fine-tuned and pegged by the world currency board. Debt balances would be calculated and stabilized by rational currency adjustments rather than on fluctuating currencies; as a result, true debt value would be paid. While the balance of trade and debts owed by one nation to another will always fluctuate, the fluctuations will reflect actual economic differences rather than trade imbalances due to speculation or, at times, manipulations of currency value that can destabilize international relations. A world currency board would be an institution of fair and just monetary value.

The current floating exchange rate system set by market bidding has an advantage over old fixed currency systems pegged to gold in that it adjusts the respective values of currencies in relation to each other based on their relative strengths (unless, in the case of some currencies, nations tie the value of their currency in ratio to another, e.g. to the U.S. Dollar). In contrast, when the old fixed currencies were adjusted, the adjustments were made by governmental actions. But neither the currency market of today nor the old versions of the gold standard were methodical systems backed by worldwide consensus. Economies grow and decline, the money supply expands and contracts, but the establishment of a world currency board that pegs and periodically adjusts currency values to the price of gold would institute objective valuation—not by market bidding, but by an ongoing and systematic review of the relative strength of each economy. Ascertaining the valuation of a currency would not be based on comparison with other currencies—which would be essentially inaccurate if not impossible—but on the basis of the evolving history of the currency's value in relation to gold. In this manner, genuine currency value for respective economies would be achieved by means of a rational monitoring process, and monetary stability will then be realized. Greater economic stability is encouraged when currencies *organically* reflect the strength of their respective economies. Poorer countries will, as today, be able to produce more cheaply (in terms of gold) than wealthier countries, but a stable foundation for growth for both rich and poor would be laid. And an organic, fertile ground of economic diversity would thus be provided that allows and encourages each economy to flourish in the context of its unique developmental dynamic. This is a prescription for world development.

Artificially attempting to unify diverse economies under the umbrella of a single currency would deplete both the weaker and the stronger economies that have been "unified." A weaker economy would endure an inflated currency respective to its true economic status and suffer higher costs and personal indebtedness. And a stronger economy will end up supporting its poor sisters and brothers whose poverty would be only deepened by the falsity of the currency integration. Broad integrations of currencies such as the "amero" would only generate problems similar to those currently being experienced in the Eurozone. And a unitary world currency would be an economic and political fiasco of monumental proportions.

II.22

On the Income Tax

The income tax is an ethically imbalanced instrument, and its only justification would be an argument that could demonstrate that there is no other form of taxation that better influences and sustains the balanced richness of the moral dialectic. Critics rightly argue that the income tax is a tax on productivity, and that consumption taxes are a far better alternative because they are levied on a pay-as-you-go basis as products are consumed or services rendered. Rather than taxing productivity, consumption taxes generate public revenue as products and services are purchased and used by the taxpaying consumer. Consumption taxes are superior to the income tax but, as will be discussed in subsequent sections, they may not be the best solution for providing necessary and sufficient governmental or public revenue.

Proponents of income tax elimination also argue that the income tax encourages wasteful governmental spending. Clearly this is the case due to the extremely poor linkage between income tax payments and the services received in return. But opponents of the income tax who want to abolish it because they are opposed to big government in order to castrate its capacity to provide needed services, argue from an ideological position equally as much as do those who argue that the income tax is "progressive." The grossly invasive and inefficient income tax, whether it is a flat tax or a tax that increases incrementally for higher incomes can never be progressive. The argument that the income tax is wrongheaded because it is the source of big government, and the counterargument that it is the progressive solution for needed social services are both deeply flawed. The libertarian accusation that the income tax is a tool of socialistic thievery clashes with the socialistic position that the income tax is the only answer or the best answer to libertarian selfishness; both positions express a morally incoherent view of economics.

The economic goal of any free society will always involve the encouragement of enlightened self-motivation for individual flourishing as well as external, socially originated motivation that encourages individuals to become self-motivated and self-empowered. But where is the motivational power produced from unearned revenue in the form of a tax that is taken or stolen from the earned income of individuals and businesses? And, so too, where is the motivational power generated by small-minded governments that allow the sick to become sicker, the poor to remain uneducated, and "justice" to be sold to the highest bidder? The income tax must go, but not at the cost of fairness, beneficence and compassion.

II.23

On Property

The notion of private ownership of land and natural resources is an audacious legalism. Is the natural habitat of all of the earth's denizens something to be owned much as someone owns a toaster or an automobile? Whatever 'God' means to you isn't *it* the real owner of land? In any case, these questions become somewhat moot because ownership of land generally does not entitle its use without restriction. Governments regulate and zone what may or may not be constructed on land or how it may be used, much as e.g. the use of the automobile is regulated.

Ego and property may be indistinguishable in some cases. But at least we are born into the world owning our own bodies, or that is the general consensus even if some extremists might contest even that right. No legitimate rule of law is going to take away an arm or a leg, even if that assumption may be called into question by ideologues. But the ownership of things is more tenuous than the ownership of our own bodies, and this is particularly the case with the ownership of real estate. The identification of material things as property is generally uncomplicated. Artwork on my wall and my laptop computer may belong to me. But even this type of ownership has limitations: they may be confiscated to pay tax or other indebtedness, and computers may be confiscated as part of criminal investigations. Therefore, even in the case of material goods there is no such thing as absolute property. Of course, the archetypal symbol of illicit property is slavery. The ownership of human beings was practiced for millennia before the institution of slavery was finally abolished in the West, although some forms of slavery still exist. Clearly, while we own our own bodies we own no one else's. We have no right to own another as a slave, nor can we own a spouse or child. A man may not own his wife or children, and it is not until human relationships expunge any notion of 'ownership' of one by another is true love and familial joy possible. And while slavery is the most extreme form of *immoral* property, it is also a reminder of the limitations of property.

Land ownership and the buildings constructed upon it are sometimes referred to as "real property," suggesting its status as the primary and most ultimate form of material possession. "Owning" one's own home does indeed have special significance. The dream of owning a home is embedded in a rich fabric of cultural metaphor. "A man's home is his castle." "It is the American dream to own your own home." However, is not the true value of property determined by the rules governing its use? Primary benefits for homeowners are the financial advantages of ownership and the use of the property that ownership entails. But real estate is also generally the first item on the lists of courts of law for confiscation in order to pay taxes or secured debts. "When the mortgage is paid, the house is yours!"; however, while you won't have any more mortgage payments you'll still need to pay property taxes, utilities, and maintenance expenses. You'll be able to renovate and remodel the property as you wish; however, you must not violate any zoning ordinances. Owning a home can provide many write-offs on your income tax. You can pass the house down to your children, and they can do the same for their children; however, the gains are reduced by inheritance taxes. You can keep the property forever; however, it may be taken by eminent domain. Real estate is a solid investment; however, this is not always the case such as demonstrated in the recent real estate collapse, and alternative investment opportunities may be superior and more secure. Qualifications aside, private ownership of real estate, by and large, seems to work well. People like it; and owning a home is a sort of *raison d'etre* for many folks.

But the real estate collapse of the past several years (beginning in 2008) is a reason to take pause, and motive enough for re-examination of the role of real estate in the contemporary economic system. We have previously discussed dogmas relating to profit, and while the profit motive is a desirable and effective mechanism respective to most spheres of economic activity, in certain economic spheres the centrality of profit can become antisocial and ethically unsustainable. In the matter of the intellectual property of patents, it has been earlier argued that the current patent system, while solidifying the notion of a patent as property, also impedes social progress and, furthermore, does not financially benefit some if not most patent holders. (§II.16) The conception of patents *qua* property in the traditional patenting of inventions stifles productivity and, almost certainly, some inventions get suppressed entirely by allowing a threatened business interest to purchase and then bury the patent for a variety of reasons. Real estate is an enormous economic sector in which the role of profit will now be critically considered from the point of view of the broad ethical perspectives that have been developed in this book. If Communism had produced superior wealth, creativity and individual flourishing it would have surely prevailed. Clearly, however, Communism was and is a dismal failure; even The People's Republic of China has adopted a largely capitalistic economy even if its repressive political system is still in force. Communism and pure socialism are not the answers and, as has been argued in these pages, they represent an ethical and social foundation that exhibits gross moral incoherence by its repression of individual rights and other moral prerogatives. The question that must now be addressed, however, is whether the conventional system of privately held real estate creates blockages in the economy that seriously impair both capitalism and democratic principles. If fundamental revisions discussed here would form a wealthier, more just and more democratic society, and if greater social harmony and individual empowerment would thereby be achieved, then these or similar revisions may be difficult or well-nigh impossible to deny!

II.24 – II.28

Ending Taxation

II.24

In the latter part of the nineteenth century a self-educated American economist named Henry George published a critique of private land ownership that is perhaps as pertinent today as when the book was first published. George and his predecessor Herbert Spencer, who in *Social Statics* (1851) advocated land nationalization, were laissez-faire economists who did not view the de-privatization of land as socialistic but only a narrowing of the scope of the free market so that laissez-faire principles could operate fairly. In *Progress and Poverty* (1879) George identifies the private ownership of land as the principal cause of cyclical economic collapse and the severe unequal distribution of wealth. In response, he advocated the transfer of lands from private ownership to public or governmental ownership and a "single-tax" based on land use that would be a replacement for all other taxes.

When George writes that his work seeks "to unite the truth perceived by the school of Smith and Ricardo to the truth perceived by the school of Proudhon and Lassalle; to show that *laissez-faire* (in its full true meaning) opens the way to a realization of the noble dreams of socialism; to identify social law with moral law..."[86] he captures the spirit of multi-perspectival philosophy in which broad cross-sections of thought become commingled as complementary incommensurables. George's reference to "the noble dreams of socialism" no doubt causes shudders of hostility in many, but the integration of oppositional viewpoints belonging to patently opposing economic and philosophical traditions becomes irresistible once obstructionist dogma is shredded and discarded. Whatever truths socialism or laissez-faireism may contain, they can only be realized in the concrete application of moral coherency rather than their respective ideologies. Ideological conflict has no possibility of resolution when the respective parties are unable to escape their ideological positions. If an end to private ownership of real estate would, *ipso facto*, be considered Communistic then the argument never advances beyond "sticks and stones" and childish name-calling. George's declaration that "The equal right of all men to the use of land is as clear as their equal right to breathe the air—it is a right proclaimed by the fact of their existence"[87] is supremely idealistic but yet on at least some level is sublimely true. What is more important, the ownership status of real estate or the advancement of freedom? If the transference of real estate from private to public ownership would eliminate the need for any other form of taxation and would create greater freedom and personal empowerment, then every freedom loving person should be for it.

The fundamental problem with the private ownership of real estate is that it concentrates vast wealth that tends to be self-perpetuating and impedes rather than stimulates economic activity. If all private wealth bottled up in the form of land and buildings were to be converted into currency by sale to public authorities and reinvested by the former owners in business, deposited into privately held bank accounts, invested in financial markets, or merely spent it would immediately begin to enrich the community as a whole. Wealth that was formerly concentrated in real estate would be freed and used by the former owners to purchase products and services, reinvested, or saved and would thereby set in motion a redistribution of capital throughout the economy. Even the dividends that the banks would earn from lending and from other banking activities would often be more vitalizing to an economy than capital bottled up in real estate that, in many cases, discourages productivity and severely limits wealth creation. It is ironic that while the private ownership of real property was necessary to amass the capital necessary to lift society to modernity, the divestiture of private real estate would create unprecedented growth and equality of opportunity that would lay the foundation for a great and empowered society. George's argument that financial speculations concerning real estate are a major factor in creating cyclical "paroxysms" of "boom and bust" seem as true today as it was in the nineteenth century.

In the end, the fate of the economy is tied significantly to the vicissitudes of the real estate markets that have little to do with the real vitality of the economy as a whole. Combined with the stabilization of monetary value (§II.21), a system of publicly owned real property could help bring an end to the destructive effects of casino-style economics and supplant it with far greater economic stability. When currencies and real estate are taken off the market other markets will soar. Radical currency and real estate fluctuations would no longer default to the whims and herd behavior of speculators. And greater economic stability combined with a deep transfusion of capital will, in time, deeply empower society as much as it empowers the individual.

In a just society, every human being born into this world should have basic opportunities. To reject this proposition is to drop the notion of justice both as ideal and as concrete value. But is the provision of basic opportunities encouraged or discouraged by the institution of privately held real estate? There will always be individuals that have the "misfortune" of being born into families less wealthy than others, but if an entirely new form of government funding facilitates the provision of higher education as a universal right then the children of less well-to-do families will be less disadvantaged by their "misfortune." Nor will children of less affluent families suffer from the sanctimonious view that it is acceptable that some parents teeter on the verge of financial ruin in order to finance their children's education. As the purchase of justice through the hire of expensive lawyers exemplifies, economics and ethics converge. An ethics that promotes poverty and discourages industry and creativity is incoherent, and an economics that disassociates the use of wealth from the guidance of ethics is perverse. The nation that first unleashes its economic potential through a union of market forces with moral forces will become a vanguard of positive historical change.

While George's arguments against the institution of privately owned real estate are still valid, there are many reasons why his proposal could not work in today's world and may not have worked when he presented it. A solution other than his "single-tax" proposal will be necessary, and the next section provides details of a proposal for the de-privatization of real estate that radically differs from George's scheme. But George's abhorrent, foolish and dangerous views opposing monetary compensation for private landholders are without merit, and would surely bankrupt a nation's spirit as thoroughly as its economy. George errs in his claim that land is "owned" by all the people by virtue of a "writ of nature" for the simple reason that *everything* that is or has ever been owned—save that of our own physical bodies, has been acquired fairly or unfairly by contract or by force. His hypothetical claim that the private ownership of property is a remnant of ancient military occupation and the feudal system is quite beside the point. In modern democracies, the institution of private property is democratically supported and, however the private system of real estate may have evolved, if it is to be changed a mythical "natural contract" invented unnaturally by philosophers doesn't qualify and cannot justify the confiscation of land without compensation! Embarrassingly, however, this is precisely what George recommends! George chastises John Stuart Mill and Herbert Spencer for even countenancing a means for providing compensation respective to the proposed nationalization of land that was debated in mid-nineteenth century Britain. In George's view, Spencer showed great temerity in even characterizing the issue of compensation as complicated and difficult.[88] But Spencer, in fact, fairly states the moral actuality in clear terms:

> most of our present landowners are men who have,
> either mediately or immediately—either by their own
> acts or by the acts of their ancestors—given for their
> estates equivalents of honestly earned wealth...[89]

This commonsense can only be criticized by an ideologue who is hell-bent on justifying his ends by any means. And that is what George does. While Spencer, like George, views the origins of private real estate as a product of theft, he is far more reasonable in considering the nature of the existing situation by declaring that the de-privatization of land must be done "with as little injury to the landed class as may be."[90] As I will argue shortly, while Spencer is vastly more correct than George on the issue of compensation, he is not generous enough if a transformation of ownership were to ever be successful.

George argues that the landholders' lands were never "theirs" but have always belonged to the collective by nature or by nature's God. George commits the egregious and dangerous philosophical error of turning a philosophical metaphor into a dogma. He writes that there is no "just title to an exclusive possession of the soil, and that private property in land is a bold, bare, enormous wrong, like that of chattel slavery."[91] The arrogance and the violent potential of this claim is a preposterous philosophical presumption that turning land into property was somehow an illegality and a transparent truth that humankind was given at its inception or, perhaps, that each human being has carved out in its brain. Any notion along these lines is, of course, an absurdity. Property rights involving the ownership and use of land have evolved differently in different cultures. George, however, wants to turn some Amerindian-like concepts about land use into a universal standard of morality. Equating private ownership of land with the wrongs of slavery is precisely the sort of absolutism that needlessly creates animosity and the potential for conflict. George attempts to further his argument for expropriation without compensation by claiming that if privately held land were to be purchased, rather than merely taken by the government, it would only perpetuate the unjust financial advantage of the landholders.[92] In other words, according to George, private property is as evil as slavery and paying to get the land "back" would be as unjust as compensating former slave owners for the loss of their slaves. George's equation of privately owned real estate with slavery is worse than a weak metaphor, it is a profound failure to understand the evil of slavery. Finally, George also attempts to further his justification for taking private lands without compensation on grounds of a justification in common law. Essentially, in common law, if it should be discovered that property had unlawfully been sold by a seller who was not the lawful owner, the innocent buyer must surrender it to whomever is adjudged to be the rightful owner.[93] The fallacy of this attempt to apply common law to private ownership of land is that the first owners may not even be known, and can probably never be known, and in the period of the first occupiers a consensus concerning landed property rights most likely did not exist. To take seriously the ramifications of George's argument, all lands constituting the continental United States should be returned to the Amerindian tribes forthwith. But justice is far more sublime than brutish solutions to complex problems. Private property is a social contract and, if its ownership is to be transferred to the public, it will become part of a new social contract. If the transfer to public ownership were to be effected without fair compensation, it *would* be robbery and would plainly convert the public authority into a crime syndicate. But the goal of the robbery would fail because it would move hoarded assets of the private sector to the public sector without any economic benefit but with vast and unfathomable harm. The public's enrichment would be unearned and society would suffer not merely on account of the wrongdoing but also because the theft would squander the momentous re-capitalization that would occur through the investment of the newly released capital. Unfair compensation to former landholders for de-privatization would attach a stigma persisting for generations and would severely sabotage the entire project while deeply wounding the spirit and depleting the nation's wealth for generations to come.

George's proposal, in addition to its ethical problems, also fails simply because it could not produce the revenue required, certainly not in our day if not in his. The single-tax proposal would be an extremely low tax based upon a calculus that sets the abstract value of land conceived of in terms of its condition prior to building construction and land development, i.e. the investment of labor. The principle, derived in larege part from Ricardo, is difficult to conceptualize as becoming anything other than arbitrary in practice. And, surely, the annual land valuation would create the very opportunities for corruption that George says that he wants to avoid. The only basis for determining the price of real estate is a free market, and market demand for real estate cannot be separated from its development. George's single-tax was proposed as a tax to end all taxes and was an ingenious idea that acquired significant political support when it was proposed, but the only way that the land transfer could produce necessary and adequate revenue is through a system that is market-driven. The income generated in a free and open market of publicly owned real estate would grow and fluctuate with supply and demand.

Henry George's single-tax proposal concerned the government ownership of *land* only. Private ownership of buildings would continue because, in George's mind, they are the products of labor and, therefore, qualify as possessions that could be sold or rented to others. In other words, while the governmental authority would collect the single-tax, wealth from privately owned real estate in the form of buildings would continue to accrue to their private owners. The tax revenue derived from the single-tax would at best—and this assessment is generous—create a revenue base for the government that might be comparable to a libertarian, small government conception in which just enough revenue would be generated for basic services meaning, for the most part, police and public works. After all, Henry George and Herbert Spencer were libertarians. Spencer, in fact, is often considered to be the first libertarian. George's "noble dream of socialism," known variously today as Georgeism, Geoism or Geolibertarianism could never—with the sole revenue of his single-tax, finance the basic network of services required by a modern society governed by morally coherent principles. On the other hand, a vision of complementary incommensurables in which libertarian and socialist ideals proudly sit side by side makes adequate public revenue possible if *market-driven* profits from all real estate including land, buildings and resources are allowed to supplant all taxation.

II.25

The proposal being set forth in this section is emblematic of philosophical freedom from the dreary restrictions of practicality and convention! It is understood that relatively few readers will greet a proposal for the divestiture and reinvestment of all privately owned real estate with much seriousness, but there is no more important function of philosophy than to question assumptions in order to facilitate a process of individual and collective self-examination. Traditional values and institutions are not justifiable in and of themselves but only by the deeper morality that they ought to express. And in this book we will continue to travel along this path.

The New York Times reported in a March 2011 article that despite worldwide profits of $14.2 billion in 2010 the General Electric Company paid ZERO income tax. ZERO! And the corporation "earned" an additional $3.2 billion in tax credits to offset taxes on future tax returns.[94] If all real estate were to become public property that is leasable by a public authority, rental payments would always generate government revenue, and even the General Electrics of the world would be unable to escape making a fair and equitable contribution. The government as landlord would derive profits from rent roughly equivalent to that of a private landlord. The GE story lifts the income tax to new levels of astronomic absurdity, but if all real estate is the source of governmental revenue, then giant international corporations, small businesses and individuals will keep every penny of profit earned because they will not pay taxes but only rent for the use of real estate. The payment of rent, a standard operating cost for business and everyday life, would replace the tax on productivity otherwise known as the income tax.

There is hardly any doubt that the divestiture of private real estate that is proposed here will produce proverbial knee-jerk charges of socialism or communism in many readers. But habitual reactions based on deeply ingrained institutional formalities, without considered self-examination, is mere deference to habit. Self-destructive habits, of course, are quite common. But personal wealth and economic productivity would experience explosive growth in a system that siphons investment away from unproductive property holdings to productive investments in both the private and public spheres. Since rights associated with land use are determined by law, a system in which all real estate is publicly owned could incorporate most if not all of the same legal rights and terms of use existing in the private ownership of real estate. While the occupiers of publicly owned real estate would not possess it as an asset, the same rights of use as existing in private real estate ownership could be built into leaseholder agreements with the public owners of the property. The principal arguments I am making here are three-fold: 1) A public system of land ownership could be designed such that the non-financial benefits and protections of privately held properties would be virtually unchanged. 2) The financial and economic benefits would be superior in the proposed system of public land ownership as the economic benefits of the proposal would unleash enormous economic potential. 3) Society would be made freer by clearing blockages that empower individual and socio-economic flourishing.

In the present proposal, tax revenue would be replaced by rental revenue derived from the public ownership of all real estate including land, buildings and natural resources as determined by market-driven supply and demand. Rent would replace tax. The elimination of the income tax would produce a dramatic increase in freedom by lifting a tax burden that is as psychologically and politically oppressive as it is economically depressing. The lifting of the oppressive burden of the income tax, and ending the wasteful expenditure of individual and corporate resources necessary for "compliance" to the threatening demands of the tax authority will redirect productive energies. The simple act of paying rent will in many if not all countries generate the preponderance of government revenues needed for desirable social services and entitlements. All real estate, with the possible exception of that which is used expressly for government administration and services, would be managed by privately owned management companies, or by individuals. The government's function with respect to the private management of property would, largely, be to a) to collect rental revenue and, b) to enforce standards of good management practiced by the private real estate management companies. Government revenue from rent would effectively be equal to the combined gross income that would have formerly been generated from all privately held real estate properties. The move to public ownership, under the administration of local dominions, would not involve privacy or security risks by virtue of the change in ownership. The law would require that private renters or realty management firms manage most if not all real estate, and renter and leaseholder rights would be no different in a prospective public system of real estate than in a private system. Governmental authority of the public real estate system would essentially concern itself with receipt of rental revenue and managerial oversight of private management firms. There would no longer be any heavy-handed, autonomous tax authority that collects owed revenue outside the purview of the court system; the collection of outstanding rent would simply become a matter of following well-established traditions of due judicial process that apply just the same as for any creditor. The authoritarian and abusive hand of tax collection agencies like the IRS can finally meet its end when government revenues are earned rather than confiscated, and the people are customers as much as they are citizens. At least as it applies to taxes, the old saw that "the only things certain in life are death and taxes" *can* in the end turn out to be false.

A large and diverse real estate management and development industry would be spawned by the requirement that third-party realty management firms manage most if not all real estate (all, that is, if private firms were to manage all properties including those that house government functions). Private investments that formerly went into purchasing real estate would be redirected into private industry, private savings or investments as well as in government bonds or securities. The argument that private ownership of land is necessary in order to motivate improvements that enhance the value of real estate properties can be addressed; leasehold property improvements could be encouraged by the issuance of government certified "leasehold investment credits" (LIC) that would be issued to leaseholders in exchange for qualified improvements. LICs would have fixed expiration dates and would be traded on a financial market or public auction; they would be offered for sale, or taken of off the market, at the discretion of the leaseholder. The leaseholder/seller would receive cash, and the LIC buyer may apply the LIC against other rental obligations up until its expiration. The seller could repurchase an LIC after it was sold, but it could not be used to offset rent for the same property for which the LIC was originally issued. LICs would facilitate the reentry of liquidity into the economy by creating a monetary return to leaseholders for improvements while simultaneously stimulating economic activity through their purchase. LICs could also function as collateral for banks. The most significant effect of LICs would be the spurring of economic activity. As the date of expiration nears the price of an LIC may be expected to fall and would, thereby, create for the buyer a means of making property improvements at significant discounts. LICs would result in a broader investment in property improvements that would be distributed throughout the economy, because they would stimulate improvements to properties rented by both sellers and buyers of LICs. In contrast to the broad stimulatory effects of LICs, tax write-offs in systems of privately owned real estate typically encourage improvements only to properties owned by the taxpayer.

The management of publicly owned real estate would be of two basic types. In the case of some properties with multi-unit or multi-lot divisions "realty management firms" would, in addition to property maintenance, be responsible for the renting of the units or lots. A fixed percentage of the rent would be counted as revenue for the government, and the balance would be used to compensate the management company. In other cases, however, there would be established "realty custodianships" in which the leaseholder's rights closely approximate standard rights of private property owners. The leaseholder would have the ability—encouraged by the LIC incentive—to modify, expand and develop properties freely within the boundaries of locally established zoning requirements for its own purpose, use and profit including that of the private subletting of property under its custodianship. Lease agreements specifying the governmental revenue generated from realty custodianships could be a fixed amount of rental revenue stipulated in the lease, or a combination of fixed rent and a percentage of rental income derived from sublet properties.

Realty custodianships could also be real estate investments. As properties are developed and their value on the rental market increases they may be "resold" to the government or to successor custodians. The government could "repurchase" a property by agreeing to terminate the lease while also paying to the custodianship a commensurate profit for the capital improvements that have increased the value of the property. The government would then enter into new lease agreements that would in turn enhance its revenues.

Additional real estate investments could occur in a new form of financial market that trades public stock holdings in "realty investment zones" or subsections of the public's real estate, including entrepreneurial opportunities that help revitalize stagnant and economically depressed areas.

Socialistic and libertarian principles are in many respects "complementary incommensurables" because the oxymoronic appearance of the coupling of these terms is the result of a confusion concerning abstract and concrete values. (§I.8) Are libertarians interested in liberty or merely an abstract construct of liberty? And, likewise, are socialists interested in raising the levels or economic opportunity and justice or is their use of the language of justice merely reflective of an ideological ideal of the centralized, bureaucratic state? The economic proposal espoused herein is a dialectical transformation of socialism and libertarianism because it is a fusion of both. The elimination of the income tax (a libertarian-friendly idea), combined with the public ownership of real estate (a clearly socialistic idea) would ignite unprecedented and sustained economic flourishing and growth. Commerce and industry would be unburdened by the elimination of the oppressive income tax, and the people will be the beneficiaries of social services that are the obligation and the passion of a compassionate society. Comparable to income tax deductions but without the loopholes, the government could soften financial downturns by helping those in need through judicious temporary reductions in rental fees. Another example of the adaptive use of rents might, in the case of "realty custodianships" that serve as primary residences, be the discretionary reduction of rents effective on the age of retirement in order to provide security for the elderly. Similarly, rent could be reduced in various circumstances of hardship. But an ironic consequence of the elimination of taxation and the gradual divestiture and reinvestment of all private real estate is that while social services would be funded far more effectively than by the invasive and regressive income tax, a more productive and more equitable economy would reduce the need for those same services.

The transitioning from private to public ownership of all real estate would require patience and time. The transition could take a generation, or more, to complete as a process of fair compensations are systematically determined and transacted in gradual steps that make the public investment of financial resources affordable and profitable over the long term. The transaction price would be fairly determined and fairly assessed (at or above market value) and tax free: Any tax would unfairly constitute a rebate for the buyer (the public entity) and a loss for the seller. The gradual transfer of private real estate to public ownership would, in stages, parallel the phasing out of the income tax and all other taxes. When the phased transfer from private to public ownership of real estate completes, so will the phased elimination of all taxes. The process would be a steady and slow public investment in a bold and empowered society.

II.26

The inheritance tax has been sarcastically characterized as the "death tax" by some of its critics. The passing down of wealth to descendants is valued by both the wealthy and those of only modest wealth because of their desire to bequeath a level of financial benefit and support to their children and offspring. And there is also a belief that wealth should be transferred to subsequent generations, generally, within the family. This belief in the transference of wealth within families may be characterized as an 'entitlement'. Attitudes about inheritance, however, would be transformed by a system of publicly owned real estate such as the one proposed. Since all real estate would be public, it could no longer be a matter of inheritance, and the transference of inherited wealth would then be a gift giving that would significantly moderate the intergenerational perpetuation of economic inequality. Certainly, passing down wealth creates unearned advantages but with the broad alleviation of inequality achieved by the divestiture and reinvestment of all private real estate, a far less dysfunctional inheritance of wealth may well be a tradition worth keeping for reasons both economic and popular. Absent the inheritance of real estate, the economy will intrinsically work towards a fairer distribution of income based upon earnings and merit. A world without private real estate but driven by entrepreneurial enterprise, inventiveness and compassionate caring for each other would be a world of opportunity and mutual self-realization.

The private ownership of real estate bottles up economic energy in the hands of the haves, and leaves both the haves and the have-nots victims of never-ending tax increases. It stifles productivity and increases demand for social services while tax revenues that are dependent upon income and commercial activity are perpetually prone to instability. Private real estate squanders economic energy and creates economic downturns born of stagnated wealth much as water might stagnate in an extended network of isthmuses and islands or, in the worst cases, a swampy morass. A progressive society that is better able to use its wealth to ensure opportunities for life, liberty and the pursuit of happiness is at our fingertips. The divestiture and reinvestment of all private real estate by its former owners would unleash a renaissance of individualism and unprecedented economic power while simultaneously creating a state of greater equality and unprecedented financial stability. Amid the tremendous but gradual release of financial energy, inheritance will be a rightful gift giving that does not impede and interfere with individual and social progress. The assets passed down, unlike real estate, will continue to stimulate and contribute to the asset base of the broader economy. And the elimination of privately owned real estate as a form of inheritance will, over time, more fairly and more reasonably distribute the wealth.

The divestiture and reinvestment of all private real estate would make it possible to eliminate all taxes including the inheritance tax. It would take a generation or more for the distribution of wealth to become fully realized. While there will always be inequalities in wealth, over time financial inequalities will largely be reflected in the differences of productivity and creativity that naturally exist between individuals. The transference of privately held real estate to the public will infuse vast amounts of liquidity into the hands of those who had owned expansive real estate holdings, and it will begin to trickle down: even the simple holding of funds in reserve has some stimulatory effect. The expenditure and reinvestment of the funds released by the divestiture will stimulate and broadly infuse wealth into the new economy. The stabilization of government revenue based on rental income will make possible a leveling of the field of opportunity as has never before been possible. Healthcare, education, and legal representation would not only be available equally to all, but its quality would improve simply because *unequal access to essential services is bad service*. Taxes would no longer be a burden on individuals and businesses because public or governmental revenue will be generated by the act of paying the basic personal and business expense that is rent. Governmental revenue would become more predictable, and taxes would no longer be a drag on economic activity.

The elimination of the inheritance tax, the income tax and all taxes is laissez-faire and libertarian, and a de-privatization of all real estate that produces a stable basis of governmental revenue for necessary and beneficent public services is socialistic. How could this utopian fusion of libertarianism and socialism be possible? It is possible because while we have been conditioned into believing that ownership of private real estate is not merely the actuality of the good life but its highest aspiration, the insanity of poverty is a spotlight on the dysfunction of the modern world. Capitalism is rational, but its rationality is not dependent upon the private ownership of real estate. Paradoxically, turning the foundational capital of real estate over to the social collective would be the liberation of capitalism.

II.27

Socialism is dangerous on multiple levels. It concentrates power into the hands of bureaucrats, and it wrecks the natural cycles of supply and demand that the marketplace needs to self-regulate and to innovate. But laissez-faireism is also dangerous because the dream of individual greatness that can be unleashed by unrestrained individual initiative has a hundred holes in it. The real imperfections of individuals interfere with the libertarian ideal. Economies collapse, jobs are lost, businesses fail, illness threatens the people and drought and famine starves them. Sometimes individuals need the help of an outstretched, compassionate hand and often the only hand to help is that of the government. But while pure laissez-faireism is a fantasy, the importance and value of fiscal conservatism is not debatable.

Good bookkeeping is good, pure and simple, and spending within a budget and borrowing not more than can be reasonably paid back is a good principle of commonsense. A government must have the capacity to provide for its people, but doing so is counterproductive when spending levels wreck the economic foundations. The proposal to limit governmental revenues to rent stemming from the divestiture of all privately held real estate would provide the funds needed to provide needed services while it eliminates the burdensome, anti-productivity income tax. Governmental revenue produced by market-driven rent derived from the public ownership of all real estate should be enough for many if not most governments to provide needed beneficent social services.

The proposed system of public rental revenue is very unlike the familiar property tax because it would represent legitimate *profit* to the public in return for its investment. A property tax confiscates money from the citizenry whereas public rental revenue would merely represent earnings from publicly owned property. Government would be run like a business, and while its rental revenues would be vast, its bureaucracy would be relatively small because the public's real estate would largely, if not exclusively, be managed by private firms. The collection of governmental revenue would be as simple as collecting rent, and the essential injustice of tax as the confiscation of income would be brought to an end. The government can live within its means, free of its unending hunger for additional revenues! And like any legitimate business, governmental or public authorities will work hard to trim and streamline its operations when the money it spends is *earned* and not stolen![95]

Governmental funding that is ample enough to serve the needs of the people but limited to revenue derived from market-driven rent will produce an additional benefit of incalculable significance. An underlying motive for never-ending tax increases is war. Military spending outpaces conventional bookkeeping. War is irrational, and there is little relationship between the taxation level that the citizenry can support and the ever-expanding spending and technology of war. While a large part of politics is concerned with questions of how much tax needs to be collected and to what ends, advocates of spiraling taxing and spending for military expansion engage in circular reasoning that attempts to justify itself by arguing that more makes us safer, even if we go broke in the process. However, the present proposal for the divestiture and reinvestment of all private real estate places a limit to the amount of revenue that can be raised. The proposal for the gradual transfer of real estate via purchase to public ownership is a proposal for progressive but limited government. It would limit government to spending only on that which it can afford, but it will be able to afford more of what is needed but less of what is not. This is a basic principle of financial responsibility. Limiting governmental spending to revenue produced by market-driven public rental revenue would return public spending to the justifiable limits of fiscal sanity. Spend only what you can afford, and save and invest what you can; if you spend more than that you will inevitably waste away and degenerate as your resources are squandered. This principle is as true for nations as it is for individuals. Fiscal sanity does not mean an end to the "noble dreams of socialism." But if government is provided with a rational basis for the collection and expenditure of revenue, overspending will become as self-evident as for healthy individuals who know that taking on excess weight generally means that it is time to put oneself on a diet.

Henry George argued that buildings are products of labor and therefore are exempted from the "single-tax." In reality, however, separating buildings and other uses of the land from its valuation is impossible because the land never had any value until it had a use, and any increase in its value is tied to the history of its use. There is little point in playing this game. *The only justifiable argument for the fair and just transfer of real estate from private to public ownership is that by so doing taxes may be eliminated and beneficent services may be fairly and compassionately provided.* A monopoly on real estate is much like a monopoly on food, and while a monopoly may at times be fairly managed and at times not, concentrations of power in the control of these resources are endemic threats to economic stability. Real estate, like food, like oil, or like currency itself should flow without artificial blockages that hinder the most basic human aspirations. And if the basic economic foundations are fractured by various self-serving blockages or obstructions then the basic issue of economic justice at its very foundation is at stake. In the case of real estate, if its transference from private to public ownership via private divestiture frees the people and its commercial enterprise from onerous tax burdens and provides for a just, beneficent and compassionate world, then a superior alternative to the divestiture and reinvestment that is proposed here would need to be tendered before it could be fairly rejected. Or does justice not matter? Or is "The haves have it, and the have-nots don't" the only principle of "justice?"

Is a country's ability to generate sufficient revenues from rental revenues a financial litmus test on its capacity for autonomy? And if the test is not met, is support from the world community or, in some cases, friendly merger with other countries desirable? If real estate would be made the primary determiner of state revenue, is it possible that natural alignments and realignments, mutually advantageous, might finally emerge that could someday supplant disastrous, unjustified, aggressive military interventions? Governmental spending limited to rental revenues (and, possibly, limited consumption fees) would limit the war machine. A state has a kind of permanence that must transcend economic ups and downs. Businesses can become bankrupt or go out of business but we cannot view a state in the same manner. There is, perhaps, no better yardstick for the economic viability of a state than the value of its real estate. If some states do not have enough value in their real estate then, at least, the income tax could be eliminated and replaced with use and/or consumption taxes. And friendly, consensual and mutually beneficial consolidation with others may be possible when the swelled egoism of nationalism inevitably converges with evolving consciousness and the realization of a future harmony.

II.28

The institution of private real estate was essential for civilization to attain its current level of economic development and its consequential industrial, scientific and technological advancement. But it is also true that stages of development must, like the stages of a rocket, sometimes fall away before success can be fully realized. It is often observed that if democracies are to have their best chance of success there must first be a level of educational and economic development, and a strong middle class as well, so that social stability may provide a firm ground for democratic traditions to take hold. The institutionalization of private real estate was almost certainly a vital stage in the development of industrial and postindustrial democratic societies, whereas Marxism-Communism grew into a nightmare whose global failure was rooted in severe moral, political and economic incoherencies. And while letting go of the institution of privately held real estate will be part of a balanced and coherent socio-ethical approach that contains some elements of socialism, Spencerian and Georgist views suggest a dialectic in which the de-privatization of real estate is also libertarian. Rugged individualism and a compassionate society are no more contradictory than a deeply loving mother who also knows and applies principles of tough love. Tender love and tough love both have their place in the human heart and in human civilization.

I will have no difficulty admitting any falsity in my views regarding the divestiture and reinvestment of all privately held real estate—or any proposal advanced in this book—should its failings be made apparent. I will happily admit my errors. Philosophy requires an open, exploratory mind or it stops being philosophy and transfigures itself into dogma or anti-philosophy. A programmatic de-privatization of all real estate is another example of the possibility of quantum convergence that was earlier discussed respective to suppressed or otherwise bypassed technologies. (§II.15) The theories of Spencer, George and others were swept away in America and Great Britain, perhaps aided by those making knee-jerk connections with socialism. The idea of land nationalization that was seriously debated in Great Britain in the nineteenth century probably came to be cavalierly dismissed as unthinkable; and Spencer's latter-day retraction of his views could not have helped the cause. Yet, George's dream of unifying laissez-faireism and socialism may well be a keen insight into opportunities now seemingly lost. As with the dismissal of nascent technology buried by the prevailing winds of history, the rediscovery or revisitation of proposals to de-privatize real estate could be modified, adapted and reinvigorated to include all real estate in an empowered form of social capitalism that reconnects the past with the future. A love-based ethics must ultimately escape rigid conceptions, preconceptions, formalities and actualities that are confused as realities. Unlike violent revolutions that destroy the good with the bad, the success of the present proposal will require farsightedness and patience for its gradual implementation over the course of a generation or more. A healthy process of integration and adaptation would ensue. But if my dream is merely a pipe dream I do not apologize for the dream. I believe that many dream similar dreams for the ultimate happiness and well-being of humanity, even if differences persist concerning the means by which they might be achieved. I am less inclined, however, to believe that I would ever discard my views concerning plural perspectivism and the transcendence of formalities that function as barriers or obstacles to intellectual truth and enlightenment. Ethics is not liberal or conservative and holds no allegiance to any political party, religious faith or conventional wisdom. The enemy of reason and progress is rigid preconception, and lest we become victims of our own delusion, it is well worth reminding ourselves that an open mind may also close in the light of reason.

II.29

What are Entitlements?

Societies that are serious about establishing fairness will distinguish wants from basic needs, and determine their capacity to procure those goods and services that qualify as basic needs. A basic need that is procurable may be characterized as an 'entitlement'.

An entitlement is or ought to be a writ of empowerment. When social entitlements are framed as the provision of basic needs for a stable, rational and ethically empowered society, the conception of what has been generally thought of as an entitlement is both expanded and delimited. For example, the stabilization of monetary value (§II.21) is a basic need as much as are good roads, running water and reliable electricity. Are not the provision of safe roadways, water and sewage systems, and electricity entitlements that every member of society has come to expect and deserve by virtue of his or her membership in society? A stable currency, no less than roads and running water, is an entitlement.

The only limitation to a consensually established entitlement is that it be provided according to principles of affordability. We have discussed in the preceding sections a proposal for the public ownership of all real estate, and it is argued that it will result in a secure and stable foundation of public funding that could replace taxation and provide funding for necessary and affordable entitlements and services. While the divestiture and reinvestment of all private real estate would likely result in the gradual diminishment in status of an elite mega-rich, the depth and breadth of affluence would radically expand.

A political system that is freed of political parties, which impede and block effective governance is, in a Washingtonian spirit, an entitlement. And, while freeing politics from these blocks that have been born out of institutionalized division and partisanship could not guarantee good democratic governance, it would empower the society by facilitating the emergence of statesmen and greater ethicality in the political arena. (§II.19) An independent, party-free political system will coalesce independent, free-thinking men and women around common goals thereby empowering them to legislate undistracted by the irrelevant maneuverings of party politics.

Closely connected to the democratic entitlement of a politics freed of the corruptive influence of political parties is the entitlement of the collective public forum structured in such a manner that it might encourage intelligent debate and discourse. The classroom and the boardroom have requirements to optimize communication, fact-finding and decision-making; *are not the voters entitled to the same?* Are slick political campaign ads really a desirable format for presenting the candidates and their positions on the issues? Or have political commercials progressively dumbed down the voter to the point that it now accepts the dumb down as the norm of political discourse? An ongoing, publicly financed discussion forum in which all candidates are afforded the opportunity to respond to questions prepared by a nonpartisan board, the recording of which would be continuously available for voter review, would augment debates and have advantages over the grandstanding that often occurs. With this media access in place, the dissemination of the views and positions of the candidates would be broadly available, and obscene and ridiculous campaign spending levels could be dramatically reduced. In addition to corrupting political discourse, the magnitude of campaign spending on idiotic "commercials"—even the term is an affront to the sacredness of the democratic process—has corrupted the very foundation of American democracy even more deeply. What is the distinction between 'lobbying' and 'bribing' when the lobbyist donates money to the politician he lobbies?

Justice based on the ability to pay is merely a system of privilege in which the best "justice" is available only to paying subscribers; but, of course, unequal justice is the definition of injustice. The clumsy justification of this system of privilege or injustice goes something like this: Lawyers deserve to be paid, and the best lawyers should be paid the most. Highly successful lawyers have earned their enormous fees because they have the right to charge whatever the market can bear, and that is all that matters. It's only fair and it's only just! If some poor schlub can't afford a good attorney it's his fault! A rich man has a right to superior legal representation in the American "justice" system. But a system in which the wealthy are entitled to superior legal defense is merely a system of privilege. The solution is clear: Demand that there be fair and equal legal representation, as an entitlement for everyone! But advocates of privilege and the status quo have a simple reply, "Justice for all would be socialism!"

The maxim that "no cost is too high to save a life" is one of those trite non-truisms that many spout but few take seriously. Since the best legal defense is unaffordable for most, there is little doubt that people have been executed who would otherwise have been saved if they could have put up the cash to pay for their "justice." People die by the thousands or millions because they have nothing to eat. But if the modern world really wanted to stop starvation, can anyone seriously doubt that it is a job that could get done? If the world truly wanted to end mass starvation it would muster the political will and economic energy to institutionalize an effective worldwide solution to needless hunger, made possible by a compassionate planet that no longer tolerates it. The question is not whether any cost is too high to save a life. The current state of healthcare in America suggests another question, "How cheap is human life?" It is all too obvious that human life is assigned a price that is trumped by profit. But the maxim about no cost being too high to save a life should be taken seriously because any human being under the threat of death from injustice, starvation or illness is as entitled as any other to receive the help that he or she needs.

While a few millionaires may have made their fortune by shrewdly investing a small sum, we can hardly expect that creating riches from practically nothing will become routine. Similarly, the self-educated man is not an argument that society should drop all efforts to educate the people. Therefore, while we have much to learn from the self-educated scholar and the self-made millionaire, it would be foolish indeed to shut down all our academies. Opportunities are like money, they beget other opportunities when they are wisely used or capitalized, and the deprivation of educational opportunity as a basic right and a basic need is a squander of vast cultural, intellectual and financial opportunity. A substandard level of equal educational opportunity deflates society and its economy at least as much as does an insufficient money supply. One of the most essential and valuable entitlements of all is the provision of opportunity.

Charity is not a substitute for entitlements. Please do not misunderstand! True charity is an expression of a giving spirit, but charitable giving will never provide for more than a relatively small portion of society's basic needs or entitlements. The end of taxation and its replacement with public rental revenues would allow charity once again to be the result of pure beneficence and compassion rather than their adulteration with desire for a nice tax deduction. But charity is not a substitute for the ethical responsibility of society to provide economically affordable entitlements.

II.30

What Entitlements are Not

The term 'entitlement' is often derogatorily used by "conservative," small government proponents because government entitlement programs are viewed by them as unearned giveaways to persons without any right or ethical claim. Entitlement programs are also viewed as the hallmarks of a paternalistic society that conditions individuals to dependency on the state rather than upon self-reliance. However, an analogy comparing citizen-to-state relationships with parent-child-familial relationships is instructive. Children are entitled to food, shelter and education and other services, but if their family is too poor to provide for them the state generally recognizes the entitlement and steps in to provide at least some of the things that the family is unable to provide. Certainly when parents provide food and shelter to their children we do not consider it to be a giveaway, and it is wrongheaded to view social entitlements that do the same any differently. A valid entitlement is not a giveaway. When a child's parents cannot provide for basic needs is the child somehow less deserving? The absolute necessity of helping children is universally acknowledged by all but the most despicable type of human being.

In order to become healthy and independent members of society children require nurture and caring, but they also need to develop the inner motivations of self-nurturing and self-caring. What takes priority, independence or flourishing? Moral actuality transcends formalities, words and preconceived notions! A partial ethical myopia that focuses on just one aspect of the human condition is badly flawed; it reflects a fragmented understanding in need of the balance that can be provided by holistic ethics. In the end, the family is a secondary or tertiary formality that ranks below the basic responsibility and duty to care for children; if a family unit fails to procure basic needs society must step in or be shamed by its collective abrogation of responsibility.

Is charity necessary in a society that is dedicated to providing basic needs and entitlements? The following passage from Nietzsche characteristically expresses his torturous, multisided understanding as it bears on the question of charity:

> Great indebtedness does not make men grateful, but
> vengeful; and if a little charity is not forgotten, it turns
> into a gnawing worm...But I am a giver of fifths: I like
> to give, as a friend to friends. Strangers, however, and
> the poor may themselves pluck the fruit from my tree:
> that will cause them less shame. But beggars should
> be abolished entirely! Verily, it is annoying to give
> to them and it is annoying not to give to them.[96]

While Nietzsche clearly struggles with charitability in this passage, when he says that, "the poor may pluck the fruit from my tree" he is arguably defending the principle of entitlement. And while his antipathy to the spirit of charity—if that is indeed what it is—is distasteful, his alacrity in having the poor take what they need reflects the noble sentiment that is at the foundation of all entitlements. Entitlements are necessary but charity is of a secondary nature, or more precisely, a distinction can and should be made between the beauty of charitable giving and the moral necessity of affordable entitlements. We witness enormous fundraising campaigns to help find cures for a variety of devastating diseases; do we view the recipients of these charities as the beneficiaries of a giveaway or, rather, as deserving receivers of acts of kindness and the beneficiaries of the noble obligation of caring and giving.

A rational program of entitlements, like the rational administering of familial duty must balance basic needs with motivational strategies to inspire greater individual independence and self-sufficiency. But the perversion of good motive is a persistent annoyance and a subterfuge of the social beneficence that is expressed in entitlement programs. Individuals who present themselves as "entitled" are often worthy of disdain, and create a public relations nightmare for proponents of entitlement programs; they are the type of individuals who Nietzsche probably had in mind in his expression of distaste and discomfort with some forms of charity. Much like the bratty little kid who is always demanding from his or her parents what they cannot afford, individuals plagued by "feelings of entitlement" suffer from a myopic and unethical form of self-love and an utter ignorance or rejection of the dynamic Self-Other duality. But a social entitlement is an honorable writ of empowerment, not a tool of greed. Those suffering from feelings of entitlement are victims of a narcissism that has contempt for others equally as much as those who prance around exhorting the oxymoronic "virtue of selfishness." And this is a phenomenon that is quite logically understood because the falsely entitled ones are nothing but selfish in their demand of unjustified assistance from others. The "virtue of selfishness" espoused by Randian self-deceivers are in truth the cousins of the "entitled ones." While entitlements are philosophically offensive to the Randians, they wallow with their cousins in their own selfishness. Both forms of selfishness, the selfishly uncompassionate or the selfishly entitled may, perhaps, be psychologically imbalanced but are clear pictures of moral incoherence heavily lopsided on the egoistic side of the Self-Other duality.

II.31

A World Society

Using the principles and viewpoints expressed in the foregoing pages, a vision of a future society emerges. What follows is an idealistic sketch of the future. As advanced nations eliminate taxes and replace them with rental revenues derived from the public ownership of all real estate, civilization will become increasingly interdependent and decentralized. An interdependent network of cities and towns will be the depositories of rental revenues to which fixed percentages would be apportioned. The broad network of social and governmental institutions receiving the funds would be designed for cooperative sharing, and would minimize excessive financial concentrations that invite abuse and corruption. The nation-state will fade in importance even as many will remain recognizable as geographic areas that reflect their cultural and sociological distinctiveness. These areas may also represent distinct economic domains in which currencies reflect the realities of economic differentiation (§II.21); a system of rational currency valuation is necessary so that exchange rates support the organic uniqueness and flourishing of diverse economies. A world currency board consisting of a broadly balanced cross-section of economic experts will be vested with the responsibility of fine tuning currency values in ratio with an objective standard such as the price of gold or other comparable criteria. Without an institution along the lines of the proposed world currency board, the value of money will continue to lose its value and, in general, cheapen all values. The world society will, thereby, have a greater respect for value.

The feared "new world order" is a legitimate and well-grounded fear that a new Leviathan or centralized world government would be a political and moral catastrophe and economic disaster of colossal dimensions that could threaten human freedom forever. The envisaged world society, on the other hand, is a dream of decentralized social empowerment, world peace and the unleashing of freedom. In the world society, nations would no longer be nation-states and their governmental structures—as parts of a greater organic whole, will be dedicated to the health and well-being of their respective constituencies and of the health of the interdependent whole. But nationalism will be dead, and both unity and diversity will thrive and flourish as never before. And the maintenance of a stable diversity of currencies will be symbolic of the rich diversity of interdependent domains that will thrive in the world society.

A dependable but limited source of revenue will end interminable political fighting over questions of whether to tax or not to tax. As a result, social services will improve, and absent the unrestricted ability to raise taxes for military spending the spending of war machines will decrease in inverse proportion to the increasing prospects for peace. Ultimately, the waning of national significance will lead to disarmament. And with the end of standing armies and a new abundance of resources freed up from the massive concentration of wealth in all things military, and by the divestiture and reinvestment of all private real estate, a realization will sweep across the world that at long last the era of nation-states and needless international conflict can be allowed to pass. In time, all former nation-states will integrate into an interdependent network of localities that together constitute an organic political holism. Competition between nations will be replaced with cooperation when a single source of governmental revenue forces local polities to live within their means, and greater sharing between them will encourage burgeoning good will that overwhelms nationalist obsessions when the obsession itself has been removed. In a world free of the nation-state and replaced with a vast network of interdependent localities there would be no need for tariffs, and free trade—with a stable but diverse world monetary system in place, will facilitate equitable worldwide economic development.

A collection of local governments unified in a cooperative mission to provide basic needs, possessing a basic consensus regarding human rights, and celebrating a healthy respect for cultural diversity will make universal freedom possible. Institutionalized political strife will finally and mercifully have met its demise. The formality of the nation-state and its egoistic connotations will wane and national identities will lessen until they are finally and proudly replaced with citizenship of the world. While political differences are part of human nature its *institutionalization* in the form or nation-states, political parties and ideology is not. A new, interdependent world society will be a human society that has been freed from its political and economic shackles, but harmonically and organically unified when it is no longer divided by the artificial boundaries and disharmonic blocks that have perpetuated unnecessary human discord since the beginnings of civilization.

A world in which taxes have been eliminated would inspire a free spirit of giving not only by individuals, but also by new traditions of interregional sharing that will evolve between the interdependent governing authorities and domains. Unused funds would be set aside by the different governmental entities for redistribution to others that are in need of additional funding. When the source of public funding is no longer taken from the wallets of citizens by taxation, governmental districts will redistribute funding to other districts that are in need after the financial requirements of giver authorities have been met. Redistributions of surplus revenue between districts and polities become second nature in a world that is no longer structured and motivated by greed. Cultural differences and national identities, at least those that possess the hallmarks of moral coherency, will be preserved as precious jewels, but these cultural jewels will no longer serve as separatist excuses to hoard revenues at the expense of those most in need. Surplus revenue from natural resources, as part of the public's real estate, would be redistributed according to need. Again, the redistributions occur only after the financial requirements of the giving domains have been met. The heavy burden of taxation would have been lifted, and basic needs will have been met not only by the sensible expenditure of public revenues sensibly derived, but by a peaceful explosion of economic activity that will fund basic social needs more efficiently than when the world endured the burdens of political polarization, taxation and militarism.

The provision of social entitlements will not be part of a monolithic Leviathan but, for the most part, will be independently operated but with necessary oversight and scrutiny, both public and private, to ensure fiscal and administrative integrity. Regulation by former executives in the regulated industries is a conflict of interest that would be prohibited by law. The insidious endangerment of government foxes guarding the henhouse—a veritable plague around the globe that shamefully protects the Monsantos of the world—can be stopped, as regulatory agencies will be effectively depoliticized. Governmental institutions will be operated like private businesses but subject to stricter oversight and conformance by independent governmental and private regulatory and watchdog entities. The partnership between government and private industry will naturally accord with "natural selection" as the most effective and efficient means for delivering services are employed. Might it not also be proposed that basic democratic principles and individual human rights are also universal entitlements that must be accepted wholeheartedly by a society, and made requisite, before any society is allowed to join the world society? Are not the responsibilities of self-government requisites that are the very basis of social entitlement? I certainly don't intend to imply that good roads and universal healthcare are not entitlements for the people of an undemocratic region, but I would like to suggest that basic principles of democratic self-governance and human rights be itself an entitlement that is required medicine for membership in the world society. A nation ill-equipped in the arts of democratic self-governance would not be ready or qualified for entry into the world society. Democracy is a necessary passage to political maturity, and membership in the world society would be a privilege, not a right, that will need to be earned.

An empowered world society will reflect an empowered ethics through its deep appreciation and recognition of the nuances and permutations of loving intention unbounded by preconception, sensitive to the nuances of the moral context, and open to reexamination in the light of wisdom. Has not the nation-state been for hundreds of years the most far-reaching of formalities? It is difficult for the modern mind to conceive of life without the trappings of the nation-state, but great thinkers such as Socrates have considered citizenship of the world the most honored of affiliations. The nation-state is the boldest form of corporate identity, but corporations also bear obstructionist qualities similar to the nation-state. While it is natural for individuals to healthily express both cooperation and competition, the same does not extend to the grand metaphor of the nation-state as collective ego. There is no benefit in competition between nations but only between individuals and the collective work of groups of individuals. The spectacle of the Olympics becomes farcical when individual metals that have been awarded are totaled up so as to turn a sublime competition of individuals into a competition for bragging rights between nations. A gold medal winner is an object of pride that should be appreciated by the citizens of all nations. And inventions and innovation should be sources of human pride even if nations and corporations seek to monopolize or corner the commercial market by turning a legitimate advantage into an unfair one. Unfair playing fields for industry could be significantly leveled by proposals such as the open patent system (§II.16) in which inventors, be they individual or corporate, would not have a monopoly but will benefit, succeed and flourish by the broad-based development of their inventions by competitors who pay them universal licensing and fees. A "cooperative competition" would in the world society replace competition whose essential purpose is, essentially, as it is in war, to bust the competition. The world society envisaged here is a cooperative society in which disharmonic blockages have been removed and institutions have been created to encourage a free-flowing movement towards individual and collective greatness.

A web of common interest binds the nation-state and the corporation together to suppress inventions, products and medicinals when it is not in their mutual self-interest. But when barriers to both competition and cooperation are removed both in terms of governmental over-regulation and monopolistic restraint of trade, the cream of innovation and productivity will be allowed to rise to the top. Greatness cannot be forced but only encouraged. Suppressions of technologies and of historical truths will become far more difficult when concentrations of power have been broken up and vested interests that drive the deceit have lost their compensation. When there is no taxation for the nation-state to levy or impose, when governmental revenue is merely the product of the government's business in its role as landlord and not tax collector, then a foundation will be laid for the world to achieve unprecedented flourishing and prosperity. And in this new world society the dismantling of the nation-state may save history as well as truth by breaking the monopoly cartel on the truth. When political and economic power becomes too concentrated lies are seen as truth; the navigation of convergent forces aided and abetted by distortion assuredly jeopardizes destiny.

How could this imaginary world society ever become a reality? Change can happen if a single nation-state in the industrialized world begins to initiate the type of harmonic unblocking discussed in the preceding sections on social empowerment. If a single nation-state in the industrialized world initiates a divestiture and reinvestment of all private real estate enormous economic power would be released. The elimination of political parties will diminish senseless and idiotic political wrangling. Social entitlements will lay the foundation for a fair and robust society. Inventors will be attracted to a society that protects their interests, as innovation, creativity and invention soar to new heights. The first nation of the new world society will usher in a realization of new actualities and will fast become the envy of others who will then join the project. One nation's success in demonstrating what the dismantling of the nation-state *could* look like, will prompt other nations to join and began to integrate into a proto world society. In the proto world society, the reinvestment of funds earned by private sellers after the sale and transfer to the public domain of private real estate holdings will stimulate enormous economic growth. A process of decentralized integration would begin. Regulatory agencies and other institutions will be reformed, democratized and self-funded by the real estate base and by interregional sharing. Step-by-step, nation-by-nation a world society will begin to take shape. In time, as the majority of advanced nations will have joined the emerging world society it will become clear that by embracing both individual and collective empowerment, by ridding humanity of the harmonic blockages that have enslaved it and threaten to destroy it, is to embrace the potential of freedom and a great destiny bounded by love. A dialectical change will follow the causal transformation that would have been in progress for some time. The evolving ethical consensus, the resolution of disharmonic institutional configurations, the reframing of values, economic success and the undeniable emergence of greater freedom will make the world society seem inevitable even if its destiny, in retrospect, was always on the bright horizon.

II.32

Incremental v. Radical Change

S ome of the most radical social changes are virtually apolitical. The digital age has witnessed a few such transformations. The personal computer, internet and mobile phone have each transformed everyday life with lightening speed, but it would be more accurate to describe the change as both incremental and radical. In the years after the introduction of the personal computer but before the advent of the internet, computer aficionados debated the question of what particular development would turn the PC into a household necessity. While the personal computer had become an item in many millions of households it was not yet as ubiquitous or as essential as the telephone, television or radio. But when the internet made its appearance the personal computer and the internet together rapidly and seamlessly ushered in the information age, inconceivable only a few years earlier. This radical transformation was the result of incremental advances that seemed to suddenly burst onto the scene transforming with ease communication, entertainment and access to information, and reshaping of the modern lifestyle. While these enormous changes have required some regulation concerning issues such as privacy and security, the political and legal apparatus have struggled *post facto* to keep up with the change. The automobile and petroleum industries in the first half of the twentieth century, not to mention the telephone and the radio, are also examples of enormous social change that fairly well happened without the initiative of politicians or legislators. These technological transformations of society are examples of very radical changes that were readily absorbed and adopted by the society without obstructive political wrangling.

However, change requiring the cooperation of the political system creates a burden for the proponents of change. They must influence the political machinery of the country, regardless of whether the country's political system is democratic or non-democratic, and sufficient political will needs to be built up before the political institutions will be moved to act, accept and execute change. Change needing governmental cooperation must be designed, planned and implemented. Unlike apolitical change in which the government and the political system are more reactive than proactive, political change requires a proactive government or political movement to support it. And unlike apolitical change, political change is something argued and debated in legislatures and other governing bodies before it is put into action. However, the phenomena of successful, broad apolitical changes such as the internet or the mobile phone raises the question of whether political change can too easily stumble over its own feet when convergent forces may have already forced its hand. It is the responsibility of the political process to interpret the convergent forces that are at work and to decide the most appropriate or the best course that accommodates causal necessity and dialectical persuasion.

The question of which is preferable, incremental or radical social change, is not answerable in dogmatic terms: at times we need to be more radical and other times more conservative. But examples of trans-formational, apolitical change indicate the great extent to which society can adapt to radical change. The hypothetical world society envisaged in (§II.31) that will have freed itself of the nation-state as we know it, that is virtually self-sufficient by virtue of public rental revenue from all real estate, in which swords have been turned into plowshares, in which freedom to pursue the highest level of creativity and inventiveness has been unblocked and unsuppressed, and that has abundant enough wealth to ensure that every human being has the basic needs that are the right of his or her humanity, is a world that could only form from both incremental and radical change. The speed of change can be deceptive. And perhaps the greatest radical changes are those managed and ushered in with patience and a long-range view, incrementally and radically.

II.33

Historical "Facts"

In 1927 Babe Ruth set a Major League baseball record when he hit 60 home runs in a single season. But in 1961, the same year that the baseball season was expanded from 154 games to 162 games, Roger Maris "broke" Ruth's record by hitting 61 home runs, even though he actually hit only 59 home runs in the first 154 games of the newly expanded season. This record follows a peculiar logic because affording players an additional eight games to break a record leads to obvious absurdities that reveal how historical accuracy is readily supplanted when it suits the needs of writers of "official" history, which in this case is organized baseball. For example, the 100-yard dash has generally been supplanted by the 100-meter sprint; what if track and field associations decided to group the 100-yard dash records together with the 100-meter sprint records? Never mind that a yard is roughly 8.5 percent shorter than a meter and, as a consequence, the 100-yard record holders would obliterate 100-meter records for the simple reason that the 100-yard race is shorter that the 100-meter race. A season is a season, a race is a race, and what does length have to do with it? Will shortening the length of a foot make people taller? Ridiculous indeed. It is perhaps understandable—and perhaps I am too charitable—that a sport might prefer that its records be "clean" and unconfused. But what if the records of political and social history were kept as shabbily or disingenuously?

The truth is that there is a good deal of history à la baseball! Columbus did not discover America and the "Wild, Wild West" was not nearly as wild or gun-happy as popular "history" would have us believe.[97] Misinformation can have insidious consequences. On January 6, 2011 the Constitution of the United States was read in the chamber of the House of Representatives. Actually, only *most* of it was read because the reading omitted parts that have been nullified by subsequent amendment. The most notable effect of this ploy was that the "Three-Fifths Compromise" of the Constitution (Article 1, Section 2, Clause 3) was passed over in the reading. The notorious Compromise counted each slave as "three-fifths" of a person in determining the population of each state. Interestingly, while the word 'slave' or 'slavery' does not appear in the unamended original form of the Constitution the reference to slavery is clearly implied. The Constitution is a living document that, while amendable, also contains within itself its genealogy so there always is a built-in reminder of the past for the benefit of future generations. The original Constitution and its amendments exist side-by-side. And the sanitized reading of the Constitution is an affront not only to Americans who are the descendants of slaves but also to anyone who cherishes freedom. Those whose ancestors have had their "inalienable rights" of "life, liberty and the pursuit of happiness" stolen from them have a deep abiding interest and right that the memory of slavery's unspeakable horrors be tediously preserved so that history is not be repeated. In the aftermath of the House reading, former U.S. Rep. Jesse Jackson, Jr. of Illinois wrote:

> Our expectation was that the new Republican majority would read the Constitution as written and its subsequent amendments. There is a broad body of law and interpretation that has developed from 1787 until the adoption of the last Amendment in 1992 that has turned our Constitution into a living document, paid for by the blood, sweat and tears of millions of Americans from the Revolutionary War, through the Civil War to even our current conflicts.[98]

Contrary to Hegel's misguided "Slave-Master Dialectic," the slave trade was never justified so why now skirt an opportunity to demonstrate, through a recitation of the Constitution in all of its organic fullness, that we honor the men and women and children that were trapped in institutionalized slavery. By reciting an evolving and *living* Constitution, we would honor the victims of slavery in a self-conscious acknowledgment of past wrongs and a solemn commitment to never forget.

The framing of historical facts, of which the reading of the U.S.

Constitution minus the three-fifths clause is an example, is common. "Russia is a country with an unpredictable past" is a well-known joke in Russia that contains much truth, and it seems that the current Russian government is attempting to institutionalize the joke into an unfunny, official reality. Differences in historical interpretation are a hallmark of intellectual freedom, but the manipulation and subversion of history is an insidious ploy that simultaneously robs both truth and freedom. The formation of the Historical Truth Commission was announced by President Dmitry Medvedev in May of 2009 in order to combat what he described as the falsification of history respective to the conduct of Soviet Russian troops during World War II. It would be wrong to entirely dismiss Russian concerns, after all "falsifications" of history occur on both sides of an issue. Much of the stimulus for the Historical Truth Commission are claims equating Soviet and Nazi policies, made by former Soviet block countries, e.g. Latvia and Lithuania, who themselves have an interest in falsifying activities conducted on behalf of the Nazis.[99] The problem for Russia in this regard, however, is that there is not much point in arguing the fact that Stalin's Russia was a colossal repression of human rights. Through purges, man-made famine (the Ukranian Holodomor), mass collectivization and other methods of brutality Stalin may indeed be compared to Hitler both in terms of his mass murders as well as the invasion, takeover and repression of conquered countries. Some have even argued that Stalin murdered twice as many non-combatants as Hitler, although the number of millions murdered is a matter of scholarly debate. Clearly, there is more than ample justification for comparisons between Stalin and Hitler, and considering the nature of Stalin's reign it should hardly be a surprise to anyone if the Russian heroism of many coincided with atrocities committed by others. After all, there is no Russian or American heroism, per se, but only the acts of individual heroes.

The overriding motivation for the intentional falsification of history, it seems, is that by sanitizing the truth and purifying the past, somehow, the collective editing of subconscious guilt will ensure a happier and more prosperous future. But this conception, this justification of falsification, is undoubtedly a prescription for future distress much as past trauma or guilt always reemerges in one form or the other if it is not intelligently and rationally resolved. The blame-shifting or avoidance is slightly reminiscent of Nietzschean ressentiment, but what is required is not avoidance, but the application of another Nietzschean concept, which is that of *overcoming*. The culpability of past generations can be overcome by acceptance of the hard truth and, in turn, by the transformational growth and wisdom gained. True freedom is not achieved through the falsification of our individual or social histories but, rather, by acceptance and the painful embrace of past disappointments, regrets or even disgrace. An individual who has committed loathsome acts will need to come to terms with his actions, and whether or not he believes that he has a soul he will need to deal with it somehow on some level. Perhaps the moral dialectic transfigures itself into a spiritual or karmic play and, if so, the perpetrators of grossly incoherent, soulless, immoral acts will have no choice in the matter. There are, however, opportunities for individuals as well as nations for redemption. We need not always look to the most heinous of acts; indeed, they can be so painful we are inclined to look away. Ongoing redemption takes form in relatively small acts of humility that in time accumulate and become transformational. Self-correction is ongoing and present and is the primary calling of the moral dialectic. Current members of the United States House of Representatives had nothing to do with the institution of slavery that left deep, penetrating and lasting wounds on the American psyche, but if they would have intentionally read the words that describe a human being as only "three-fifths" human they could have reminded all of us of how far we have come. The United States of America is a great nation and the Constitution is a brilliant document, but there is far too much chest pounding and conceit that sours the taste of freedom. A good dose of humility will *always* serve us well as a collective reminder of how far we have come and, echoing Frost, of the many "miles to go" before we sleep.

II.34

The Right to Know

He who controls the past controls the future, and
he who controls the present controls the past.
George Orwell, *1984*

Truth and ethics are joined at the hip. The subject of conspiracy theories provides an illustration of the relationship between truth and ethics. Conspiracy theories are often criticized for using an inadequate or incomplete examination of the evidence that, through selective thinking, forms an inordinate bias or antipathy against conventional perceptions of events, institutions and power relationships. Ironically, however, conspiracy theories also represent a form of skepticism. They offer skeptical views about official or generally accepted narratives concerning events, discoveries and institutional relationships most typically in respect to governments or other organizations that are perceived to have decisive and controlling influence. In an actual conspiracy, the truth may be hidden or manipulated by conspirators who seek, as it were, to hijack history by taking control of elements of the political-socio-economic apparatus. A conspiracy theory is an assertion of fact or a set of facts that, from the point of view of a presumed right to know is something to be either substantiated or disqualified as groundless or, perhaps, something in-between. An actual conspiracy could be described as a dysfunction of the exteriority that obstructs both the vital process of truth-seeking and the right to know. And if a claim of serious dysfunction is true there is a clear moral imperative and right to know.

Often, the right to know is declined in favor of the right *not* to know. There are many legitimate ethical restrictions on the right to know from simple promise-keeping and privacy issues in personal life to the security issues of a nation. But the right to know is as much psychological as it is philosophical or ethical. A complex array of conscious and subconscious defenses may be constructed within both the interiority and exteriority that act as a shield against truth-seeking, and the right to know may be affirmed or denied because of the preconception, convention or fear of nonconformity. An ideophobic basis of the right to know can be seen in both the bias of conspiracy theorists and defenders of the conventional wisdom. Conspiracy theorists may believe that the truth is cloaked in secrecy that denies them their right to know the truth, while defenders of the conventional wisdom my believe that the cloak is either fantasy or delusion, that there is nothing new to know, and that conspiracy theory is merely a case of pseudo-knowledge, in which case, there is nothing to know. The ideophobic bias reflects the subconscious and non-rational aspects of pre-conditioned hypnotic thinking that may include fears that foundational beliefs may be wrong, or simply formalities and habits of thought that close the mind to challenging perspectives. Both conspiracy theories and the conventional wisdom can be biases that thwart objective inquiry. Not infrequently, both may become continuing intellectual suppressants that lead to dogma and ideology. However, by unblocking intellectual blockages in the interiority of our minds we begin the process of removing external barriers that disempower the exteriority or social mind. As with all belief there is no neat division separating conscious and subconscious belief, and the exteriority reinforces the interiority and, therefore, as with all duality the boundary between the conscious and the subconscious blurs.

There is perhaps no better exemplification of the social implications of the right to know than the 1960 NASA commission report prepared by The Bookings Institution entitled "Proposed Studies on the Implications of Peaceful Space Activities for Human Affairs." The Report's findings included the recommendation that studies be undertaken to evaluate the "emotional and intellectual" reactions to the hypothetical discovery of extraterrestrial life, and famously remarked that,

> Questions one might wish to answer by such studies
> would include: How might such information, under
> what circumstances, be presented to or withheld from

the public for what ends? What might be the role of
the discovering scientists and other decisionmakers
regarding release of the fact of discovery?[100]

Would there not be a presumed right to know in the eventuality of such a
momentous discovery? While some might dismiss this subject as the stuff
of science fiction, The Brookings Institution gave the matter enough
credence in 1960 to consider the ramifications of whether or not the public
would have a right to know if it should come to pass that the existence of
extraterrestrial beings are discovered or—we can conjecture, if contact had
already been made. Rightly or wrongly, the Report has helped to frame the
attitude of ufologists and others interested in UFO phenomena that there
has been a U.S. government cover-up. Has evidence been suppressed? And
if so, why? Is it because the government believes that we can't handle the
truth? Or, on the contrary, are UFO believers merely victims of their own
beliefs and conspiratorial suspicions. The answer may be unclear, but it is
difficult to describe the attitude expressed in the Report as anything other
than one of disempowerment. An environment in which the possibility of
extraterrestrial contact is openly discussed in the mainstream would
empower society to come to grips with the very implications and questions
that the Report raises. In general, it is true that truth empowers, and it is
highly questionable that fictional alien invasion movies can do the job!
Nonetheless, if there has been a suppression of information relating to UFOs
or extraterrestrial intelligence science fiction may be the only contact that
the public has with this enormously significant subject.

Everyday life presents diverse phenomena of which scientific
verification is not required in order for it to be believed. Thousands of UFO
sightings have been reported by many persons whose testimony, were it to
be presented in a court of law, would be accorded serious consideration.
Anyone qualified to sit on a jury to decide guilt or innocence is qualified to
judge whether evidence supporting extraterrestrial contact has been covered-
up, hidden or intentionally muddled. The analogy breaks down for many
on the grounds that unlike ten people testifying that a man robbed a
convenience store, an excellent description of a UFO sighting is not
objectively identifiable. In other words, what are the criteria for establishing
that a UFO sighting was actually an extraterrestrial spacecraft? But the

evidence is compelling nonetheless. Observed phenomena of something darting this way or that, which then whiz away in the blink of an eye, and that was of a certain size, color etc. creates an environment of disbelief, but the multiple repetitions of similar phenomena make 'unidentified' an unsatisfactory identifier. It is much like an interesting color that becomes repeatedly used on signs, clothing, etc. and soon enough it will be given a name. The mere volume of UFO sightings has produced enough commonalities, in many cases, to warrant a more serious and less dismissive tag than 'unidentified'. Does the unidentified status of a sighting negate the quality of the evidence? If the quality of the perceptions are good and are corroborated by others and, at times, detected by radar, does the 'unidentified' tag suffice? Conventional anti-UFO bias is not merely one of skepticism, which is appropriate, but is too often an attitude of easy dismissal and condescension. The conventional wisdom on UFOs is deceptively constructed by simple syllogistic reasoning that rigs the conclusion:

major premise: All flying objects are either manmade objects or
                  animals or natural phenomena such as meteors.

minor premise: A flying object was sighted.

conclusion: Therefore, the flying object was either a
                  manmade object or an animal or a natural
                  phenomenon such as a meteor (though meteors
                  are from outer space).

As is the case with most syllogisms, the argument is logically correct but empirically insufficient. The quality of evidence is disregarded; it is not taken seriously because the possibility of extraterrestrial origin is excluded in the major premise. The conclusion is rigged; there was no extraterrestrial craft sighted because its possibility is arbitrarily excluded from con-sideration. This is over-simplistic syllogistic reasoning, you say? No, the only simplicity here is the manner in which the conventional wisdom and its governmental enforcers have cavalierly dismissed high-quality evidence! The fact that an object is not identifiable does not mean that evidence for it should be dismissed and disregarded. Rather, the only rational attitude towards UFO sightings, when accompanied with creditable evidence, is to acknowledge that they represent the plausibility of alien or extraterrestrial contact. That's it in a nutshell. We do not need to believe that the aliens have arrived, but the preponderance of evidence strongly suggests that it is not unreasonable to suppose that they may have arrived. Knee-jerk rejections by skeptics of claims that UFOs are extraterrestrial craft are seemingly motivated by an ideophobic need to defend their exclusionary major premise at all cost, apparently in order to exercise their right not to know. Or is the drive not to know merely to save a current paradigm? Certainly, the discovery of intelligent extraterrestrial beings who conceivably have been observing or interacting with human beings might conjure a deep fear that could shake the anthropocentric order to its foundations.

Fear of upsetting the apple cart of convention combined with the fear of losing money can explain many impediments to legitimate rights to know. Much like the suppression of technological development, (§II.16) unless there is a demonstrable threat to the physical welfare of the community, suppression of knowledge and technology is a failure to preserve, protect and defend the public's right to know. Alongside the predictable denigration of conspiracy theorists is the broad dismissal by mainstream science and academia of a class of thought derisively referred to as "pseudoscience." Ufology is certainly one of the subjects most frequently targeted by priests of scientific convention, but there are many other fields alleged to be pseudoscience, perhaps most notably in health and alternative medicine. Merely mentioning the Rife Microscope would prompt jeers and laughter by mainstream experts in medical science. (§II.15) Perhaps the Rife machines have little merit, however, it is a simple matter to retain a smug attitude when formal testing has never been carried out, and intimidation and harassment is never mentioned. There seems to have been a powerful motive by the old AMA and its minions not to know. And Big Pharma and others are today lobbying for increased regulations to control the distribution of herbal and dietary supplements despite the fact that the safety record of these products is vastly, exponentially safer than pharmaceuticals. It would be a truly stupid argument to say that pharmaceuticals should not be developed, but what is also stupid—and malicious, is interference with the natural supplementation industry for reasons of greed and desire for monopoly control over all medicinal substances including natural dietary or herbal supplementation. Asserting the right *not* to know can be very lucrative.

Syllogistic exclusions exemplify the hypnotic process of selective thinking. (§I.4) Paradigms of conventional thinking in the various fields of thought selectively embrace a body of belief and all exceptions are discounted and minimized. Through selective thinking, findings that conform to the accepted principles (the major premise) are endorsed while findings that do not conform are conveniently ignored. Anomalous phenomena don't really matter because if they are anomalous, they are of no interest. There is much evidence that T. Henry Moray invented something truly remarkable, witnessed by many, and affirmed by an esteemed physicist near the end of his life, but the conception of zero-point or "free energy" is that it is impossible, so power elite in charge either didn't take him seriously or could not afford to. (§II.15) And the new plebeian class of know-nothings and ask-nothings have a genuine right to know but, for the most part, don't know it. Nonetheless, in science as in all fields of knowledge some of the greatest advances are those that succeed in radically overturning old orders of belief. The disparaged and ignored "pseudosciences" are a large and disparate body of material that is ignored by the powerful because of ideophobia or other more mundane fears such as, e.g., losing market share. Eventually the fear of alternative technologies may deepen the ideophobia into a sort of "hysterical blindness": the traumatic prospects of integrating beliefs that would turn accepted principles on their head become so distressful to the psyche and to the intellect that the anxiety is converted into blindness to truth.

The desire not to know can be self-deluding, but the suppressors of the truth may also be suppressing information because they really believe it does not prove what is claimed, and then take upon themselves the mission of defending the public from what, in their view, is delusion. Never mind that it is they who may be the deluded ones who do not realize the significance of the evidence; their selective thinking has decided the matter and justified the repression. The submission of truth into the service of a wish fulfillment, arguably, finds a supporter in the venerable William James in this passage from Pragmatism:

...truth is one species of good, and not, as is usually

> supposed, a category distinct from good, and co-ordinate
> with it. The true is the name of whatever proves itself
> to be good in the way of belief…'What would be better
> for us to believe'! This sounds very like a definition of truth.
> It comes very near to saying 'what we ought to believe':
> Ought we ever not to believe what it is better for us to
> believe? And can we then keep the notion of what is better
> for us, and what is true for us, permanently apart?
> Pragmatism says no…[101]

But we cannot go along with James here unless we all agree that it is always better for us to believe what is most epistemically justified; but James seems to be suggesting that "what would be better for us to believe" goes beyond epistemology. The truth of the matter is that we do not always agree on what is best. And it is clear that vested interests have an insidious way of spinning for us what is best. Sometimes, as the saying says, "the truth hurts" and therefore if we are to be swayed by the pleasure principle we will invariably avoid the truth. Truth made subsidiary to any other impulse than a good faith assessment of what is objectively judged to be true will inevitably suffer from moral incoherence; an ethical life is impossible without the notion that ethical choices are predicated on due diligence in determining the true facts or the truth as best we are capable of comprehending it. But our concern here is not about what is true or the grounds for judging it but, rather, when there is and when there is not a right to know. The lines of demarcation blur. The distinction between truth and the right to know the truth blur because beliefs about what is true influence our assessments about whether there is a right to know. The line of demarcation blurs between conscious ethical deliberations and subconscious fears that prefer that things stay the same. Fears often disguise themselves as reason. The blurring also occurs between the interiority and exteriority, when ethical deliberations concerning whether there is a right to know interlace our moral sense with the representations of society, culture and the world in which we live.

Documents released under The U.S. Freedom of Information Act often have large swaths of text blacked out or deleted, even on records that are over 20, 30, 50 years old. Shouldn't there be an oversight committee to limit the overly liberal use of the magic marker? Does it really make sense that the suppressors of information—in this case particular agencies of government, should also be the final arbiters of what should be released? Is this not a conflict of interest? There should be an impartial oversight board to help ensure that the spirit of The Freedom of Information Act is enforced without prejudice. Establishing the collective right to know is a pathway to individual and social empowerment that needs to be honored. Everyone has the wool pulled over their eyes from time to time, and it can also happen to societies and even to humanity in its whole collectivity. But knowledge and wisdom deserve a fair shot. Without the right to know, recalling the sense of Orwell's words, we cede both the past and the future. We would lose our freedom to our controllers or, perhaps we we should say, the manufacturers of truth.

II.35

Philosophy of Conspiracy

Conspiracy theories typically allege secretive and illegal plots that seek to change or maintain political, economic or socio-cultural conditions. If true, many conspiracy theories, e.g. the JFK assassination or the 9/11 attacks, have momentous significance not only for our understanding of history but also for the future. And if the conspiracy theorist is vindicated, he will most likely be redeemed and viewed as an enlightened thinker who forewarned the ignorant masses of their folly. But if the conspiracy theorist is not vindicated he will generally be seen as just a kook. The tides of change are gentler for the skeptics who love to dismiss and ridicule conspiracy theories because all will likely be forgiven and soon forgotten as the conspiracy theory soon becomes part of a new conventional wisdom and the new actuality.

Historical accuracy is profoundly important. Is it preferable to leave shameful events buried in the recesses of individual or collective unconsciousness? In the case of individual persons, the answer is certainly in the negative. The repression of unpleasant or traumatic memories will continue to fester and disturb the mind until they are dealt with, brought to the level of consciousness, sometimes reframed but ultimately resolved in such a way that the truth can be accepted; then, with the realization of wisdom gained the past need not continue to haunt and disempower. Similarly, if left uncorrected, false histories also haunt and endanger a repetition of a covered-up and distorted past. Surely, there are no lessons to be learned from history that never happened. And a sugarcoated history that has been distorted by myths lingers like a ghost awaiting closure until the truth is finally revealed. But with truth comes freedom and opportunity to both learn and also detach from the past.

Close-mindedness is not a virtue. Arbitrary rejections and the discouragement of inquiry are in-and-of themselves disturbing and are the very sort of attitude that should be universally discouraged. David Aaronovitch has written a good book about conspiracies that makes a case that virtually all of the major modern conspiracy theories are false, and that the hidden motive for many if not most of them are scapegoatism, blame shifting or vengefulness. Aaronovitch applies "Occam's Razor" in his favoring of simpler explanations over those that are more complex. However, Occam's Razor is a very fallible principle and is not a law of nature. Sometimes shaving too close can shave away what we would have been better off keeping! But Aaronovitch, at times, seems to want to make Occam's Razor universal law and relishes putting the kibosh—if I'm not mistaken, on every conspiracy theory that he discusses in his book. His approach, however, results in a fundamental contradiction. Aaronovitch documents the fictitiously conjured conspiracies detailed in the so-called "Protocols of the Elders of Zion," and also in the kangaroo trial conducted by Stalin's regime against alleged Trotskyites. The "Protocols" was actually a plot by a Czarist Russian spy to scapegoat Jews so as to take pressure off the Czar's economic problems at the time. And the Soviet's kangaroo trial was used to wrongly incriminate certain individuals in order to set the stage for Stalin to orchestrate his purge and program of mass murder.[102] Counter to the thrust of Aaronovitch's book, while accusations of these conspiracy theories had no grounds, the accusations were themselves conspiracies of the worst kind! The "Protocols of the Elders of Zion" was not a conspiracy by a Jewish cabal but was instead a conspiracy by anti-Semites conspiring to scapegoat, defame and incite violence against Jews and to promulgate lies made fertile in an environment of latent anti-Semitism. And Stalin's kangaroo trials were equally contrived and malicious. The real conspiracy in both cases was not what was falsely alleged but was, rather, the promulgation of the falsehoods themselves. In a word, both organized deceptions were conspiracies to deceive. And so Aaronovitch has, counter to his anti-conspiracy bias, effectively demonstrated that at least two conspiracy theories are true: 1) It is true that there was and still remains a conspiracy to promulgate the myth of the "Protocols" and to incite anti-Semitism and 2) It is true that there was a conspiracy to wrongly allege and convict Trotskyite co-conspirators in order to facilitate the subsequent atrocities of Stalin's regime.

Conspiracy theories, as with any beliefs, should be judged by their evidence and plausibility. There are certainly many conspiracy theories that are patently absurd and warrant no more serious consideration than would a critical examination of comic books. For example, I have not seen or read any evidence suggesting that the Royal Family of England and U.S. presidents are descended from a line of shape-shifting reptilians intent on dominating humankind. Unfortunately, there are more than a few ridiculous conspiracy theories out there that are taken seriously by many without any evidence; they are nothing more than fantasms created by imagination or fear or both. But the dismissal of all conspiracy theories is nearly as unbelievable and foolish as the belief that all of them are true. Dismissing evidence that clashes with the conventional wisdom can be a tragic fault if the denials and the suppressions produce a false reality that seriously endangers both the present and the future. And the easy dismissals profoundly disempower society by blunting opposition to conventional belief by intellectual ostracism, political marginalization, threats of financial ruination and other tactics. Aaronovitch makes a good point when he argues that many people experience dissatisfaction with "the untidiness of reality" respective to tragic events and that the adoption of conspiracy theories helps them to avoid painful self-examination about themselves and contemporary culture.[103] The alternative worldview that conspiratorial forces behind the scenes are controlling our lives and our collective destiny may be, for some, a better alternative to "the untidiness of reality" than Occam's razor. But this simple broad brush or Occam's razing has its limits to be sure. What competent crime investigator would ignore motives of power and profit?

The Stalinist conspiracy and the "Protocols of the Elders of Zion" are examples of government sponsorship or complicity in conspiracy. McCarthyism in America in the 40s and 50s is another example of a conspiracy to deceive, i.e. to accuse others of conspiracy. Joseph McCarthy's accusations of widespread Communist conspiracy, primarily within the U.S. government, had little substantive evidence even if, not surprisingly, there were *some* spies who were guilty of crimes. The only widespread organized conspiracy was, in fact, an informal consortium of McCarthy's Senate committee, the House Committee on Un-American Activities and a broad spectrum of supporters. A reign of terror orchestrated by fear, intimidation and paranoia attempted to prevent the free association and freedom of speech that are the very foundations of American democracy. It occurred during a period of rising fear at the height of the Cold War and, indeed, the possibility of enemy infiltration by Soviet spies was a legitimate concern. In truth, however, the McCarthyite conspiracy and its blacklists and false or unsubstantiated allegations were doing the dirty work for the Soviet government by assisting it in its efforts to wreck American democracy. McCarthy was Soviet Russia's best friend.[104] Good evidence and logic are the only bases for weighing the merit of a conspiracy theory. The McCarthyite accusations of a widespread Communist conspiracy that infiltrated American government and society was a failed conspiracy theory because its shabby claims were largely groundless and entirely reckless. Its defamations were criminal, but who among the perpetrators of the very real McCarthyite conspiracy to defame and ruin lives was ever prosecuted or charged with crimes?

The McCarthyite conspiracy suggests how conspiracies can be undertaken by highly public persons loosely unorganized around common goals. It is claimed by some conspiracy theorists that the group of important business and political leaders known as the Bilderberg Group is a front that exists in order to create a world government or "new world order." The Bilderberg conspiracy theory may well be fueled by elements of paranoia, however, concern that an extra-governmental convention of powerful business and political leaders could circumvent legislatures and constitutionally established leadership is not without warrant. The claims that the Bilderbergers, the Trilateral Commission, the Council on Foreign Relations and other interrelated associations are seeking to achieve world dominance reflect fears that increasing globalization and concentrations of corporate, political and military power are becoming a threat to the political and economic autonomy of nation-states. It is not unreasonable to suppose that a worldwide organization of powerful business and political leaders might develop or evolve, out of mutual self-interest, into closer alliances that ultimately run contrary to fundamental aspirations—the will of the people—that could undemocratically supercede democratic institutions. Whether or not these groups have conspiratorial intentions, there is at least a theoretical threat posed by extra-governmental cooperation by elite capitalists and power brokers that, through extra-constitutional means, could maneuver the world political and economic systems into irreversible configurations leading to repression or monopoly or both. As Lord Acton said, "Power tends to corrupt, and absolute power corrupts absolutely." But Acton's quote also went on to articulate a view that the writer does not share, that "Great men are almost always bad men." Gatherings of the world's most powerful people are not necessarily bad. There is no denying that monopolies form and that human nature is such that the powerful tend to grab more power if they can get away with it. Monopolization is a natural occurrence in business, and without antitrust laws monopolies would dominate economies more than they already do. The paranoiac quality of many conspiracy theories is duly noted, but paranoia much like phobias often exhibit underlying elements of rational fear elevated to irrational extremes. Accordingly, the mere existence of some irrational conspiratorial fears should not erase a fundamental concern over concentrations of power, any more than, say, resolving phobic fears of flying should lead to disinterest in airline safety. Therefore, it is possible to monitor groups such as the Bilderbergers without descending into unreason.

The fear of concentrating political and economic power into the hands of a few is surely something that any man or woman who cares about freedom should fear. The Framers of the U.S. Constitution understood quite well that the fear of tyranny is a rational fear requiring institutionalized protection. Today, the world is in dire need of new protections from oligarchy and tyranny, and other concentrations of political and economic power that suppress freedom of expression and inquiry. There is no doubt that a centralized world government is a terrifying *1984* nightmare that must be prevented. Arbitrarily rejecting conspiracy theories is staying in the darkness of ignorance, like Plato's cave dwellers who interpreted shadows as reality. Are we living in caves of darkness because our minds have been *willingly* closed to the light of truth? Most conspiracy theories may well be mostly wrong if not flat out wrong. But the arbitrary closing of minds to alternative explanations that are counter to conventionally embraced wisdom is a modern re-creation of Plato's cave. Why is there such resistance and fear by so many to the serious consideration of conspiracy theories and other affronts to the conventional wisdom? Some conspiracy theories are patent nonsense while others are worthy of serious consideration, some more so than others. The anti-conspiracy theorist is very popular in conventional society and it is very comfortable to lightly dismiss conspiracy theories.

It is acceptable in conventional "polite" society to dismiss conspiracy theories as the preoccupations of not-very-serious people, and wackos out of touch with the real world. Questioning basic truths is bad etiquette in conventional society and is a display of bad manners that may be viewed as suggestive of an unstable mind. However, indoctrination and over-reliance on the formalities of the conventional wisdom may produce far greater instability. In periods of change and moments of crisis, the closed mind is the least stable form of existence.

Is not a governmental investigation in itself a spectacle profuse with conspiratorial potential? Fear and ignorance are closely allied. Ignorance breeds fear and fear breeds ignorance. Fear creates resistance to the objective pursuit of knowledge thereby breeding ignorance, and ignorance in turn breeds new fears that impede the pursuit of the truth. Indeed, knowledge is the cure for both ignorance and irrational fear. And while governmental complicity is hardly a requisite for a conspiracy, government and its agencies are in a formidable position to manage the fear and ignorance that are the essence of conspiratorial misdirection. In our present day, a painful example of the synergy between fear and ignorance may be the disturbing cloud of doubt that concerns the 9/11 attacks against America. The tragic events of September 11, 2001 have transformed life in America and have profoundly impacted world politics and international affairs, but it has also been targeted by conspiracy theorists as, essentially, a staged misdirection most likely managed by a conspiracy from inside the U.S. government. But, as we might expect, the investigations, reportage and evidence have all been well managed by agencies of the U.S. government and aided by the natural proclivity of the public's conventional wisdom to reject conspiracy theories. Therefore, the accusations against the government—habitually dismissed out of a normal bias to begin with, have been weakly and neglectfully investigated and sheltered by the government, i.e. the hypothetical conspirators themselves.

Many troubling questions haunt the investigation of 9/11 that impartial, non-governmental authorities ought to investigate. When the government itself is the accused, then it should be routine for the government to recuse itself or be recused, and replaced by officially authorized but independent bodies. Otherwise, governmental denials of plausible evidence suggesting its direct or indirect culpability in the attacks are almost without worth. What is the behavior of the government that makes the government itself a suspect in 9/11? A compelling presentation that raises doubts about the official version of the 9/11 tragedy is the PBS broadcast of the documentary *9/11 Explosive Evidence – Experts Speak Out*.[105] A litany of expert witnesses are interviewed who make claims that cannot be easily dismissed and certainly warrant further investigation. A conspiracy theorist has a good rule of thumb for suspicion: If evidence is covered-up, hidden, manipulated, or destroyed, and if barriers to investigation are erected, then there is cause to suspect some type of conspiracy. But governments often justify these behaviors by asserting the need to protect "national security." The bottom line is that if national security is invoked as the motive for obstruction, then principles of democratic governance should require strong oversight to justify and verify the merits of the claim, and that they have not been contrived. If there is an ulterior motive for a conspiracy, the seriousness of the conspiratorial charges increases by degrees. Key points made in *9/11 Explosive Evidence – Experts Speak Out* cannot be lightly dismissed, and the skeptic who dismisses the uncomfortable evidence *oh so lightly* reveals a complete absence of skepticism with respect to his own beliefs. Bona fide evidence dismissed by investigators without due process and consideration bears the mark of an incompetent, a fool, or a coward; the exception, of course, being that of the investigator who is threatened with dire consequences if he fails to toe the line or breaks the code of silence.

In the hours and days after the 9/11 attacks 400 truckloads per day of steel rubble were removed from ground zero and promptly shipped off to China for recycling. By so doing evidence was destroyed and protocols for crime scene investigations were blatantly violated.[106] Should this gross disregard of governmental responsibility and civic duty be simply passed off as poor judgment? Hardly. Can this malfeasance in investigating the most heinous crime in American history be a mere oversight? Most unlikely. And should the government be simply let off the hook and allow this wanton and massive destruction of evidence escape without judicial investigation, or better yet, by an investigation comprised of a panel of impartially selected private experts empowered and authorized by Congress? Clearly, an empowered investigative body free of any conflict of interest involving government or its agencies—or of any other party, is absolutely necessary.

The Twin towers and Building 7 appear to have been brought down by controlled demolition. As a boy, I was fascinated by television coverage of controlled demolitions of revered iconic buildings that needed to be cleared to make way for new and modern structures, and I was amazed by the surgical precision and elegant orchestration of the clean and safe collapse. But apparently two airliners can smash into huge, super modern steel framed high-rise towers and achieve the same remarkable results as a controlled demolition! So much for the science of demolishing buildings! And Building 7 also collapsed, again with the precision of a controlled demolition after only a few limited fires, and no collisions with aircraft whatsoever. How about that! While the nearly perfect domino-like collapse of the twin towers does indeed strongly suggest controlled demolition, the case of Building 7 is an even more starkly suggestive. Building 7 had relatively little damage from the falling rubble coming down from the twin towers, and yet the collapse was a perfect, accelerating freefall not slowed down by impact with the enormous mass that lay in the path of descent. Without explosive intervention to clear a path, the freefall would be a violation of the "laws of physics."[107] The only means to account for this type of acceleration is to remove the interference created by the massive weight from the lower floors of the building by planting explosives at critical points in the structure, i.e. by controlled demolition. Apparently, the scientists at the National Institute of Standards and Technology (NIST) who insist there were no anomalies in the collapse are guilty of practicing pseudoscience. Further evidence that the collapse of the twin towers and of Building 7 was the result of planned demolition consists of over 100 reports of secondary explosions reported by people present at the scene.[108] Even more striking are the notorious horizontal ejections that appear to have proceeded in orchestrated procession as the twin towers were collapsing. Human tissue was discovered on a 40-story building 250 feet away almost as if launched by cannon fire, i.e. by explosive horizontal ejection. How are these systematic, rapid cannon-like explosions to be explained?

Among evidence that may have been destroyed when the steel rubble was melted down in China was the presence of the high-tech, highly incendiary nano-thermite explosive/accelerant. Despite the hasty, mad rush to evacuate almost all the steel rubble to China, a number of private investigators have found evidence of the presence of the nano-thermite mixed in remaining dust samples and other debris,[109] some of which were curiously melted. These findings contradict the National Institute of Standards and Technology's (NIST) denial of the existence of any evidence of explosives. Should credible, non-government scientists be ignored? Meanwhile, the heat in the Twin Towers as well as in Building 7, even in consideration of the jet fuel dumped into the twin towers, was far too low to melt steel or induce total structural collapse of the steel structures. No steel framed high-rise building has ever collapsed because of fire before or since 9/11.[110] In the case of Building 7, there was no collision by aircraft and there was no jet fuel involved; nonetheless, the limited fires in the building brought down the entire 47-story structure exactly in the manner of a controlled demolition. For reasons of building safety alone, a new investigation is necessary.

NIST has produced a computer model to explain the collapse of Building 7. But the model radically departs from the video recording of the symmetrical freefall collapse. The agency has refused to provide the variables for the computer model and, furthermore, there has been no reasonable explanation for how relatively minor damage could have caused a steel framed high-rise like Building 7 to collapse. Evidence for a cover-up, the manipulation and destruction of evidence, and the controlled demolition of the Twin towers and of Building 7 is sufficient to warrant a reopening of the investigation. The inexplicable evacuation of the rubble and its frenzied shipment to China for recycling and melting, and the apparent fabrication of a false computer model of the Building 7 collapse are reason enough in and of itself to proceed but, of course, this short discussion only scratches the surface. The convention of an impartial, extra-governmental body to re-investigate the evidence of the 9/11 attacks has not lost its urgency.

What does virtue require in the matter of the 9/11 attacks on America? The answer, of course, is that virtue requires much action and concomitant reflection by a people who have undergone the magnitude of pain, destruction and ongoing danger that was precipitated by the 9/11 attacks. But all virtuous efforts are compromised if the truth is not known or has been inadequately investigated. No matter how strong the evidence of conspiratorial wrongdoing may be, it is wrong to assume the truth of the conspiratorial claims; the only virtue in this matter would concern the diligent investigation of facts to the extent that due process and ethical considerations allow. But up to this point, in terms of investigative behavior, the word 'virtue' to characterize the official investigation of 9/11 is a word that does not appear to have much applicability. There is little mystery of why there is antipathy towards conspiracy theories when they question prevailing paradigms and the conventional wisdom, but the resistance to conspiracy theories can become overwhelming when it is aided and abetted by government. Thus, it is vitally important and imperative that when the integrity of fundamental governmental institutions comes under suspicion, efforts to thwart impartial reinvestigation should be forcefully rejected and, with urgency, investigation should be allowed to proceed. There is no escaping the enormity of pain in tragedies the likes of 9/11 and the JFK assassination; they have left deep scars on the American psyche. The question that needs to be posed is whether scars of ignorance inflicted by inadequate or suppressed investigation will be longer lasting, even more dangerous, and ultimately more destructive than the criminal and heinous acts were in themselves.

II.36

Destiny

Destiny is a plenitude of potential outcomes that is in part a product of freedom and, therefore, freedom helps shape destiny. While Marx was correct in his recognition that economic conditions in mid-nineteenth century Europe created the potential for qualitative change, he also manufactured a false necessity by insisting that the plenitude of possible changes had only one outcome, synthesis or resolution. Marx, like Hegel, rejected a multilinear dialectic by which dialectical thinking can help to reveal multiple possibilities and more than one acceptable path. However, if dialectic is viewed as intrinsically moral (§1.8) and under the guidance of loving intention the violent, morally incoherent and disharmonic implications of Marx's program become clear. Marx foresaw, at least through most of his career, a communist utopia that would necessarily involve violent overthrow of the bourgeoisie when "the material productive forces of society come into conflict with the existing relations of production."[111] But whether the impulse for an overthrow came from the working class or through meddling by Marxist revolutionaries, its necessity was a contrivance spun by the imagination of Marxian theorists. To be sure, big changes were in the works for the new industrial age and fundamental inequalities were going to be encountered in one way or another, whether proactively or reactively, however the necessity of violent revolution was created by the promulgation of Marx's ideology and the chain reaction it produced amongst political activists inclined towards violence.

Marx believed that consciousness and free will are charades and mere epiphenomena of the material conditions of society, and destiny is merely the pawn of causality. What we believe or think is inconsequential; they are, rather, only the consequences of the material and economic forces in play. In his preface to *A Critique of Political Economy* (1859) Marx rejects free will, writing that:

> It is not the consciousness of men that determines their
> existence, but their social existence that determines their
> consciousness. At a certain stage of development, the
> material productive forces of society come into conflict
> with the existing relations of production or—this merely
> expresses the same thing in legal terms—with the property
> relations within the framework of which they have
> operated hitherto. From forms of development of the
> productive forces these relations turn into their fetters.
> Then begins an era of social revolution. The changes in
> the economic foundation lead sooner or later to the
> transformation of the whole immense superstructure.[112]

Marx dismisses philosophy, law, religion and art by saying that they are merely the variant forms in which underlying material conflict is made conscious and that "this consciousness must be explained from the contradictions of material life…"[113] Apparently the philosophic view of Marx is the exception because it is what drives the material foundations of consciousness; after all, Marx's views are in harmony with the revolutionary necessities that he himself "discovered!" But Marx's position is no less perspectival, i.e. just a perspective like any other, and his thoughts have no more necessary truth. Marx is perhaps the iconic representation of Nietzsche's paradox that any statement of a truth is just another perspective on the truth.

Yet, we must give Marx partial credit when he says,

> No social order is ever destroyed before all the
> productive forces for which it is sufficient have been
> developed, and new superior relations of production
> never replace older ones before the material conditions
> for their existence have matured within the framework
> of the old society.[114]

Clearly, the conditions for change need to be in place before changes are implemented, but who is Marx or his followers to deign with certainly *what* new "superior" material conditions will emerge? It is precisely because he believes that his method both ascertains *and* creates Truth that the entire methodology of "dialectical materialism" is ultimately a form of prophesy and that, when all is said and done, goes the way of other failed prophecies of political change. Contrary to Marx's view, as conditions of society evolve to support change the legitimate question becomes, What is the shape of the required change? The moral spectrum is often conducive to a variety of ethical alternatives. With respect to our discussion of a prospective world society, (§II.31) it is a vision of a harmonic fusion of principles, some of which might be endorsed by libertarians and some by socialists. Of course, the third element of convergent causality and dialectic is freedom and, therefore, any path of convergence can shift because elements of free will that enter into decisions are always indeterminate and fallible. Destiny is not fate, but the realization of great potential can be produced with the engagement of freedom. Fate, on the other hand, simply is and ought not be a cause for celebration unless, like Nietzsche's *amor fati* (love of fate) it is the joyful acceptance of what is or must be. Destiny is much more than fate and is indeed the epitome of a thing to be celebrated: it is the success of a partnership between freedom, dialectical persuasion and deterministic causality. Without freedom there is no destiny, which is why true victories of the spirit are celebrations of the creative will in its shaping of an existentially fulfilling future.

Sufficient material conditions are clearly necessary if changes are to be successful. But the critical factor of whether individual or collective destinies are realized or become only failed destinies may largely be freedom both in terms of collective and individual decision. Forces set loose by human acts or by acts of nature are simply what they are, but the extent to which free choice exists is the margin of exception that decides destiny. The world society speculated and conjectured in this book is only a particular viewpoint or collection of viewpoints on a positive path for human destiny. Clearing blocks and barriers to freedom and self-realization make possible the evolution of the finest individuals and the finest society but, of course, views on how to get there and the nature of the blockages in need of clearing differ widely. The basic sentiment of clearing away blockages so as to clear a path to human destiny is consistent with Herbert Spencer, however, my conception of what constitutes harmonic blockages, as presented in this book, differs widely from Spencer's and is often in direct opposition to him. For Spencer and libertarian thinkers individual freedom and government are most generally viewed as being in a state of opposition, with excessive government the source of disharmonic blockages in society. For Spencer, the individual would adapt or evolve to his full potential if only government would get out of the way so that "the perfect man in the perfect society" could be realized. The views presented here, in contrast, express the view that the destiny of humankind rests in a harmonic balancing of nature and nurture, of equally strong individualism and interdependence, of tutelage by society and self-reliance, of self-interest and concern for others, of moral toughness and universal compassion, of loving intention and moral action on behalf of both Self and Other. However, the ideological basis of political thinking often leads to knee-jerk condemnations of positions that embrace complementary incommensurables or mixed ingredients of libertarian or socialistic thinking. Spencer himself took up a position in favor of the nationalization of land but—perhaps in part for reasons of ideological purity, would eventually reject it late in his career. Arguments advanced here in favor of *some* positions such as the divestiture of all private real estate will be condemned as socialistic or even communistic, but the more libertarian and laissez-faire leaning proposals (e.g. the elimination of taxation or the unfettering of the patent system) will also be dismissed by libertarians who might otherwise be inclined to support them, were it not for the impurity of complementary incommensurables that may contain elements tilting towards socialism. The fear of change cannot be exaggerated.

Destiny is generally thought of as an unstoppable outcome. But destiny is a destination. There are fits and starts, twists and turns, layovers and detours and destiny's destination can remain in doubt almost to the point of its arrival. The interplay between causality and dialectical forces and their convergence modified by the imposition of freedom is evolving and, indeed, at a certain point a positive or a negative destiny may be cemented; then, there may be no turning back. Of course, regardless of how dire the situation, it is the nature of free beings to never wish to surrender to fate and, after all, who but the Universe or God can know whether a final destiny has been cast. But the very notion of a positive destiny and self-realization that incorporates the interplay of free will with causality and dialectic, and that does not include free access to the truth is a foolish absurdity. Being kept in the dark has not often illuminated the way to greatness and, therefore, there is perhaps no greater block to the unfolding of human destiny than the pernicious suppression of truth. Can a great destiny have a narrative that is based on lies? What is destiny without a consciousness of who we are and of the *means* by which we have reached a glorious destination? Surely, the moral unfolding of destiny requires the truth of how we may have gotten there for the simplest of reasons, namely the need to know ourselves, knowing also that in whatever form destiny arrives it is not the end of the journey and that new destinies await us. And this never-ending journey, this self-realization cannot be a wisdom founded on ignorance. Consequently, despite the arrogant derision and cocky presumption of the priests of conventional wisdom who assure us that conspiracy theories are the occupations of fools, the positive realization of our highest destiny will never be realized by means of wearing blinders. Accusations of the suppression of knowledge and invention are mocked and dismissed as mere fantasms of the ignorant who simply do not understand, you see, because the claims have been forever squelched by the superior state of our conventional knowledge. There is no need for further questions! Ah, but if we stop asking questions we are done, finished and utterly without hope.

A deep and appreciative openness to self-examination is as essential for societies and the entire human collectivity as it is for individuals. The formation of institutions of higher curiosity e.g. of "contra-paradigmatic research" (§II.15) are essential so that the conventional wisdom is continually challenged and reevaluated to help clear disharmonic blocks and hardened formalities. It is a logically sound presumption that significant quantum convergence (§II.15) can be attained if looking backwards is both allowed and encouraged to dynamically augment the spirit of discovery. The human mind and human progress are inevitably and ironically sidetracked by their successes, and inroads to vast domains of knowledge may be lost as a result. We should not allow the many successes and achievements of the modern world to be reasons for suppressing vital leads that may have been buried in the sands of history; the uncovering of lost or hidden truths could unite them with truths of the present and new vistas may well emerge.

Karma and Heaven are religious destinations that may say something about the nature of destiny. Is destiny the result of self-correction or reward? Or may it be both? A great and flourishing destiny would seem to be its own reward, and a successful life that has been occupied with good work and loving intention is a destiny each person who strives for goodness deeply desires. But an ostensibly successful life is not truly successful if it has been corrupted by wrongfulness and bad intention. And whether we take the karmic viewpoint of multiple corrections afforded by a soul's journey over many lifetimes, or the belief that a Divine Judge decides whether we are to be rewarded in an eternally beautiful afterlife, it seems clear that from the perspective of religious wisdom both the means and the ends of life are the moral and spiritual fiber that comprise the essence of destiny. In contrast, from a purely empirical perspective, destiny is the judgment of history, but we should always remind ourselves that 'history' is a word that can be used to denote the actual past as well as the past as it has been reported. It *may* seem unlikely that destiny can be shaped by the reportage of history contradistinguished from the actual truth of history. It may seem that only the actual truth of history shapes the destiny of an individual, of a nation and of all humanity. And yet, by altering our understanding of the past history has the potential to ennoble both the present and the future. Thus, the reporting of historical truth and its corrections can help shape destiny.

Power

and

Humility

II.37

Ethical Holism

Attempts to isolate a single, unitary motive for human behavior have long occupied philosophers and psychologists. And it should not be surprising if these attempts have resulted in a good deal of dogma and many dead ends for the intellect. Nietzsche's "will to power" is less susceptible to hardened ideology. It is difficult if not impossible to deny that human beings, if not all forms of life, manifest what could be called a will to power. Every rational being wants to see the world organized or structured in accordance to his or her will. Needs for pleasure as well, almost certainly, are subsumed by a presumptive will to power and therefore Freudian thinking, as in Adler's case, need not be inconsistent with the will to power. Nietzsche idealized a noble class that to him evoked Homeric ideals such as courage, strength, self-reliance and self-realization. It embodies a philosophy of overcoming adversity and saying "Yes" to life, and a "master" or noble ethic that he contrasts to a Judeo-Christian ethic that he argues is based upon 'ressentiment' or a perspective of victimization. Nietzsche attempted to compensate for the absence of compassion and altruism in his ethics by rationalizing the necessity of noblesse oblige. But the rationalization reveals fundamental flaws in Nietzsche's conception of morality; like other philosophers who overemphasize the ego at the expense of concern for others he is often blind to the dualistic nature of morality and the need for a thorough balancing of the moral elements. The balancing of the diversity of moral elements and principles may be described as holistic ethics.

We all have a will to power. It is natural and good that individuals strive to influence or change the world in a manner that they perceive as positive and constructive. But maximal power is comprised of actions that are morally coherent and that are within the realm of possibility as framed by freedom operating in convergent reality. Convergence limits the field of ethical action, but many viable free choices remain, individually or collectively, that help shape human destiny. Nietzsche is almost apologetic in his explanation that the noble or master morality is in part designed to uplift the weak masses from their self-enslaving ressentiment, but his begrudging acknowledgement shouts to the heavens for the need to reframe unitary theories of human motivation. What I call 'holistic ethics' is a reframing of unitary ethical motivation and ethical principles in general, and expresses the harmonizing and powerful potential of moral intentionality and effectuality. The terms 'holistic ethics', 'social harmonics', 'love-based morality', 'moral coherence' and 'ethical empowerment' all have much in common and refer to the overarching themes of this book.

As with health, morality is holistic. It is not necessary to subscribe to any one particular dietary routine, exercise regimen, meditative practice, or therapy in order to practice "holistic health." And certainly, good holistic health practices can and, at times necessarily must, be inclusive of pharmaceutical preparations and other treatments that "holistic" purists would eschew. The term 'holistic' simply refers to a consideration of the whole, and is closely aligned with the harmonic science of clearing disharmonic blockages. The practice of ethics is analogously in need of a holistic approach because a broad spectrum of factors and considerations must be harmonized if *moral health* is to be achieved and maintained. And just as the practice of a presumptive "holistic" health regimen that categorically rejects any use of pharmaceuticals or conventional treatment is foolhardy and dangerous, the same may be said about a "holistic" ethics that ignores all convention, rules and formalities. But, at the same time, acknowledging the profound worth of convention and traditional ways must not stand in the way of the clearing of blockages that can endanger and impede human flourishing.

A holistic ethics constantly deliberates and harmonizes intentionality and effectuality, the oscillating permutations of the Self-Other duality and its subsidiary dualisms, and the impact of moral coherencies and in-coherencies on social institutions. A failure in any part of a holism may range from minor to catastrophic. A malfunctioning organ, an imbalanced diet, biochemical imbalances, emotional stress or turmoil, inadequate physical activity or overuse and excess dependency on drugs and pharmaceuticals can result in bad health. Moral health, likewise, is subject to dangerous and degenerative imbalance. Maximal health begins with a nutritious and balanced diet, and moral health begins with the everyday sustenance gotten by the reinforcement of good intention. Moral health, like physical health, is a complex balancing of many principles, and both moral and physical well-being are frequently compromised with misapplications of the conventional wisdom. The struggle to find equilibrium between the competing claims of Self and Other expressed within the basic ethical dualisms is not a unitary principle of human motivation but, rather, an ethical resonance that modulates and transforms the "enslavement of the passions" into moral understanding and, if we are fortunate, into wisdom.

The holistic perspective humbles as much as it empowers. Within each individual resides the potential for both humility and greatness. The surrendering of and detachment from possessions that to some may define their very being can paradoxically empower and enrich. But empowerment can bring with it new attachments in the form of formalities and possessions that are both material and intellectual. Heraclitus was right when he said that the world is in a state of continuous change, but Parmenides and the Eleatic philosophers were also correct because in another sense nothing changes: without a sense of changelessness, change becomes incomprehensible. Some moral philosophers have called this unchangeable essence the soul or the world soul but I don't have a metaphysical conception of it, except that I know that the only constancy of experience is love and it is the task of ethics to better understand it. Love is the crown jewel of consciousness. Theoretical physics has not yet conclusively answered the question of whether the ultimate basis of matter is divisible or indivisible but, nonetheless, the nature of the human mind is to analyze so that we capture some level of understanding regardless how meager. I suspect that love is indeed indivisible, and so the basic ethical dualisms (§I.7) are merely a meager effort to analyze the basic moral essence, or love.

To summarize, I am quite comfortable describing human motive as a striving or acting out of a will to power. But maximal power itself must of necessity embody the breadth of morality because morally incoherent motives will in the end implode or cancel each other and disassemble. Morality, as Aristotle said, is the flourishing of humanity both individually and collectively, and from our view is also the harmonic expression of the basic moral forces. Humility is required. Only a consciousness of humility can avail itself to the breadth and scope of human wisdom. Through humility we open our minds as well as our hearts, detach from egoistic obstructions, and tap into the potentiality of greatness. Through humility, wisdom from the ancient past can be accepted and future awakenings will emerge.

II.38

Abraham and Isaac

What sort of God would position itself as higher than the Good itself? In Genesis: 22 God commands Abraham to kill his son Isaac by sacrificing him as a burnt offering, but just as Abraham is about strike his son to death an angel suddenly appears and stops the execution by telling Abraham that, "Now I know that thou fearest God, seeing thou hast not withheld thy son." Abraham has proven his loyalty, so now Isaac is allowed to live! Perhaps this exercise of terrorism was merely a pedagogical device employed by God in order to instill upon a primitive people the necessity of obedience to moral authority, but this interpretation is surely too charitable.

In *Fear and Trembling*, Kierkegaard makes a distinction between "the ethical" and "the religious." He argues that "faith begins precisely where thought stops,"[115] and since ethical reasoning is a form of thought there is a "suspension of the ethical" in favor of faith. But Kierkegaard cannot hide behind his faith any more than Hegel could hide behind his cold master-slave dialectic, which allowed him to justify slavery's existence even while he was repulsed by it. Short of the dubious argument that God's command or threat was a necessary display of tough love to facilitate the birth pangs of humanity's moral development, there does not seem to be any benevolent way of looking at the Divinely ordered murder. Would a parent—and parents are like gods to their small children—who uses a similar technique be worthy of receiving love from his child? If a mere mortal had given the command to kill he would be described as a terrorist. Some argue that God did not act as a terrorist because he did not actually allow Abraham to carry out the murder, but if a terrorist takes a hostage and releases him only after his demands have been met, or even releases him because he has a change of heart, would we drop the usage of the term 'terrorist'? Certainly not, and a government committed to fighting terrorism would do everything it could to apprehend or kill the terrorist.

If Abraham refused God's order to kill Isaac, what would God's reaction have been? "Just kidding; I didn't really mean it?" If Abraham had mustered the bravery to say "No! Dear God, I love you with all of my being but not even you are above The Good! If you must, take *me*, but please allow my son to live!" In this case, God would have found "himself" in the awkward position in which Abraham's courageous and loving defiance of his tyrannical demand would show him to be *more* moral than He himself. Arguably, Abraham's behavior can be viewed as the "courage" to save his own skin at the expense of his son's. Abraham pleased God because he proved himself to a God-fearing subject, but if he instead had stood up to God and shown willingness to sacrifice himself in place of his son he would have become a model of heroism for all time, and of indomitable courage in doing what is right by acting out of no other motivation than pure love for his child. But taken literally, the moral of the biblical story is that we *should* surrender our power to fear!

There is an alternative interpretation if the primitive nomad we call Abraham is viewed as being in no position to challenge the wisdom of God and, therefore, following God's command was for him tantamount to acting in accordance with The Good. For Abraham, morality equaled the word of God. We modern humans continually require a strong dose of humility to remind ourselves of our innate fallibility. However, our fallibility and ethical limitations do not entail the surrender of reason. For modern humans, whatever your religious or theological views happen to be, even if they include a truly personal God that you communicate with telepathically or through the medium of your holy scripture, human beings possess the power to reason and make rational choices and reach decisions that are in harmony with whatever conception of God you believe in or subscribe to. Nietzsche proclaimed that "God is dead," but he did not say this on the basis of some personal knowledge of the Deity's demise but simply because—regardless of whether morality is learned or revealed, we must choose for ourselves. If God speaks to you or you believe that he speaks to you and he commands you to kill your child because he is God and therefore what s/he says is Good and right, your true obligation dictated by any legitimate *moral* faith based on loving intention can only command that you to tell *that* god to go straight to Hell.

But Kierkegaard adopts a different perspective. He defends Abraham not because Abraham was a member of a primitive tribe and in no position to question the word of God. No, Abraham's status is immaterial; Kierkegaard, as a man of faith, believes that ethical reasoning must be suspended in matters of faith. While the deeply existential quality of Kierkegaard's philosophy is admirable, there is no escaping morality and ethical judgment. Suspending the entire ethical enterprise on the basis of what you believe God is telling you or says in scripture, when it contradicts the rational intelligence that God supposedly gave you, is perhaps the gravest of sins and the root of much evil in this world. *My* God, the one I cannot describe or even comprehend what it would mean to comprehend it, that represents all that is and all that is not, that God I deeply believe must in some sense be affronted and saddened by our modern day Abrahams.

Kierkegaard also says that, "subjectivity is higher than actuality," because 'subjectivity' is profoundly personal and achieved by a dialectical encounter of the individual with God that is beyond comprehension, and that "subjectivity is incommensurable with actuality."[116] While, of course, Isaiah Berlin's value pluralism (§I.8) is a very different philosophy than Kierkegaard's, nonetheless, in the case of both philosophers the incommensurability argument is a fallacious *reductio ad absurdum* that denies the possibility of moral reasoning because, whether the concern is value in Berlin's case or religion in the case of Kierkegaard, significant moral content is viewed as beyond the framework of reason. Both arguments attempt to justify rational arguments with irrational premises and thus have the force of *faux* reasoning. Arbitrary, pre-defined ethical limitations do not limit the scope of ethics but only create an ethics that is impotent and dangerous. Relinquishments of humanity's moral will to power and moral sense are simply and quite purely unethical.

II.39

Mirrors of Self-esteem

A mirror's reflection is not independent of the viewer's perspective. The most objective self-reflection is at least to some extent intermingled with what the viewer wants to see. The very important sort of self-reflection known as self-esteem consists of reflections on oneself hardened into beliefs relating to self-worth or self-unworthiness. The mirrors of self-esteem are composite perspectives of the interiority and the exteriority reflected upon oneself.

Self-esteem can be compared to the work of an artist. An artist may view her latest work as a masterpiece that will wow all the critics only to see it fall flat, or she may think the work to be a dismal failure until pleasantly surprised with many accolades. The breadth of artistic expression today encompasses a diversity of form that would appear thoroughly alien to bygone ages. Yet, while some may cavalierly dismiss some art as "not art," the subjectivity of art has ample room for consensus respective to "artistic appreciation." Self-esteem entails a balancing of self-reflection and introspection with the broader opinions of others. Moral toughness is a characteristic of high self-esteem that sometimes requires the ability to follow a lonely path of staying true to one's convictions, but it also requires enough self-esteem and a mind that is open enough to acknowledge errors and make corrections.

There are three basic types of low self-esteem. *Conditioned low self-esteem* commonly is the result of negative, discouraging language from parents or others, whether direct or misconstrued, that develops an inferiority of being "just not good enough." Sadly, this form of low self-esteem may be demonstrably untrue but sufferers find it extremely difficult to believe themselves to be good and valued individuals. *Performance-based low self-esteem* may rest on an accurate assessment of low performance that may be caused by a bad fit of an individual to a particular job or activity. Correcting the bad fit will solve this particular type of low self-esteem. Performance-based low self-esteem can also result from anxiety-related self-sabotage, but this too can be corrected. Still another form of low self-esteem is *masked low self-esteem,* which is a suppression of initially recognized wrongful patterns of behavior that are perversely masked by a self-perception of high self-esteem. Criminals often exemplify masked low self-esteem, but others as well can develop it when they have fallen into longstanding patterns of unethical behavior and begin wearing the mask as hurtful and wrongful behaviors become accepted as their self-identity. If masked low self-esteem is caused by something other than genetically driven compulsion, perhaps it is possible that prolonged gazes into the flawed mirror of self-esteem might catch a glimmer of the moral sense that still remains and, if so, a process of recovery might begin.

The lapsing self-esteem movement has been criticized for coddling when a good dose of honest criticism would have been more effective and appropriate. Surprise! Surprise! Praising mediocrity in order to build self-esteem does not generally work very well. At least one study has concluded that praising children when the praise is unwarranted has a contrary effect. But do we truly need studies to tell us what common sense has always understood? Do we require a hyperactive scientism that researches commonsense wisdom or the lack thereof? Indeed, the excessive coddling of children is not a prescription for individual success or for high self-esteem. A rational approach balances self-motivation and external motivation with constructive criticism when necessary, and the likely if not inevitable result would be a society rich in self-esteem in which the individual and the society reciprocally enrich each other. Modern-day conservatives tend to think of self-esteem with an emphasis on individualism and self-initiative. Modern-day liberals, on the other hand, tend to emphasize the need to rectify social and economic inequalities that hinder the development of good self-esteem in persons who live under disadvantaged and disempowered conditions. Certainly, self-esteem will flourish best when both self-motivating and externally motivating factors are optimized. The severe economic recession that began in 2008 surely has taken its toll individually and collectively. An economic depression is at least in part also a collective psychological depression rooted in the doldrums of low self-esteem. But building self-esteem, collectively and individually, is probably as good for the economy as it is for the individual; is not a good economy often accompanied with an expanding climate of good self-esteem?

It is true that a strong national culture will maintain good collective self-esteem even during difficult times, but beware the condescension of Stoic-like philosophies of acceptance of unsatisfactory and unrewarding existential conditions. While serenity amid suffering that cannot be changed is noble, there is nothing inspirational about "living in harmony with nature" when the existing state of affairs is rotten and something can and should be done about it. We are reminded of the "courage" segment of the Serenity Prayer. If you don't have the courage to change what in your own mind should be changed, I would like to submit that you are suffering from low self-esteem. It is unfortunately true that the suffering of impoverished children is today accepted by virtually the same rationale as used by traditional Stoicism. And while it is true that in most modern societies the notion of upward mobility and individual advancement beyond the circumstances of one's birth is accepted as a birthright, the fact remains that opportunities doled out to persons born into the world are far from fair. The fundamental imbalance in the world is not of income in and of itself, but of an imbalance in opportunity. The disempowerment caused by drastic differences in income and financial status will remain a force for lowering self-esteem for large segments of the population until equal opportunity becomes viewed as a basic need. It is not necessary that there be forced redistribution of wealth, but it is necessary that all individuals have opportunities afforded to them to gain wealth and to flourish. But wealth and other forms of material success do not guarantee high self-esteem. Self-esteem is the inner conviction of moral authenticity that the self bestows upon itself, and this authenticity emanates from within the exteriority as much as from within the interiority.

Disharmonic blockages in society function as breeding mechanisms for low self-esteem for society and its individual members. For instance, Nietzsche correctly identified the political party is an incubator of low self-esteem:

> The most common lie is the lie one tells to oneself;
> lying to others is relatively the exception.—Now this
> desiring *not* to see what one sees, this desiring not to

> see as one sees, is virtually the primary condition for
> all who are in any sense party: the party man necessarily
> becomes a liar.[117]

At least in democracies we do not have the pantheon of the thoroughly vomit-producing giant murals of dictators that become plastered on the psyche of peoples groveling at the feet of their enslavers. But the democracies manage to demean themselves and lower their collective self-esteem by turning politicians into the vicarious representations of their collective will while perpetuating needless division and vitriol. The parties with their cadres and rubber stamped support create plastic posters rather than true leaders and, as Nietzsche says, the party followers see what the party wants them to see. Let leaders emerge as independent men and women rather than as party men or party women. And these politicians and leaders will lead by the power of their ideas, and they will themselves be empowered by the mutual interchange of thought when the disharmonic block that is the political party is finally cleared. The self-esteem lowering spectacle of needless governmental paralysis can be reversed and lifted by the institution of meaningful political dialogue.

Any social disharmony is likely to damage collective self-esteem. For example, I suggest that the current patent system is not an especially good booster of high self-esteem; it inhibits inventiveness and creativity that could take society and progress to a new level. And collective self-esteem would soar if the development and marketing of new inventions were facilitated and inventors, rather than monopolists, were properly rewarded. (§II.16) Everything possible to encourage invention should be a high social mandate, and unaffordable costs for the small inventor is an outrage. Suppression can and should be eliminated. When the focus of inventors is invention and not monopoly, and when commercial entities owning inventions are only one of many pursuing their development and production, then greater inventiveness and commercial success will follow. A patent system like the proposed open system would encourage businesses to create and to be innovative without encouraging a monopolization of the market and, as a result, the proposed system will be a boon to society's collective self-esteem. And great good redounds to those who help build the collective state of self-esteem.

It would be a brilliant turn if national chest-thumping becomes seen for what it is. Pride is a desirable and wonderful thing, and there can be no good self-esteem without pride. But how does one feel about someone who attends a social gathering and says to anyone who would listen that, "I'm better than you. I am the best. You're not a bad Joe, but you can't compare to me!" High self-esteem, whether it be of an individual, a group or a nation is a mirror image of grace and humility.

II.40

Alone and Together

An object of love is a projection of a lover's self-loving desire. And hence, love is an attachment of one who loves that may or may not be reciprocated by the beloved. Moral incoherence is, in a sense, unreciprocated love and, therefore, an imbalanced love resulting from disagreement or confusion. A perfect love, should it exist, is a perfectly coherent union. Self-love and love are, in essence, the same. A perfect universe, the best of all possible universes, would be a perfectly loving universe in which each part "desires" each other because each is a complementary part in the harmony of the whole. The notion of a loving universe may or may not be construed to be exclusive of rational beings or of living beings, however, consciousness and only consciousness has the capacity for love. If the universe itself is indeed conscious, then it could potentially become a loving universe. But to conclude that the universe *could* become perfectly loving would necessitate that it could also become imperfectly loving or perfectly *unloving*.

It follows that a peaceful and loving relationship within oneself can be preferable to relationships with an other in which the moral forces are so badly imbalanced that they may rightly be said to be *un*loving. It might be thought that nothing is being said here that is outside the realm of the obvious if it weren't for the fact that so many friendships, familial relationships and conjugal or sexual relationships are maintained when quite clearly their dissolution would be a far preferable outcome than their perpetuation. And why do morally incoherent and unloving relationships have the trenchancy to continue over long periods or even a lifetime? The answer may be that often the self-loving relationship within oneself is so weak or the self-esteem is so low that self-abnegation prevails and any sort of friendship or union is viewed as better than being alone. And this is a tragedy of our time: anything is thought to be better than being alone.

Is the foregoing said in praise of the virtue of solitude? Yes and No! Solitude and togetherness can both be either virtues or vices. A person may not recognize and acknowledge that she is very capable of going it alone for a time in order to heal and rebuild relationships with others not to mention the relationship within the interiority of the self. Modern society seems to be weakening the interiority of love so that many people just can't stand being alone. By now the reader knows that I am not a great fan of Ayn Rand, however her books that caricature the autonomous self, most boldly depicted in *Anthem* in its simplistic contrasting of total individualism and total collectivism, provide some insight into the importance of individualism and the ethics of selfhood that expects love and strength from the self as much as it does from others. Clearly, Rand would not state her case in this way; Rand's views are incoherently imbalanced in favor of self-regarding instincts. But today we see cell phones and smartphones seemingly attached to the ears and mouths of people, especially the young who are growing up with them, and it seems that many people just cannot tolerate solitude or the absence of constant, empty chatter or "texting." Oh, young girls in particular! But everyone sees that. If even a glimmer of Rand's nightmarish vision of a collectivist society that has obliterated the word 'I' should come to pass the human race will certainly be doomed and its pathetic destiny sealed.

What matters, and really the only thing that does matter is that the flourishing of love and the ethical means to achieve it be continually nurtured, sustained and strengthened. Togetherness in the form of friendship, family, camaraderie, marriage or family is natural for human beings. But while I am not attempting to refute biology, I am arguing that the human social animal also needs time alone in order to develop strong relationships within the interiority of the self. When healthy relationships between inner "selves" and inner "others" that populate the interiority are impeded or stunted greater social harmony suffers. I recall a study that found that the health of single men, statistically, was catching up with the health of married men. The conclusion of the study was that better social support and income levels were reducing stress levels and improving the overall health of single men. The finding exposes the indoctrinating quality of the everyday formality or cliché that "Married people are healthier." Health and marriage have no necessary connection except in the context of a good marriage that encourages health by easing burdens, lessening stresses and increasing happiness and joy. The needs that individuals require may or may not come with marriage but when those needs are met people are healthier. But this is obvious, and it exemplifies hyperactive scientism, which is dedicated to the belief that any proposition, no matter how obvious, needs to be confirmed by the obligatory "scientific" study. The conventional wisdom has contended that one of the reasons men should marry is to increase their longevity, but it is reasonable to think that the conventional wisdom *should* have always been that if a single adult can attend to his needs and wants with a satisfactory measure of psychological homeostasis then longevity would be roughly the same for married and unmarried adults. If moral coherence and a healthy lifestyle prevail in a person's life, then health and longevity are likely to be better than it would be otherwise, regardless of marital status. The single point of these remarks is that the fear of aloneness can and should be dwarfed by the fear of a dysfunctional togetherness that can mock the idealistic values of friendship, family or marriage. Moral coherence and empowerment, both with respect to the relationship of the Self with itself and with others, constitute life's higher meaning and aspirations.

Distinguishing moral actualities from the wide array of ethical formalities is the fundamental purpose of ethics. Moral actuality, like all actuality, is the product of our rational understanding of what is the case. In ethics as well as in science and factual reporting, confusion and conflict are common. Physical actuality has plentiful everyday examples, e.g. the weekly weather forecast. Uncertainty in solving crimes is another example of everyday physical actualities that may be unclear. Diagnosing disease is another. In ethics, too, the ascertainment of moral actuality has ongoing challenges. With respect to moral actuality, truth-telling routinely conflicts with promise-keeping because upholding one principle may well involve rejecting the other. And a good measure of political, cultural and even economic disagreement in the world is rooted in conflicting ethical perspectives. The greater truth resides in the deeper and more transcendent principles of reasoning that are the substratum of seemingly incommensurable values or principles. Moral confusion also applies to the ethics of aloneness and togetherness. Friendship is certainly among the highest of all values, indeed, it may well be the highest value of all even superceding that ubiquitous maxim that "if you have your health you have everything," because if you have no friends then all the worlds riches and the best of health could become meaningless. Yet, without a loving relationship within the interiority of the self the possibility of true friendship is quite likely also destroyed. Can someone truly love another if he has no capacity for self-love?

Marcus Aurelius writes that, "Nothing is more disgraceful than a wolfish friendship (false friendship)."[118] And I am in agreement with Aristotle when he says that friendship must be associated with virtue, but Aristotle seems to find all of the sources of other-regarding virtue embedded in community. In Francis Bacon's translation of the *Politics*, Aristotle says that, "Whosoever is delighted in solitude is either a wild beast or a god." But Benjamin Jowett may have captured Aristotle's sense more accurately: "…he who is unable to live in society, or who has no need because he is sufficient for himself, must either be a god or a beast: he is no part of a state."[119] This passage illuminates the absurdity of Ayn Rand's intellectual infatuation with Aristotle for he would have rejected her "virtue of selfishness" with utter dispatch. But Aristotle's view is also imbalanced in our view since his conception of virtue is one of a harmonic association between the individual and the state, whereas the argument maintained throughout this book has been that a dualistic harmony holds sway equally with respect to the individual as well as the community. Accordingly, while an inability of an individual to live in society or for whom solitude is a perpetual state of delight may say as much about his or her sanity as about virtue, it must be admitted that the serenity of solitude and nonconformance to the state *can* be a great and powerful virtue when the state of society is so sadly decadent and incoherent that one's highest duty becomes honoring one's self with solitude. Submitting to an environment in which virtue is everywhere in a state of decay is surely not the path of virtue. Indeed, in dire times we must strive to become like gods. And, therefore, it follows that Aurelius and the Stoics are right in contending that few things are more woeful or self-destructive than false friendships. The addict sometimes feels that the addicting substance is like a friend even when that "friend" is his consort on the journey to a hellish demise. All, or nearly all, of the great philosophers warn us to be careful with whom we surround ourselves and select as friends. First and foremost, be worthy to yourself, be worthy of self-respect and deserve the love you can reward to yourself, and then take seriously the mission and the responsibility of choosing friends who are worthy of you and you of them.

There are great families with traditions that inspire their progeny's continuing commitment and dedication to a good life and, yes, to greatness. Great families of great wealth may use their fortunes to foster a culture of greatness that perpetuates and furthers philanthropic endeavors as much as they further the development of themselves individually. But there is overwhelming evidence that money is not enough. Wealth can clear a pathway to greatness, but whether or not that road is taken is purely a choice. A morally coherent and harmonic societal condition is almost certainly dependent upon a foundation of strong and loving families that embody high self-esteem and, conversely, deeply embedded low self-esteem may be imparted to children by parents who were similarly affected by their parents and so on intergenerationally. Wealth will not of itself remove the moral encumbrances of low self-esteem or substitute for an interior relationship that is founded on true self-love that both nurtures and inspires. However, while healthy self-love and self-esteem are often a parent's greatest gift to a child, even when parents fail to bequeath this most precious gift it does not mean that the inner Mother and the inner Father cannot be restored. Regardless of our station in life or the state of our relationships or lack thereof, at the end of the day one's truest friend and benefactor is the Self whose internalized self-love has either been most significantly passed down by parents or has, through its own power, been given to itself by itself in a dialectical act of self-creation.

II.41

Mother and Father

The living heritage passed down from parents to their children cannot be simplified as a set of values. Fundamental beliefs and values—even if only rarely—can change but the heritage conveyed to us by our parents transcends them. The "karma" passed along from parents to children is more than a causal chain between actions and their effects or consequences. Parents *can* pass along to their children the spirit of loving intention, clothed in their behavior, deeds, teachings and traditions. Arguably, the expression of loving intention is the most important gift that a mother or father can give to a child. The word karma (in the above) is placed in quotes because it is used here metaphorically as "a karma of intentionality" that transcends its traditional conception as the law of cause and effect. As the origination point of conscious human action, intentionality shapes and influences a person's karma.

Values and customs change, and if only values about this or that, or of money and possessions are passed down, the ineffable legacy of Mother and Father will disappear with the ever-changing cultural or political environment. It has been said that, "A man does not come to know himself until he has lost everything." We become attached to many things in life, but the meaning of loving intention and the unerasable sense of self-worth and individual authenticity that it builds from within cannot be destroyed. If the interiority of self-esteem is not imprinted or reinforced with a parent's love then it can still be created with intelligence and will power. A parent's tutelage can become the model of a transformative partnership of the self with itself as a self-consoler, a self-encourager, a constructive self-critic, a self-jester, a self-nurturer, a self-guided spirit that connects this physical life to a sense of something beyond this worldly plain that is self-transcending. But whether or not self-esteem and the moral coherency of the interior life come from parents or are generated from other sources, it is something that ultimately detaches from exterior things and becomes the essence of self-sufficiency and moral integrity. And this is not to say that the sense of self is anything other than a psychological adaptation by the ingenuity of the complex human brain, but it is also not to say that a deeper or more transcendent explanation is impossible or implausible.

The validity of an authentic self that yearns and strives for the moral coherency of a good and harmonious world cannot be denied once you realize that you have it. All of our possessions, beliefs and values become trivial once we comprehend that our actualities are only projections onto our interiority and, therefore, are necessarily imperfect. Exterior existence is also imperfect, as many great philosophers who know the world as constant change (or illusion) have understood: Siddhartha Gautama (the Buddha), Lao-Tzu, Heraclitus (everything is change) and the Eleatics (change is an illusion). For Schopenhauer, impermanence and the constant change of experience are cause for pessimism and despair, although he thought that philosophical ideals were a refuge. But there is a sort of perfection within ourselves, such as Jesus and the Buddha and other spiritual masters have taught, that is not a perfection of things but of the pure loving intention that is possible even if only few have ever realized it. This does not trivialize life in the world, but the moral project seeks to create or shape the world so that it can conform to the multiple possibilities of the pure love within each rational being. These interior possibilities of perfection are layers of emergent hope or higher aspiration that contrast existing actualities with what might be.

With unquestioning, children receive the wisdom that their parents may convey that each human being is an important part of the whole of humanity. Sometimes this recognition of individual significance in the context of a grander holism is thought of in terms of love of country or of a particular religion because by so doing the incomprehensible is made to appear more comprehensible when scaled down to human terms. My mother gave to me a sense of self-worth and indefatigability when situations seem hopeless. Everything that happened somehow, she believed, was in some sense meant to be, and I now view this as part of the convergent flow of an individual life. Her spirit continues to speak to me and guide me and seems more authentic with each passing day. Faith comes from within. In my eulogy to my mother I noted that she loved to quote Shakespeare's famous passage from *Julius Caesar*: "the valiant never taste of death but once…" and when she was dying she greeted death with serenity even while I was too cowardly to let her go because I loved her so much. I eulogized that my mother had a passionate faith in the ultimate victory of wisdom, truth, goodness and mercy, and at the age of 16 or 17 she wrote an essay called "Goodwill" about a mystical experience "full of unexplainable joy" as "each person, each little bird, each flower" radiates God's love, and she then concluded that "goodwill" is nothing else other than the "love of all living things." Continuing my eulogy, I said that my mother "possessed the courage and serenity that is the reward of those who live a life undaunted and graced by the goodwill of a loving heart. Live life this way and as individuals we will have done what we can to help wisdom, truth and good to emerge victorious. And when death comes, the valiant bow out gracefully as the curtain falls. This is how my mother greeted death. I often feel as though I see the world through my mother's eyes, so strong has been the influence that she has had on my life. We shared a mystical or quasi-mystical view of the universe. Now that you have escaped the suffering of your failing body you can rest in peace, but I suspect that your strong, restless spirit is an active soul that is now part of the implicit order working—as you wrote long ago, to give Creation a chance to reveal itself."

I wouldn't describe my views in Jungian archetypal terms; I don't see a Mother or a Father archetype, but I see a void that the mother and father—in traditional families, are in an ideal position to fill, or have the opportunity to fill, but which in any case needs to be filled. My father is a picture of faith insofar as his children are concerned as he projects onto them his own decency, and this decency and faith is the kernel of integrity that on some level is understood by each of us as a duty to emulate and aspire. His unwavering effort to support and provide for his family with a joyful sense of humor was a quiet model and an example of the essence and the meaning of loving support. And in his retirement years my father has thrived as a man as he seemingly has become younger in spirit despite an eight-year long period of tireless, unyielding care for Mom during her long illness, and at the time of this writing he is 92 years young. My self-esteem has grown simply in knowing who my parents are, and they have always been a source of faith for me because I knew that they had faith in me. I believe that much of the early childhood development stuff should be taken with at least a few grains of salt in some respects; we never lose our ability to grow, evolve and change and in a very real sense we can become stronger with age. I am now in my late middle age, and I deeply understand that my parents continue to teach me the inner essence of right.

My mother and father, to be sure, instilled their values into my upbringing. At the same time, I think it very likely that my dad will not be in agreement with some of the ideas and proposals put forth in this book. But specific values, or particular positions on political or social issues are ultimately transitional. Values frequently clash but, as I have argued, they are not incommensurable but, on the contrary, beautifully commensurable because of the transcendent essence of morality that unifies them. There is and always has been only one hope for this world, but its realization will require far more than merely mouthing the words "all we need is love." We need to acquire a deeper understanding of how basic loving intention is translated by ethical deliberation into increasingly coherent moral actuality. After first accepting that each of us must learn to "love thy neighbor as thyself," it becomes necessary that we understand better what fairness, beneficence and compassion mean and how these basic concepts might be applied in terms of both their other-regarding and self-regarding aspects and ramifications. Apparent egoisms and altruisms need to be continually flipped so that the dualisms reveal corresponding intentions, actions and effects in the full dimensionality of the dualism (and polarity) between Self and Other. But building self-worth and self-esteem is where the process must start. And as a general rule, it starts with mother and father.

II.42

Vegetarianism

I remember that when I was roughly five or six years old I had amused myself by smashing anthills with a rock. I don't think that this is uncommon childhood behavior, but whether I was an especially cruel child or merely typical I think that my life reflects the development of compassion. But I admit that I still kill insects in my home when it is not practical to shoo them outside and I do so without suffering great remorse. Some persons exhibit greater compassion and will not kill an insect in their home. Compassion may be endlessly expanded, but complexities in the justification of some killing can at times make killing compassionate as, for example, in the merciful euthanasia of a terminally ill or suffering pet.

Most thoughtful individuals will profess that they value life but at the same time are quite capable of providing examples of when it is justifiable to kill. If "Thou shalt not kill" is more than a mere formality then there can be no controversy because, in that case, every killing is an outrage. However, given the reality that most people would and should kill in certain specified circumstances (e.g. an unprovoked attacker who is about to kill you and/or your family if you don't kill him first) the question of, "What is the value of life?" must be answered with, "It has its price." While most people value human life over animal life and do not prohibit themselves from eating meat or using the byproducts of animals that have been killed, most persons also recognize that killing animals can sometimes be wrong. For example, I think that most people would find the needless smashing of an anthill to be bad behavior and wrong. Compassion itself is without limit, but it can be supervened by the countervailing forces of the other basic ethical elements that may offset or modify its role or function in specific circumstances.

Any killing, needless to say, requires ethical justification. Some anti-vegetarians make the claim that scientific instruments that measure responses in plants prove that they suffer as much as animals do and, therefore, vegetarianism and veganism are pointless from the standpoint of the ethical treatment of animals. However, the argument is specious and a prima facie absurdity because it ignores the enormous import of compassion. The word 'pain' used to describe the "experience" of a plant that does not possess a nervous system or exhibit behaviors of pain is a meaningless term. In order to make the argument that a vegetable feels pain its proponents, ironically, would need to become mystics in order to make an empathic, compassionate connection with the suffering plants. But these skeptics-become-mystics present quite an irony by justifying animal suffering with idle speculations that broccoli or apples suffer in the same way as cows or dogs or human beings. These casual equations of suffering between animals such as cows, and plants such as broccoli are either the mark of disingenuousness or pure idiocy. Let the compassionate defenders of suffering broccoli watch films of farm or lab animals writhing in pain on the floors of slaughterhouses or in laboratories, and then let them contrast the animals' all-to-real and true suffering with the imagined "pain" and "suffering" of broccoli. I have already wasted too many words on the moronic broccoli defense and its attempt to justify the perpetuation of animal suffering; however, one should never shut up when it comes to protestation against cruelty. But our premise is that some killing is justified and, therefore, pointing out the position of the broccoli defender that is in equal parts radical and laughable, and also the positions of radical vegetarian or animal rights advocates against all killing of animals do not help us solve the dilemma. A more cogent argument is one that accepts a hierarchy of life forms that, while also being wary of the potential for its abuse, can be part of a reverence for life that can distinguish between a cow, a horse, a dog, or a fruit fly. The oft-quoted statement by Ingrid Newkirk, the founder of People for the Ethical Treatment of Animals, that "When it comes to pain, love, joy, loneliness, and fear, a rat is a pig is a dog is a boy. Each one values his or her life and fights the knife,"[120] while admirably expressing compassion for all animals ignores any sort of hierarchy as a means for valuing animal life. It is doubtful that rats and most non-human animals feel love or joy because those emotional states are a bonding of reason with emotion. But rats certainly do experience pain and, indeed, deserve our compassion, and the needless suffering of any animal is surely wrong. But the equation of the value of a human life to the life of a rat devalues any sense of value. And the wrongful death of a rat is not equivalent to the wrongful death of a human being. Rats and people do not possess the same intrinsic value.

The substance of Schopenhauer's simplistic argument that compassion alone is a guarantor of moral conduct has been rejected previously in my discussion of the basic ethical dualisms, but compassion *is* a starting point. Morality, as a feature of consciousness, would not be possible without compassion. While the same may be said for the other dualisms, compassion is the purest aspect of loving intention. However, it is largely the complex permutations of fairness and beneficence, rather than the simple purity of compassion, that accounts for the exceptions to the biblical command that "Thou shalt not kill." But it is nonetheless essential that we embrace the power and the beauty of compassion. Some of the greatest minds and moral souls have not been vegetarians, and so on that basis alone I believe that my fellow vegetarians need to take pause before over politicizing our cause. With some exceptions, meat eaters do not eat meat with malicious intention. While vegetarians, such as myself, ultimately view meat eating as a form of ignorance, any belief that I hold it is only one point of view or perspective and vegetarianism is not an exception. And ignorance is not so much a fault as an indication that there is a need for some enlightenment and, of course, meat eaters may have another point of view, e.g. that vegetarians and vegans deny the way of nature and live an ideal that does not reflect a correct perspective on moral actuality. Radical vegetarians and animal activists do not do themselves or animals any service by turning what is a *moral* issue or controversy into a *political* issue. Yet, the depoliticization of vegetarianism does not mean that it will not ultimately, as it already has done to some extent, result in political change. Vegetarianism, or more specifically, ethical vegetarianism and veganism grounded on principles of compassion and reverence for life, because they relate to the basic existential function of food and sustenance, is a gateway to expanded compassion. Much more than compassion is required for ethical empowerment and the attainment of elusive virtue, and vegetarianism is hardly a guarantee of overall goodness, but as part of a holistic ethics that embraces compassion it will continue to usher in positive political and economic change through the medium of a kinder and more compassionate evolving consciousness.

How is the practice of compassion to be cultivated and nurtured by a civilized society and a civilized world? Abstract values are necessary before they are made concrete by the dialogical interplay of the moral forces and their dialectical engagement in the world. The abstract principle of compassion is the basis of reverence for life. The reverence for life is a value that embodies the compassion for all life, but if compassion is left in its pure abstractness it will fail to fulfill its purpose. In its pure abstractness, the compassionate treatment of all living creatures may miserably miss its mark through twisted rationalizations that allow incoherent fairness and incoherent beneficence to be deemed compassionate. Uncompassionate justice is no more justifiable, or sensible, than unjust compassion. The values that embody a reverence for life are those religious, spiritual, civic rituals and the breadth of personal behavior that reminds us that the compassionate treatment of all life is a solemn responsibility for any moral being. *There is no more effective ritual for transmitting the values of reverence for life than the practice of vegetarianism.* Someday, perhaps, vegetarian diet and nonviolence in all aspects of civilized life will prevail. But in the meantime, those who are engaged in the transmission of nonviolent values that express a reverence for life continue to build and reinforce the ways of compassion in concrete and coherent ethical form. As Gandhi said, "The greatness of a nation and its moral progress can be judged by the way its animals are treated." The practice of reverence for life by means of dietary choice is perhaps *not* the first step towards individual or collective greatness. But it may be one of the final steps symbolizing humanity's completion of the circle of compassion.

II.43

Pro-Life / Pro-Choice

There are no rules that can help us through the abortion muddle. "Abortion is murder" and "A woman has a right to control her own body" do not illuminate but are only pretenses of illumination. They are slogans whose repetitions hypnotically deepen the intractability of the controversy. These slogans are pseudo-principles and have no value: they inform us of nothing regarding the ethicality of certain forms of killing, or of the substance concerning any particular right that a woman might have with respect to control over her body. Wrongfulness in the *moral* sense, as distinguished from the legal or statutory sense, is not determined by referring to a preset codification or set of definitions, let alone cute sloganeering. With respect to a woman's right to "control" her own body, comparing abortion to, say, body piercing would be stupid. And, with respect to the question of "murder" in the moral sense, only ethical reasoning concerning the facts and circumstances of a killing can meaningfully reach a judgment of whether it is wrongful and constitutive of murder. It is quite plausible that in a particular situation the killing of a human being may—according to legal definition, be properly ruled by a jury or a judge as a commission of murder, but from an ethical perspective the killing may have been justified and therefore was not an act of murder. But having said that, only a lunatic or a reckless anarchist would want to leave the societal determination of murder up to personal ethical decision! The boundary between law and ethics defines the abortion controversy.

To understand the abortion issue it is necessary to throw most ethical rules out the window because they don't apply. The issue of abortion may be viewed situationally from the perspective of the basic ethical dualisms. Most certainly, one can feel compassion for an unborn child and, clearly, the further along in the birth cycle the more profound the compassion becomes. While it is a stretch of imagination to speak of genuine compassion for a one week old fetus without also projecting religious or spiritual beliefs about selfhood that have little scientific or empirical grounding, as a fetus develops in its mother's womb the feelings of compassion may naturally develop and evolve. So while we can imagine compassion that is abstractly felt for a one week old fetus, the meaningfulness of compassion grows as the baby develops. From the standpoint of elemental fairness, it appears wrong to terminate a new life; but it may also be argued that in some cases it is unfair to force a mother to carry a child to term. Likewise, from the standpoint of elemental beneficence we can see arguments in favor of defending an embryo's right to survive as a clear case of beneficent action; but on the other hand, a woman's life may be such that the consequences of carrying the child are so negative that the beneficence to the mother outweighs or takes precedence over that of the unborn child. However, from the position of elemental compassion if would seem that the balance shifts back to the unborn child. As with arguments in favor of vegetarianism and the treatment of animals, applying the principle of compassion seems to favor a reverence for life and this sacred value may be an overriding argument against terminating a pregnancy. But then, as in the vegetarian argument, more than compassion is involved in making ethical judgments and the moral equipoise shifts in accordance with circumstances.

A mother's ethical deliberation concerning a possible abortion can end up on one side or the other. In the question of whether or not a pregnancy should be aborted, different situations can produce different choices as perspectives concerning fairness, beneficence and compassion are weighed. In some cases, the mother will find that the compassion she feels for her unborn child is overwhelming and will overrule any consideration of abortion. But regardless of whether or not the mother has compassion for her unborn child, it is an a priori ought for her to foster some form of elemental compassion. Thus, in the matter of pregnancy, regardless of the choice made, the matter of compassion needs to be considered as something that is owed the unborn child. And, in general, for a *mature* mother to simply have an abortion without first subjecting herself to serious ethical reflection would be an *a*moral abdication. Since we cannot escape ethical choices because not choosing is a form of choosing, is the failure to ethically deliberate the question of whether to abort a pregnancy wrongful? It would not seem so in the case of teen pregnancies in which a teenage mother is given complete legal authority over making the decision. It would be quite unreasonable to suppose that a teenager is fully capable of deliberating complex ethical issues, or possesses the maturity to adequately assess the ramifications of aborting her pregnancy. The teenage mother is in many respects not ethically empowered, i.e. not fully capable of making the decision. A decision will be made one way of the other, but in the case of pregnancies in which a teenage mother is given full legal authority, the ethical issue will necessarily be decided on practical consequences that are more easily grasped than complex and intangible ethical reflections. The latter statement is virtually a statement of fact, unless ideology is substituted for reasoned assessment.

However, for mature individuals competent to engage in ethical reflection, *not* deliberating the moral implications of an abortion can only be described as an ethical abdication and, hence, wrong by default. However, if a failure for a woman to make a good faith effort in deliberating the question of whether to carry her child to term is indicative of moral incoherency, is it not equally incoherent for the state to make itself the moral agent by expropriating a woman's right to choose? The question of whether to end a pregnancy may have many permutations and indeterminacy, but a law forbidding a woman's right to choose is an interference with her personal freedom that may be justifiable only by means of ignoring the self-regarding components of the issue. But to ignore the self-regarding components is as incoherent as it would be to ignore those that are other-regarding. While the state does have an interest in the abortion issue, it is the pregnant mother, not the state, that is the principal moral agent, and it is her choice whether or not to carry her pregnancy to term. The state has no grounds to interfere with the woman's choice and rob her of her freedom. However, society can act in such a way that makes conditions more bearable for a woman to carry an unwanted pregnancy to term and, thereby, empower her self-realization. There is social resistance to making teen pregnancies *too* acceptable and, therefore, we can see that the much vaunted "rights" for mothers to choose, on the one hand, and for unborn fetuses to be born, on the other hand, may serve to mask a general insecurity on both sides of the issue. There may be a secret or subconscious preference by some pro-choice proponents that abortions are a more preferable option than the stigma of teen pregnancy, and pro-life proponents may have an ulterior interest in opposing programs such as sex education in the public schools because they believe that public sex education leads to greater promiscuity. Rather than taking freedom of choice away from mothers concerning the most personal of matters, it would be far better if society were to actively facilitate and create opportunities to help women make the right choices for themselves. Rather than making teen pregnancies seem too acceptable on the one hand, and encouraging abortions on the other an enlightened social program would do neither. An enlightened culture of sex education and compassion that is dedicated to developing greater understanding of reverence for life, as well as compassion for women who are contemplating the possibility of terminating a pregnancy, would both reduce teen pregnancies and reduce the number of abortions. And this type of social policy is reflective of a culture that empowers women.

The pro-choice argument emphasizes freedom whereas the pro-life arguments emphasize the value of reverence for life. Who does not want freedom? Who does not revere life? Yes, there are opponents to freedom and there are those who do not revere life, but I am not addressing those individuals here. Freedom, in the pragmatic sense, is merely conduct that is guided by reason and wisdom that is inclusive of respect for the opinions of others and the humility that acknowledges human fallibility. This pragmatic conception of freedom is almost certainly the most fundamental human value other than life itself, and could human life without basic freedom be something we could revere? If the reader accepts my argument of the primacy of freedom for human beings, then you will be able to accept the premise that a woman's decision to abort or to not to abort her child is an expression of her freedom regardless of the choice that is made. Is there any more simple statement of desire than, "I just want to be free!" Indeed, most of us want that, but freedom is enormously challenging for individuals as well as for nations and societies. Challenges and difficult choices ironically make us freer, and there is no freedom without the possibility of choice. If choice has been forcibly removed then there is no freedom. Human beings have a hand in creating their own destiny, but a radical pro-life position that condemns all abortions is a position that denies to a woman the freedom that helps shape her destiny.

The maxim that "God acts in mysterious ways" is appropriate. Right choices may be elusive despite our best efforts. We may even be unsure of our own good intentions because subconscious beliefs, needs or desires may be hidden and, thus, decisions may be grounded by motives of which we are unaware. The abortion issue is far too intertwined with the big questions about the meaning or purpose of life to ever justify casting aspersions and demeaning the views on either side of the controversy. And so, to those who consider themselves religious or spiritual, if you say that you believe in the existence of a soul within each human being, how can you be certain whether the divine plan for a particular soul is to be born as a result of a particular pregnancy, or that in actuality it is the termination of the fetus that is part of the plan? Perhaps not every birth is meant to be. And to scientists or deniers of all things spiritual, are you certain within the context of the finitude of your knowledge that there is not an infinite wisdom that might contravene the rightness of a particular abortion? The entire abortion controversy comes back to questions of freedom and personal destiny. Each individual has a destiny that is not predetermined but is the potential for positive self-realization. Certainly, the questions surrounding the issue of abortion are among the most difficult that any woman (or person) can contemplate. But if we continue to develop our capacities for self-realization and reverence for life, then a dialectical interplay may emerge that allows the controversy between Pro-Life and Pro-Choice to transition from an ideological debate between incommensurable conceptions of Life and Freedom into a deeper understanding that is grounded in mutual respect and genuine compassion.

II.44

Beyond Disunity

Authors of Utopian visions have imagined a world or societies in which harmony and peace reign and harmonic potential flourishes. However, a closer look reveals that the basis of Utopias is often a morally incoherent and harmonically imbalanced communistic (e.g. *Looking Backward*) or laissez-faire (e.g. *Atlas Shrugged*) vision of a perfect society. I have little doubt that some of my readers may interpret many of the ideas presented in this book as Utopian or impossibly unrealistic. However, while I believe that the changes that I have proposed can be refined, implemented and phased in, I have no illusions that the world's problems would suddenly vanish. I do not necessarily believe in Utopias or their desirability, but I do believe that ethical empowerment and virtue are attainable by removing disharmonious blocks that stand in the way of human self-realization.

Unity is sometimes confused with homogeneity, but more generally a unity suggests the harmonious integration of disparate parts whereas homogeneity tends to suggest thoroughgoing conformity. For example, he human body is a paradigm of harmonic unity that is a symphonic-like coordination of diverse bodily parts, organs and biological, chemical, and electrical systems and, no doubt, still more than current knowledge comprehends. The present section discusses three broadly recognized features of civilization that disguise themselves as forces of unity when, in fact, they are deep historical sources of disunity. I speak here of political parties, religions and nation-states. The language of these disunities is filled with the ideals of unity while, in truth, they have been both cause and object of conflict and disunity throughout history. The simplified explanation for the disunifying nature of nation-states, political parties and religions is that while they posture themselves as forces for peace or prosperity within a transcendent unity, they inevitably become divisive and polarizing because universal agreement with any single ideology is not possible without coercion. They are forms of forced unity and, therefore, prescriptions for disunity.

The only path for achieving harmonic unity is the healthful flourishing of a multiplicity of perspectives that conform to the underlying moral unity that binds conscious beings together. Uncertainty is the only certitude, but when human intentionality finally frees itself from the triadic disunities of political parties, religions and nation-states, when that day comes humanity will have cleared many obstacles to its positive, self-realized destiny. Abraham Lincoln's statement that he prayed not that God is on our side but that we are on His epitomizes the sentiment of assured uncertainty under the guidance of faith. But absolutists who reject as mentally deranged anyone who does not share a particular political orientation, or proclaim that "God is on our side" and damn all others who do not share their ideological or theological viewpoint, or who nauseatingly and constantly proclaim that their country is "the best and the greatest country in the world," profoundly diverge from Lincoln's sentiment and expose their "good intentions" as nothing but egoistic attachments to dogma.

The process of convergence away from the triadic disunities has already begun. In the United States the number of "unenrolled" or independent voters who do not declare allegiance to any political party has grown significantly. The phrase "spiritual but not religious" has become commonplace for many folks who do not associate themselves with atheism or any particular organized religion. Non-religious spirituality generally reflects faith in some form of existence beyond conventional notions of physical reality, but is also for many a rejection of the disunifying impact of organized religion. And in many respects divisions between nation-states are seemingly becoming less important thanks largely to technology that has made the world a vastly smaller place. The twentieth century witnessed aviation shrink the distances between nations, and planet earth has never seemed smaller in this nascent period of the space age. And during the late twentieth and early twenty-first centuries distance seems to have almost been made obsolete by the instant multimedia communication of the internet. People now have the ability to interact with others on the other side of the globe almost as if they were next door. And then there is globalization that for all its dangers and negative ramifications is a glimmer of the increasing insignificance of national boundaries. And yet, despite the weakening influence of political parties, religions, and nation-states and some slippage into irrelevancy, in other spheres their divisiveness and disunifying influence and destructive force have become more severe and threatening.

Discord over policies and decisions about how to lead a country are natural but discord for the sake of discord is both pointless and destructive. Getting rid of the parties (§II.19) may become a model and a precedent for tearing down other needless social divisions. The formulation of public policies that *emerge* from the natural flow of different perspectives will always be associated with temporary alliances, but they need not become permanently institutionalized political divisions that force division for the sake of party politics. Once electoral politics has been freed from the distortion and corruption of unfair campaign spending, the influence of temporary issue based alliances will be rightfully earned because they will represent the interests of voters that they represent, rather than a de facto form of institutionalized bribery otherwise known as campaign contributions by political lobbies. An independent non-party based democracy, freed from the corruption of excessive private electoral campaign spending, would be a powerful symbol of unity that reflects the harmonic unity of *e pluribus unum*.

Paralleling the increase in the United States of independent or unenrolled voters, large numbers of Americans and Europeans are detaching themselves from formal associations with religion. More people than ever before consider themselves to be atheist, agnostic or "spiritual but not religious." Linking independent or non-party democratic politics with the growth of atheism and non-religious spiritual practices may seem to be forced, but both represent an unblocking of divisive dogma and an unleashing of potential for a new and empowered politics and consciousness. Of course, we are at the same time witnessing a growth in religious extremism and fundamentalism and increasing partisanship and polarization in politics and, most disconcerting, the conjoining of religion and politics. The "Arab Spring" has produced the overthrow of dictators but at least some are being replaced with dictatorial Islamic regimes. The world seems to be in a mess as the forces of unity bump heads with the forces of disunity.

Nonetheless, the decline of political parties and organized religions, where it has occurred, is a hopeful trend.

While separation between church and state helps to protect government from control by any particular religion, government should actively promote comparative religion in the schools to cultivate understanding of the theology, philosophy and history of the world's religions. But learning and understanding the religions of your neighbors near and far should not end in the schools. Let there be established "eclectic temples" or "eclectic churches" that regularly sponsor religious services and prayers of a wide diversity of traditions! And further, imagine religious congregations inviting members of other faiths, on a regular basis, to attend their services. Imagine Jews praying at mosques or Muslims praying at synagogues! Imagine the mutual commingling of Christianity, Judaism, Islam, Buddhism, Hinduism, Zoroastrianism and other traditions. Thusly, the world will open up the doors of its collective consciousness to a new unity and a new harmony that would hold the promise for a spiritual synthesis, a spiritual empowerment and a spiritual flourishing the beauty, wisdom and magnificence of which *can* be imagined. For the sake of peace—which is the presumptive purpose of all great religions, the commingling of traditions should be *state sponsored!* There will come a day when state sponsored peaceful sharing and exchanges between all religions will supplant the ugliness of state sponsored terrorism and religious extremism. This is a dream of the nation-state transforming itself into a unifying force, and if statesmen are brave enough the dream can become reality.

The disunity of the system of nation-states perpetuates gross moral incoherencies. On all scores: dualistic fairness, dualistic beneficence and dualistic compassion the nation-state is failing and it is failing badly. On the face of it, the notion that each nation-state has autonomy and, therefore, that criminal and grotesque injustices are allowed to continue for years or even generations would be comparable to a hands off attitude by police to domestic criminals because, after all, they are autonomous human beings. This may sound like an advocacy that America or, if not America, some other nation act as the "policeman of the world," however, this is not the case. America's hyperactive military policies, both when they are right and when they are wrong, are bankrupting the nation and helping to drive its economy into a shadow of its former self. America can no longer (and never could) afford to be the policeman of the world. But we do need to recognize that the system of nation-states in itself tends to justify the unjustifiable. National sovereignty is a filthy joke when it becomes the protectorate of evil.

Harmonic unity emerges from internal diversity; a harmonic unity is much more than a federal integration of states but, rather, a unified organic whole that is a process of mutual support and self-interest. Reducing the entrenched disunity of the nation-state will move us closer towards a free and empowered world society that will be more like a network of cooperating communities than a collection of nations. (§II.31) The nation-state is a formality because its continued existence matters not a wink if the individual and collective lives of human beings are freer and more flourishing without it. Self-realization and free association, i.e. true freedom, within the context of a harmonic, morally coherent and flourishing social universe are the essential goals of any free polity, economy or society. But a world society would not mean the end of cultural uniqueness and self-governance. Cultural and national identities and their proud heritage would continue to evolve. What *would* change is the actuality of institutionalized disharmonic blocks and disunities that have been fostered by the old system of nation-states, political parties and religions. In time, institutionalized barriers to peace and freedom will be removed. In this unity, diversity will flourish.

The political party, organized religion and the nation-state have each had enormous influence on world history and, despite their disunifying force in the contemporary world they were necessary for the political and moral development of civilization. But like rusty old habits that have outgrown their usefulness, they have become impediments and barriers to a greater future. Progress may have been impossible without what I have called the triadic disunities, but much like privately held real estate, they are stages of development that can now enter into a harmonic process of transition that reflects the advancement of consciousness. The unleashing of human potential, blocked and trapped in the institutional corpses that now unnecessarily divide humanity, can ultimately reshape the planet in the peaceful and productive diverse unity of its self-realization.

II.45

A New Overman

Could you *create* a God? Then do not speak to me
of any gods. But you could well create the overman.
Perhaps not you yourselves, my brothers. But into
fathers and forefathers of the overman you could
re-create yourselves: and let this be your best creation.[121]

A new Overman will emerge who embodies the harmonic unity
between Self and Other. This new Overman, which does not refer
to a single individual but to a class of men and women who would shake
the conventional wisdom to its foundations, is a radical departure from the
Overman or *Ubermensch* of Nietzsche's *Thus Spoke Zarathustra*. Nietzsche
was no fan of democracy or of the virtue of altruism. In democracies, he
quite rightly observes, individuals are often dragged down to the lowest
common denominator of the herd mentality. In addition, Nietzsche targets
the Judeo-Christian ethic as the seat of a particular form of the herd mentality
called *ressentiment*, his term for an ethics in which the powerful are blamed
by the weak as the cause of their suffering or perceived victimization. While
Nietzsche's ressentiment certainly has a point because some individuals or
disempowered classes can descend into a culture that excessively or
exclusively blames others, he profoundly fails if he seriously wants us to
believe that the vulnerable or the weaker classes never have anyone to
rightfully blame for their misery. Reading Nietzsche is far more rewarding
when the reader knows when to read him with a few large grains of salt.
But Nietzsche is surely on target with his critiques of the herd mentality.
The herd mentality can form in any groupthink environment and, therefore,
the citizen whose mentality transcends the knee-jerk or "rigidly hypnotic"
thinking of the conventional wisdom always remains an urgent and desperate

need. Like Ayn Rand, Nietzsche glorifies the self, but the individual greatness of the Overman has vastly more subtlety than Rand's John Galt character in *Atlas Shrugged*, a cartoon of rugged individualism and radical laissez-faire capitalism. While it is true that Nietzsche, like Rand, celebrates self-regarding qualities and disparages those that are other-regarding it is also true that the Overman represents man *overcoming* himself and, as such, is intrinsically self-humbling. The power of the Overman is in large measure the power of humility.

The greatness of the Overman is his ability to acknowledge his limitations and then to overcome them. The subtlety involved in portraying a selfish person overcoming his miserable limitations is expressed by Nietzsche's fascinating dialectical relationship between good and evil in which evil is a necessary ingredient for the germination of good in human existence. In the following passage from *Thus Spoke Zarathurstra* Nietzsche expresses the internal contradictions of overcoming in a meeting between the prophet-like Zarathurstra and "higher men" who don't quite make the grade for entry into the class of the Overman:

> When power becomes gracious and descends into the visible—such descent I call beauty. And there is nobody from whom I want beauty as much as from you who are powerful: let your kindness be your final self-conquest. Of all evil I deem you capable: therefore I want the good from you.[122]

As discussed previously (§I.7) Nietzsche believed in a sort of noblesse oblige. Here, again, the confusing concept of "beyond good and evil" needs to be clarified. The noble and strong must overcome evil by going beyond good and evil. I don't defend Nietzsche's language; it is notoriously susceptible to both misinterpretation and distortion such as, for e.g. by the Nazis roughly a couple of generations after Nietzsche wrote, who twisted and manipulated his words with evil intention and thoroughly vacuous understanding. But Nietzsche courageously confronts the existentiality of beauty and good in terms of a dialectical understanding of their respective polar opposition in which the moral sense is sharpened by an acquaintance with what it is not. And the overcoming of ourselves is, in this sense, a profound reality that some sugar sweet mentalities wound rather avoid. Indeed, while we can learn much about who we are by purely experiencing the best within ourselves, we can also learn and go much further by understanding what is the worst within ourselves…and then overcoming it.

The new Overman will overcome the mediocrity of mass culture both individually and collectively; s/he is a leader in a free and democratic society of leaders. The new Overman will celebrate the strength, boldness, creativity and power of the harmonic unity of Self and Other without which true greatness is severely stifled and limited. This harmonic unity of which I speak is nothing less than the guidance of love in the fullness of both its intentionality and its effectuality. The new Overman will both emerge and be part of the transformation of the exteriority into a society that empowers individuals who in turn empower society. The new Overman is represented by men and women who are boldly courageous *both* in their support and in their overthrow of convention, and in their will to invent and create out of compassion and desire for the betterment of themselves and others. Downgrading the significance of others while upgrading arrogance as a form of empowerment is comical; a major difference between Nietzsche's Zarathustra and Rand's John Galt is that Nietzsche intended his hero to be half comic. Fantasies of super autonomous individuals are merely reflections of a detachment from reality because there are no purely autonomous individuals. But the increased moral status of the individual also lifts the moral status of the social body, which in turn empowers the evolution of the Overman and the building of a moral actuality lovingly expressed in the harmonic unity of Self and Other.

Only by "going under" and engaging a deep understanding of the negative can the Overman illuminate and inspire and wholeheartedly embrace the positive. In many ways, negative emotions are our friends because they can remind us of how far we can stray and of that which we never want to become. But the exteriority also must overcome itself! The will of the Overman is in large part born from the ribs the social body. It is no slight against individualism to say that individuals are always indebted to others. The latter comment is reminiscent of the "death of the author"[123] argument that states the very interesting but obvious truth that any author is indebted to other authors and the overall wealth of her total experience. "I stand on the shoulders of giants," said the great Isaac Newton. But indebtedness to others extends beyond the relatively straightforward influences that we have all received from others to the overall effect of our collective influences on the exteriority of the human mind that, perhaps as an emergent property, has a life of it is own. But the emerging exteriority is not always a positive development. The exteriority, as much as the self's interiority, must dialectically overcome its own negativity of self-sabotage and self-destructiveness and its lack of compassion if it is to become empowered, and if it is to collectively empower a virtuous society of great individuals. The Overman is the projection and the embodiment of ethical and social virtue in the interiority and in the exteriority, in the individual consciousness and in the collective consciousness, in the life of an individual and in the life of a society.

Only a lopsided and ethically imbalanced view of virtue could laud a titan of industry such as a Morgan or a Rockefeller and dismiss selfless heroes such as Florence Nightingale, Clara Barton or Mother Theresa. And of the two groups, which represents the stronger or more courageous individuals? I doubt that any serious commentator would describe the industrial titans as stronger or more courageous than any of the three aforementioned women who gave of themselves so tirelessly and effectively to ease the suffering of others. Which is not to dismiss the industrialists except, of course, when they were using their might to cheat the little man or unfairly wipe out competition. A great society requires great achievers in all walks of life and the new Overman will walk along all of these paths even if some pathways seem self-regarding while others are other-regarding; both paths can be opportunities for empowerment and a diverse reflection of virtue. I have previously mentioned the case of the great Nikola Tesla who was far too generous and other-regarding towards George Westinghouse (II.7), and the latter was probably not nearly generous and beneficent enough in his dealing with Tesla. Sadly, history has paid a harsh price for the stymieing of Tesla's work. That Nietzsche exalted Homeric strength and denigrated selflessness and compassion are, in the end, paradoxical contradictions of his own perspectivism. Selflessness and self-interestedness concerning personal achievement are two perspectives on greatness, and the new Overman finds greatness along the many pathways of both.

The Overman is no emotionless Stoic sage; s/he can be full of mirth and passion provided that the emotions are tempered in accordance with reason. All else is a matter of taste, and the new Overman has good taste.

A new Overman will emerge who overcomes selfishness, and who also overcomes altruism. These overmen and overwomen seek true power by saying 'Yes!' to the *will to power* through the only authentic basis of power that exists: love-based ethical reasoning shaped and tuned by a diversity of perspectives.

A new Overman will emerge who knows the value of values in both their abstract and concrete forms, and concrete good—like concrete beauty, can only be understood in terms of a plurality of perspective. The new Overman is a curator, a scholar of diverse perspectives and a reframer of all values. The Good and what *is* good requires bountiful perspective. While an Overman can and will revere the diversity of particular schools or systems of philosophic, religious and spiritual wisdom s/he will never idolize, idealize, iconify or dogmatize any of them.

The new Overman will oscillate between attachment and detachment, and knows how to balance the value of money and the value of life. And these overmen and overwomen will build a rational foundation for monetary or currency value that is worthy of culture inspired and led by the example of the Overman. An Overman is a citizen of the world; s/he is a moral agent that attaches to good things and good actions. But when good is no longer served by attachments, be they material things or stale dogma, they are purged from the mind when, for e.g., nostalgia becomes unaffordable or retrograde. An appetite for wealth, however, that does not become a blinding attachment can sharpen the moral sense in the Overman. The new Overman will not lose his or her way in the dualistic moral jungle by losing sight of the forest for the trees; when the only tree cared for is the Tree of the Self intellectual and ethical blindness have surely set in.

The new Overman will thrive in a society in which artificial blockages, barriers and disharmony that have made him or her a rarity have been removed, and in its place fertile soil will have been laid for a democratic class who leads by example and with compassion so that, in the end, the Overman may be most everyman. For example, unencumbered by a patent system designed to monopolize inventions rather than facilitate them, and unburdened by fees unaffordable to many, the inventor will invent. And society will have inspired itself with greatness born of the seeds it will have sewn. And so too, the political Overman will be unattached from political parties and finally freed from arbitrary and institutionalized divisiveness. The new political Overman will always be a statesman and a citizen of the world.

The new Overman will transcend and go under and then with the wisdom gained lead and go over the disunity of nationalism and the nation-state. How can the Overman transcend the nation-state if s/he is also a statesman? The state is an ideal that becomes less desirable as it recedes into history. But it is now becoming possible to see the diverse unity that ultimate harmony requires. The new Overman *as* statesman love's love more than statehood, and the transcendent power of love as the essence and the basis of morality requires that it supervene every other human motive. The new Overman as statesman may overcome himself or herself and become the first citizens of the world society. Above all else, the new Overman will creatively and tirelessly search for alternatives to war. The knowledge that the disgrace of war is embedded in every man and every woman will allow those who are Overman to lead humankind to overcome the decadence that is the acceptance of war and, thereby, allow humanity to achieve peace by overcoming itself.

*   *   *   *

Discussion about Nietzsche's Overman is suggestive of the subject of evolution. There is some comparison between Nietzsche and Herbert Spencer, the nineteenth-century philosopher of evolution whose publication of *Social Statics* antedated the publication of Darwin's *Origin of Species* by eight years. Spencer, often considered to be the first libertarian, believed that the evolution of a perfect man would require a perfect laissez-faire society with almost no governmental interference. In contrast, Nietzsche saw moral convention as blockades or barriers to greatness and by tearing down these restraints the Overman could attain his moral perfection. Both Spencer and Nietzsche viewed moral progress as contingent upon freeing humanity from negative and obstructive barriers so that it could then "adapt" or "overcome" the challenges of freedom to achieve greatness.

Man is something that shall be overcome...What is the ape

> to man? A laughing-stock or a painful embarrassment.
> And man shall be just that for the overman: a
> laughingstock or a painful embarrassment. You have
> made your way from worm to man, and much in you is
> still worm. Once you were apes, and even now, too, man
> is more ape than any ape.[124]

The herd mentality is as suggestive of aping as it is of following like sheep. The questions surrounding notions of the Overman, as well as Spencer's views on perfection give reason for pause on the relationship between freedom and the future realization of humanity's full potential. With respect to the relationship between the individual and society, Nietzsche and Spencer radically part ways. Nietzsche's political views were not fully developed but he favored an aristocratic or noble form of government that would reward the "higher rank" of strong individuals. Spencer, the coiner of the phrase "survival of the fittest"—while not the ruthless advocate of "Social Darwinism" that some commentators have claimed, advocated a free and open society that would encourage competition and strengthen and perfect the individual. However, both approaches exhibit severe moral incoherencies that skew the balance between Self and Other radically towards the Self. Spencer's ideas have no answer for the repressive nature of monopoly capitalism, and the anti-democratic features of a Nietzschean society would inhibit those not in the "higher rank" from ever gaining the knowledge and skills to escape and overcome a life of mediocrity and suffering. The visions of human perfection of both philosophers are decidedly imperfect; whether it would be the inevitable monopoly capitalism in the case of Spencer or the rigid class structure of Nietzsche, both visions are hard views of social and individual perfection and highly imperfect from the perspective of a holistic and coherent ethics.

Zecharia Sitchin, in his *Earth Chronicles* series argues that, based on his interpretation of ancient Sumerian texts, the gods of Greek myth and the God of the Bible were inspired by the legacy of ancient visitors from a distant planet who bio-engineered the human species by hybridization of terrestrial and extraterrestrial DNA and subsequent crossbreeding. It is interesting to observe the fallibilities and sensitive egos of these gods. It may be conjectured whether the true mission of humanity is to perfect or complete the moral project because these gods were also gods of vice. When Nietzsche wrote that, "God is dead" he was simply commenting that the human race has reached a point in its development in which it is no longer possible to rely on ancient writings to solve humanity's contemporary problems. The gods themselves were all-to-imperfect, and the time may have arrived for humankind to overcome itself and to fulfill its mission. Now is the moment to overcome our all-too-human flaws and improve upon the amorality of the gods. Now is the time to broadly potentiate our ethical empowerment and pave the way for a flourishing of individual and collective virtue.

II.46

Convergence in the Middle East

Is there a dialectic working its way to peace in the Middle East, or is the region plodding towards a grim destiny?

The Jews were expelled from ancient Israel by the Romans in the year 70 CE and thereafter embarked on their Diaspora and nineteen hundred years of recurrent persecution. "Next year in Jerusalem," the perennial dream of *aliyah* or return to the Jewish homeland became immortalized in traditional prayer. Despite the Diaspora, significant Jewish communities would continue to exist in Palestine (the name adopted for the territory of ancient Israel after the Roman expulsion) up until the reestablishment of modern Israel. Social and political activity for Jewish immigration to Palestine increased in the nineteenth century as anti-Semitism again began to deepen in Europe. The growth of anti-Semitism produced a dialectical reaction: the ancient dream of aliyah was politicized and led to the formation of the Zionist movement to form an independent Jewish state. Then came the Holocaust and the extermination of six million Jews—or about two-thirds of the Jewish population of Europe; in its aftermath, large-scale immigration of Jewish refugees flowed into Palestine and political pressures for the reestablishment of a Jewish homeland greatly intensified.

The existence of any ethnic, cultural or politically distinct population creates an *existential imperative*. The reality of any human population is a moral actuality that *is*, and while there may be natural shifts in population due to migration, birthrate and death rates forced exile or relocation would require the most extreme and rigorous ethical justification. The contemporary illegal immigration issue in the United States has some basis of comparison to the situation that existed in the Middle East prior to the establishment of the modern State of Israel in 1948. Illegal immigrants have entered the United States through avoidance of the immigration laws and, at the time of this writing, their total population appears to number over ten million. Who is to blame? The immigrants who came to America desperate to provide food and shelter for their families? The businesses who have illegally employed them? The pros and cons of proposed legislation to deal with the illegal immigration controversy are outside the scope of this section, but only the most cold-hearted sort of person would demand that the non-documented immigrants be exiled en masse to their native countries. While the problem clearly needs to be contained and certain restrictions that fall short of full citizenship could be reasonably considered, shipping these people out of the country would be a horrible wrong. Fairness, beneficence and compassion, when focused in broad human terms, require that the immigration issue be dealt with in both a humane and pragmatic fashion. Another case with some relevancy to the Arab-Israeli conflict, and one that exemplifies how *not* to deal with an existential imperative, is the manner in which the British and, subsequently, the American governments dealt with the indigenous Amerindian populations. Aggressive relocations to reservations and other assorted injustices occurred that obliterated the Amerindian cultures and subjected these peoples to much death and suffering. A strong argument can be made that undocumented immigrants in contemporary America, and the European settlers in the New World both demonstrate an existential imperative. Which group, the Israelis or the Palestinians, holds the existential imperative in the Middle East?

The preceding question involves a dilemma that may be called the *Arab-Israeli antinomy* because it contains equally compelling arguments on both sides of the controversy. An antinomy consists of a pair of contradictory arguments of which both appear to be valid. It can be argued that the non-Jewish residents of Palestine in 1948 had a right to live their lives as in the past, which since 1516 was under the authority of the Ottoman Empire and since the aftermath of World War I under a British Protectorate. And it can be argued, in turn, that the Jewish population that had returned to Palestine, which had fairly and legally purchased land from the existing residents, was also a refugee population rebounding from immense atrocity and genocide. Did not the Jews as well as the Palestinians both have an existential imperative to remain in Palestine? Antinomies are often flawed and inconclusive due the to the limitations of their defined terms and the exclusion of vast countervailing considerations. For example, consider this paraphrasing of one of Kant's famous antinomies that opposed two arguments: 1) Matter is divisible into simple parts and 2) Matter is indivisible and is not reducible to simple parts. Kant argues that the arguments that comprise the antinomy are mutually exclusive, and the logic of both arguments is equally justified. But imagine a modern-day quantum physicist using Kant's logic! Kant's antinomies don't work because the truth is embedded in the nature of physical reality and not in a philosopher's definitions. Ethical and political controversies are no different because the language of an antinomy may not account for critical factors that are outside of its terms and assumptions. This incompleteness also applies to the Arab-Israeli antinomy.

In the matter before us, three critical elements are not addressed by the narrow logic of the Arab-Israeli antinomy: a) power, b) "compassionate correction" and c) the role of religion. We should consider what the existential imperative meant in 1948 Palestine in terms that both include and go beyond the narrow limitations of the antinomy. The Arab-Israeli antinomy simply pits one land claim against another and without supervening arguments there can be no resolution. Power may be dismissed as ethically irrelevant by ethicists, but politics without power is not politics, and power that is not morally coherent is ultimately not true power and cannot by itself stand. *Within the Arab-Israeli antinomy, and in the reality of the existential imperative there is a stark contrast*: the creation of the modern nation of Israel was a dialectical reaction against anti-Semitism and also the result of longstanding aspirations of Jews to return to their ancient homeland, while the political movement for Palestinian statehood was both a political and an anti-Semitic reaction against the increasing Jewish population in Palestine. In the nearly two thousand years after the Roman expulsion of the Jews, there had not been a political movement for a homeland or nation-state for non-Jewish Palestinians. The power in Palestine had shifted to the Israeli/Jewish side. And the authenticity of motive was also on the side of the Jews. And yet, the ramifications of power are multifaceted and involve more than original motives that set the stage for historical processes. Israeli power would not be true power and cannot be ultimately successful without also being a moral power in all respects. And so it is for all nations.

Compassionate correction is introduced here as a form of affirmative action. Affirmative action is compensation for injury inflicted by a more powerful social group upon one that is weaker; however, sometimes the unequal distribution of power is in itself constitutive—even without any culpability, of a need for compassionate correction. Compassionate correction is a demonstration of manifest compassion and a statement that vocalization of sympathy for peoples on the short end of a political or military struggle is insufficient. When the continuing state of war between Israel and its Arab neighbors finally ends and peace emerges, both sides will have the opportunity to willingly enact affirmative actions to compensate for wrongs suffered by innocent victims. Mutual acknowledgment of wrongdoing is a powerful healer. But at the current time, Israel is the dominant power in the area. Israel could take dramatic actions that convincingly demonstrate compassion by ensuring that Arab residents of the occupied territories receive the same quality of social services had by citizens of Israel. These policies will hardly end the crisis, but it could certainly help to transcend differences by the pure force and positive effect of their humanity. Indeed, a 2008 Harvard University study, entitled "Coexistence in Israel: A National Study" found that seventy-seven percent or Arab-Israeli citizens would prefer to continue living in Israel rather in any other country. The study also found that the great majority of both Jewish and Arab Israeli citizens believe that increased investment in coexistence programs is urgently needed.[125] It is not a far reach to believe that similar initiatives in the occupied territories would encourage a process of peace that could slowly defuse the continuing momentum towards war. The return on the investment of high-cost programs that engage deep compassionate corrections would be at least as cost-effective as is Israel's impressive military. There are two categories of courage (§II.9). One category of courage is to stick to your guns and conform to formalities or traditions when they are warranted but may be unpopular. The other category of courage is one of stepping outside the accepted principles and the conventional wisdom when moral conviction mandates that accepted norms are not acceptable; these are the instances in which heroes reverse the tide of the conventional thinking "led" by the stupefied herd. And the quagmire of violence and hatred in the Middle East is a paradigm of the herd mentality. Programs that implement inspired policies of compassionate corrections can, with persistence, begin to penetrate the hatred that is perpetuated by the herd mentality.

Any vision of peace in the Middle East must begin with the irony and the hypocrisy that "The Holy Land" has been consumed with hatred and interminable fighting between Jews and Muslims. 'Hypocrisy' may not be the right word, yet there is no denying that the conflagration would be far less dangerous if it were merely another political dispute over territory rather than a confrontation between two different religious faiths and their perceived conflict and disharmony. And so the word 'hypocrisy' in fact is appropriate and the magnitude of the hypocrisy is a paradigm of shame. But the leaders of the two religions *could* survey the ugliness and their direct and indirect roles in perpetuating the conflict, and they could miraculously do what political negotiations and military actions appear incapable of doing. Judaism and Islam and, in fact, all of the world's religions can simply and boldly decree that there shall be peace! It would be an epiphany and a self-realization that—in the insanity of the seemingly endless conflict, the whole blessed point of "the world's great religions" has been missed! The world may now be poised in a moment of history forced by an insane perversion of religious principle; a dialectical opportunity now exists to reverse the perversity of our times. Here we are, at the crossroads, and it is not too late for religion to inspire the loving spirit that in spite of everything lies at the core of all authentic spiritual faith. If the world's religious authorities, from the most reform or progressive to the most fundamentalist, emerged from holier than thou mouthing of doctrine they could position themselves to reverse the tide of history and its grim destiny. The religious authorities may yet save religion and inspire peace. They can demand that cultural programs of mutual education in the schools, as well as for adults, be commenced without delay and with massive and overwhelming insistence. If such a program were to be instituted fundamental political and economic changes would begin to emerge. A culture of reconciliation that today seems inconceivable would become possible. And it will not be the first time that the impossible will have become possible. If large numbers of Israeli children were to attend Arab schools for significant portions of their schooling, and if Arab children were to do the same in Israeli schools, and if adults were also mandated to participate in exchange programs so that meaningful friendships could form and ultimately flourish the culture of violence would begin to change. Indeed, possibilities beyond mere peaceful coexistence to mutual flourishing, perhaps only slowly, will emerge. Most view this sort of vision of peace as impossibly idealistic and with utter disbelief only because hypnotic, dogmatic and theocratic formalities of religious separatism have been impressed upon mass consciousness as the substance of faith. The dogmatic slumber of religious hatred is accepted and embraced by more than a few "religious" people. If peace, survival and salvation amount to more than doublespeak and empty words, religion will ultimately come to respect the collective wisdom of humanity in all of its diversity as the bulwark of its faith.

Religion, if it will only come to its senses, can be a critical stepping-stone to peaceful cooperation between Israel and its neighbors. It is a critical moment for Israel because it finds itself threatened by an internal threat that may, ultimately, threaten its survival as much as does its external threat. Israel is the hope of the Middle East because it has been, for the most part, a moderate secular state that has rejected governance by its religious orthodoxy. But if Israel becomes a just another Middle Eastern country dominated by orthodox religious dogma—and this is possible based on current population trends, and if the centrality of toleration and diversity is overwhelmed by separatist ideology, then it may become a sad reality that the freedom of Israel and all that it represents could be destroyed from within. It is has not generally been recognized that one of the great missions of Israel is to overcome its religious symbolisms while simultaneously embracing them. In the end, the religions of the world must represent the spirituality of freedom if they are to help the world survive and thrive. Contrary to the conventional wisdom of the Arab world, Israel is the best hope and the best opportunity for human flourishing throughout the Middle East. But Israel itself must remain free. Democracy, denied to almost every other country in the region, and the progressive wave of modernity, will be encouraged by the joint survival of Israel and its neighbors so that they can experience together freedom and peaceful flourishing throughout the region. The dialectic of peace in the Middle East can emerge from a critical mass of loving intention and good deeds, including transformative policies embarked not only by Israel but by its neighbors as well. When that critical mass of good will finally forms, an environment of fairness, beneficence and compassion will emerge that transcends and overcomes itself: a momentous, historic overcoming of the nation-state. As evolving trust and mutual flourishing abounds, new and brilliant possibilities will become impossible to ignore.

Ultimately, a strong, free and just Israel would be in a unique position to overcome the nation-state. In time, when false convictions of impossibility collapse into belief in what is possible, Israel and its neighbors will be able to take steps together that gradually dissolve the disunity of the nation-state in order to build a democratic, free and cooperative region that becomes the harbinger of a great human destiny. A flourishing and enlightened, ultimately borderless region in a land formerly plagued with endless bloodshed would demonstrate that the nation-state is no longer necessary! Like "Wittgenstein's ladder" on a political scale, the day may come when Israel and its neighbors can cast away their statehood and Israel can be just Israel, and Egypt just Egypt, Lebanon just Lebanon, and Jordan just Jordan. Thereafter, the nation-states of the world will begin their detachment from statehood and usher in the rise of true freedom as they witness the astounding and soul-penetrating spectacle of a region once absorbed in its self-destruction transformed into the hope of the world. When humanity truly learns to live in peace, life without national borders becomes possible, and what better training ground for peace could there be than in overcoming and transforming the morass that is the Middle East. Israel and its neighbors *can* become part of a proto world society; a stateless, harmonious and decentralized union. This spectacle would herald the obsolescence of the nation-state. This scenario is just a fantasy. Right? Well, the actuality of the nation-state has been embedded in the human mind as a vital part of the nature of things. But a new, convergent political actuality is emerging.

If the Jewish people had not endured two thousand years of deeply embedded persecution, their peaceful integration into European society would have been a model of how religious diversity and minority peoples can thrive within nation-states that support and protect the liberty and rights of all its citizens. But, facts being as they are, the Holocaust is the reason why the State of Israel became a necessity and will remain a necessity in the age of the nation-state. As long as there are nation-states there must and always will be a Jewish state. But the Middle East can become a glimmer of the nation-state's ultimate fate, that is to say, an expression of why the nation-state disunity is in the early stages of a radical transformation if not demise. The creation of Israel was a necessity that is doubtable only by the unreason of its enemies, but without needless divisions the world will someday be able to finally unite in the loving spirit that binds it together. But to replace the nation-state with an interdependent free association of communities while internecine and hateful behavior retains strong footholds could only be the fulfillment of a collective death wish. Basic fairness, human rights, political equality and justice for all citizens built into the fabric of society are only the necessary first conditions for a borderless society. Clearly, the moral incoherence and social disharmony that perpetuate the Arab-Israeli conflict will need to be addressed and resolved before any evolution of the region into a proto world society could be conceivable in any reasonable sense; nonetheless, the establishment of lasting peace in the Middle East could become a surprising opportunity for taking infant steps towards the harmonic unity of a world society.

A unified Middle East that has overcome the disunifying forces of religion, political parties and nation-states, that lives in peace and that celebrates the religious and spiritual diversity of all, that supports the rights of all to live and pray and work as neighbors, and then becomes the fulfillment of the "love thy neighbor" injunction certainly is only a dream from the perspective of our current day. Need I state the obvious! But if the interiority and exteriority of consciousness in the region should become inspired by spiritual callings no longer twisted, corrupted and perverted by hatred, then the land that has been paradoxically deemed Holy could be miraculously and forever transformed into the world symbol of dreams, hopes and prayers realized.

II.47

Ritual and Reverie

It is not uncommon for hard-nosed scientists to be regular churchgoers and practitioners of their of respective faiths. To their credit these scientists do not allow science to get in the way of their faith; as Emerson crisply and insightfully observes, "Consistency is the hobgoblin of little minds." The truth is not easily packaged, and the reconciliation of the seeming incommensurability of scientific objectivity with religious ritual and faith is both an inspiration and a symbol of faith itself. In contrast, so-called "freethinking" is not any freer than other types of thinking. "Freethinking" pretentiously inverts the notion of freedom so as to exclude other forms of thinking. Freethinkers hold that nothing is worthy of belief except the doctrines and evidence of Science! Science! Science! They are generally self-described skeptics whose core belief system is that skepticism is the only valid belief system. Excepting, of course, atheism, naturalism, moral relativism and, of course, science. Right, uh huh. Freethinkers! You think that you are free but you are perhaps more enslaved to dogma than most other ideologues. To be precise, "freethinking" is an absolutism.

Thinking holds the potential to set us free, but freedom is relative to the size of the intellectual pond in which we swim. Slaves to science or to atheism swim in ponds that, arguably, are not much bigger than the ponds in which religionists do their swimming. If you don't believe in the conventional wisdom of the current state of scientific knowledge then some of your beliefs may be easily dismissed, if not derided, as pseudoscience and without value. (§II.15) Freedom does indeed require a rational basis if it is to resist excessive bias, but which pond will produce greater freedom: the local swimming pond or the great oceans of the world? The inlet to the ocean of freedom is not a closed mind but, rather, a multi-perspectival attitude of plural perspectivism that encourages a good faith effort to overcome the limitations of our thinking; in that way we are made relatively freer. Spiritual thinkers, freethinkers, and all of us self-described thinkers must overcome our own thinking and the only way to do that is to muster the courage of self-examination and scrutiny by exposing ourselves to a plethora of perspectives. And so I am not really castigating "freethinking" any more than other preconditioned and pre-conceptualized forms of thinking. But the pretension of the word "freethinking" makes freethinkers an easy target.

Mea culpa! I confess to having committed an intentional hyperbole in suggesting that science is a small pond, but it is no hyperbole to say that what science does not know dwarfs what it does know. Swimming in the big pond of knowledge hardly requires the hubris of he who thinks he knows everything, but it does necessitate the humility in knowing that we know very little in the total scheme of things. This fundamental intellectual humility was articulated by Socrates and Lao-Tzu twenty-five hundred years ago, and the vast increase in the storehouse of human knowledge has not altered its relevancy even an iota. Not only is our knowledge tiny compared to what we do not know, but the more that we learn the less we know relative to the whole of knowledge because new knowledge creates new doubt, uncertainty and many, many new questions. The ever-growing volume of our unknowingness fills another whole pond of wisdom: the knowledge and awareness of not knowing. The universe is a very big pond indeed, and the moral universe, as well, is filled with never-ending uncertainty. I wasn't going to begin this section with a discussion concerning "freethinking," and I was even teetering on the idea of calling myself a "freethinker" but I then recognized that the current usage of the term—particularly its unhyphenated form, is very unlike the plural perspectivism that I advocate. Plural perspectivism is a far freer form of thinking than "freethinking" because it is intended to persistently encourage a consideration of alternative perspectives, and a constant reconsideration of presumed limitations. In contrast, "freethinking," as do all forms of dogma, forms barriers to emergent actuality by arbitrarily shutting out all unwelcome, paradigm-shifting perspectives.

Plural perspectivism is the anti-dogmatism, but it still must be prepared to overcome itself. It has an advantage because of its friendship with a multiplicity of perspectives that finds wisdom in many quarters, but a suspension of belief in one's own perspectives is necessary in order to adequately comprehend another's perspective. Then, with subsequent reattachment to multi-perspectival philosophy greater wisdom through the enlightenment of many ways may be realized. The significance of ritual is an example in which plural perspectivism must overcome itself. A person who practices meditation will often take great pains so that each meditation ritual is exactly alike: the room, the preparations, perhaps the time of day, the repetition of each breath, audible or silent vocalizations, or visualization are designed to make each session the same *in form*. This repetition hardly seems like fertile ground for discovering the uniqueness of experience, but the quieting of the mind can produce a fertile mind that, like a rich soil, produces creative insight and sensitivity. Thus it happens that ritual—the icon of traditionalism, can also be a fountain of change.

Intense focus on spiritual or ritual practice and prayer may very well reap a spiritual empowerment that an authentic plural perspectivism cannot ignore. Buddhism has been described as atheistic or non-theistic because it does not posit a deity, however, there is a distinction between God and divinity and Buddhism can be very well described as an expression of sacred divinity that is nonetheless atheistic. Some atheists consider themselves spiritual and are comfortable with the mood of some forms of Buddhism, although I think that this is less the case for self-described freethinkers. Some forms of Buddhism posit metaphysical principles such as the intermediate Bardo states of reality (in Tibetan Buddhism) that would not likely be supported by a freethinker who claims to be bounded by purely empirical and scientifically grounded reasoning. Some "freethinking" skeptics even think that hypnosis is impossible, but even if it is not always clear exactly how hypnosis works it quite clearly does work. And if hypnosis is rejected in a knee jerk, it is also quite unlikely that the implications of meditation rituals would be taken seriously. To a very large degree we create our own spiritual actualities. If you believe that nothing beyond the narrow confines of individual experience and strict empirical and scientific methodology can provide a basis for rational belief, then meditative and mystical reveries or speculations concerning reincarnation, for example, are hardly going to be granted admission into the proceedings of the rational mind. Of course, it is always possible that something profoundly unexplainable and spiritually suggestive could occur that awakens the freethinker from his or her dogmatic slumber.

I need a little ritual in my life; my plural perspectivism needs it; so does my soul and so I will work to overcome this deficiency.

As is the case with the *I Ching*, there are parallels between the three basic ethical dualisms and the Kabbalistic "tree of life." The Kabbalistic tree of life, as it is generally depicted, features three basic dualisms and its corresponding six poles ("Sefirot"), but there are also an additional four Sefirot configured along a central column or path. A total of 22 columns or paths interconnect the ten Sefirot. The tree of life represents the energy flow of the universe that enters into the uppermost Sefira on the tree of life called the Crown or *Keter* and descends to lower levels of Sefirot. The driving tension in the Kabbalistic tree of life, however, consists of the dualistic separations from the nonduaity that is Keter, which is the pure and indescribable emanation of *Ein-Sof* or God. The tensions between the dualistic oppositions must be overcome in order to attain greater consciousness so that a return to the unity or singularity of Keter, the highest level of human consciousness, is attainable. A consciousness of Keter may be compared to Kundalini consciousness and its complete unblocking of the Kundalini energy in yogic practice and meditation. Higher consciousness in Kabbalah is achievable by reconciling or repairing (tikkun) the dualistic separations from Keter in meditation and ethical practice. As in other mystical and spiritual practices a higher consciousness is achieved by harmonic balancing. With respect to the ethical principles discussed in this book, meditation can be a helpful tool in reflections that seek moral coherence and equipoise (§I.7). For example, exploring the myriad permutations of the basic ethical dualisms configured to the sixty-four *I Ching* hexagrams (§1.8) can help clarify a multitude of ethical perspectives in terms of intentionality, effectuality and the influence of convergent factors (§1.10). While I am not interested in making an excessive connection with meditation and the principles advanced in this book, I would like to suggest that meditation rituals can become powerful adjuncts to any creative enterprise including the art of living an ethical life.

Mystical traditions may or may not produce a deep insight into the nature of reality, but they certainly have the capacity to clear the mind and also to make it more receptive to creativity and novel ideas. Kabbalah, Gnosticism and Sufism in the West, and the *I Ching*, philosophical Taoism,

Zen Buddhism, Kundalini Yoga and Tantra in the East are prime examples. They tend to be unconventional but, of course, they each have their own rich traditions. While unconventional practices readily become traditional for their practitioners, an interesting thing about mystical traditions is their capacity to help resist conventional thinking. It was an old custom in the Kabbalistic tradition that only married men over 40 years of age were allowed to practice, because sufficient stability and social status were deemed essential for the practitioner of Kabbalah in order to deal with radical departures from traditional Judaism that it could potentially eventuate. From the perspective of multi-perspectival philosophy the value of mysticism is clear. The mystery, the immense size, the immense smallness, the grandeur, the violence, the beauty of the universe is awesome beyond description or understanding. It is understandable that such incomprehensibility sometimes finds its best expression in paradoxes such as Zen koans that convey truths in the form of seeming nonsensicality.

While rationality is, in the end, the greatest hope for human survival the question that must continually be asked is, "What is rational?" It is probably best not to answer that question *too* rationally because there are many correct answers and, yes, the irrational can sometimes be rational. The key to rationality, I think, has something to do with being able to see both "the forest and the trees" because in a great forest there may be a great diversity of trees, but it is also true that each tree has something special to say about the forest as a whole. So we should not be too quick to denounce a particular nonsensicality as irrational because in the end we may yet discover that it has utmost rational value. In the same vein, mystics are sometimes prone to prophesy. Prophesy may perhaps be relatively uncomplicated for a civilization that is capable of perceiving long-range developments through an understanding of convergent forces, and the relative balance or imbalance between technology and wisdom. But, no! Do not accuse me of suggesting that we throw away our philosophy books and our science and study only Nostradamus and biblical prophecy! I give you the extreme case for good reason. Prophesy is a byproduct of overly confident and overly linear thinking, and its claims are often laughable. But an open mind balanced with a healthy skepticism will not arbitrarily reject opinion without first subjecting itself to rational principles that are themselves free of arrogance and fake certitude.

II.48

Speculations on Time and Spirit

The speculations on time that are expressed here are no more than the fantasy of a non-scientist. And my speculations on spirit are in part based on a "what if" scenario should my fantasy on the nature of time have some affinity with the truth. This disclaimer aside, I freely admit that in my opinion the following falls into the category of reasonable speculation.

Imagine how time travel could—should it ever become reality, alter our view of history and, in turn, our moral and spiritual conceptions. The past would meet the future, fictions of the past that have been hardened into "history" would be corrected, and the present would more completely reflect from within itself the truth of the past. One does not need to be a conspiracy theorist to acknowledge the probability that some important and critical historical "facts" are false. How would the moral actuality of the present respond to dialectical pressures created by changes to our understanding of the past? Corrections to false history and the enlightenment that results, of course, have often changed human consciousness both gradually as well as with great turbulence and rapidity. Should the substance of this speculative fantasy concerning time ever be realized, however, the shift in consciousness would be most dramatic.

Modern theories and speculations concerning time travel often begin as an attempt to explain or resolve the issue of the "grandfather paradox," which poses the question of what would happen if a time traveler were to travel to a time before his parents were born and then kill his grandfather. The point of the unlikely situation posed by the question is to boldly exemplify the problem of contemplating the consequences of changing the past. Some have speculated that if the grandfather paradox were to someday be put to the test the result would cause the negation of the time traveler's own existence. Others have speculated that by altering the past we could potentially tear the fabric of space-time and cataclysmically put an end to the universe as we know it. A current popular view of the grandfather paradox and, I think, the view favored by most physicists, derives from quantum theory and explains away the awkward difficulties of the grandfather paradox. According to this theory, if the past were to be altered the timeline would split so that one timeline would preserve the existence of the time traveler, while the other timeline would produce a completely distinct but parallel reality in which our wayward grandpa killer would cease to exist. For all practical intents and purposes, the possibility of timeline splitting would create a parallel universe of which, it is theorized, could be unlimited in number. In any case, the splitting of timelines would neutralize the grandfather paradox. Arguably, however, timeline splitting would not truly constitute "time travel" because once any alteration to the past occurs, no matter how slight, it would bump the time traveler off his current timeline and he could never return to the home that he left because, for e.g., if he killed his grandfather he would be separated from the timeline of his origins and, perhaps, he would find himself on a different timeline in which he would have no lineage. The slightest, most incidental change would bump the time traveler onto another timeline that would prevent him from ever returning to the home from which he had originally departed; for him, the home or his origins no longer exists even if the changes are minute or insignificant. If absolutely no changes of any sort were made no parallel timeline would be created and then, and only then, could the time traveler return to his home in the same timeline from which he had originally made his departure.

Infinite time splitting into alternative realities seems unlikely. However, there is another theoretical approach to time travel that could avoid the grandfather paradox. I believe that the grandfather paradox is a part of a more general problem that could ultimately make information gathering from the past possible. If, in the year 2011 a chair manufactured in 1960 were to have been transported backwards in time to the year 1962, the same atomic material would co-exist in the form of two distinct chairs that are also the *same* chair! There will be some slight atomic decay in the chair coming from 2011 compared with the chair vintage 1962 but they would be composed of the *same* atoms and the *same* subatomic particles.

This would appear to violate the physical "law" of the conservation of mass-energy because the total mass-energy in the universe would be increased. In terms of the theory of quantum time splitting, would the mere transportation of matter into the past *by itself* be sufficient to produce a new timeline? The speculation becomes even more compelling when the ramifications of quantum "entanglement" are considered. The principle of "non-locality" suggests a fundamental interconnectedness in the universe. When two subatomic particles come into contact with each other they seem to influence each other irrespective of the distance that separates them. However, John Gribbin points out that, at least in accordance with the Big Bang theory, all particles may have been entangled from the very start, and each particle of existence "knows" about the others since they were all in contact with each other at the moment of the Big Bang![126] It seems to follow that if time travel were to occur so that it places a person or other object in the past, it would result in the occurrence of duplicate atomic and subatomic material that would not merely be copies of each other but would be *un-individuated duplicates* that have the same cosmic identity or imprint. Whenever an object is transported to the past the un-individuated duplication would occur. What would happen to the quantum communication or information sharing between entangled particles when, suddenly, some of them lose their unique identity? Would the cosmic communication become confused, thereby messing up the cosmic order and the fundamental structure of spacetime?

A solution to time splitting, i.e., for addressing problems involving the grandfather paradox, the law of the conservation of mass-energy, and quantum entanglement might be an alternate reality that is quite different from that which would, theoretically, be produced by time splitting. What if un-individuated duplicates were ejected into another dimension rather than a new timeline? If that were to be the case, perhaps inter-dimensional *observation* of the past would be possible even if interaction with the past is not. The introduction of un-individuated duplicates would have to be dealt with somehow. The law of the conservation of mass-energy would be either disproved or otherwise explained. An "observers dimension" would preserve the singularity of our particular universe rather than require an infinite potential for splitting into alternative timelines. The introduction of un-individuated duplicates would be ejected into an observers dimension that is not a separate parallel universe but, rather, a sort of extra-dimensional receptacle for rejected mass-energy that is incompatible with the coherence of the dimensions that we occupy. In this extra dimension a time traveler could "see" but not interact with the past. Nature has endowed the body of animals with the ability to reject foreign matter or invading organisms that enter into it; perhaps there may be some analogy with inter-dimensional ejections within the cosmic body itself?

This hypothetical extra-dimension could be an observatory of the past and of the physically possible future? Is it the fifth dimension? Is this "observatory" a physical dimension of mind or consciousness? Knowledge of the past and to a lesser extent of the future would approach the empirical status of the present. The essence of intelligent consciousness (or mind) is self-correction. Time travel would be a journey into the extended mind in search of the empirical past and the empirically possible future making it possible to self-correct the present. But the dimension of mind is the realm of the real, the possible and the imaginary. Time belongs to the physical world, but the contents of mind are free flowing and timeless. Mental phenomena can be characterized by free-flowing interactions between images and ideas, but it is also the realm of logic and reason. But physical law has no authority over mental phenomena. In the dimension of mind reality, possibility and imagination are indeterminate and exist side-by-side.

History is the collective self-reflection of our past. This is another way of saying that history is the relationship between the collective present that is the *Self* with its collective past that becomes its *Other*. Understanding the past empowers the understanding of ourselves by enabling us to better know who we are and what we may become. If someday it becomes possible to send a human being or surrogate recording devices via time travel to a specific time and place in order to observe the past or the future, humanity will be enormously empowered with undreamed of wisdom, compassion and justice. The knowledge and the wisdom gained would afford an opportunity that would be no less welcome than the correction of a person's faulty gene: the defense of present conditions justified by false history is no more credible than the failure to correct a genetic defect on the absurd grounds that a person's biological history has some sort of intrinsic justification. Historical truth could clear the path for a happier future, and the fantasy imagined here, were it ever to be realized, would help to heal history of falsehoods. Consciousness and historical truth would become unified and a new moral actuality would be born. But we cannot wait for the development of a technology of this hypothetical glorious end times, or what is perhaps better stated as a new beginning for time. We must make due with the knowledge that our truths are never more than pragmatic truths and that some of them, perhaps comprising important and critical domains of our knowledge, are likely to be false. But the purpose of this little foray into science fiction is not to pin human destiny on hopes that time travel may in the future become reality but, rather, to reflect upon the fragile relationship between history, possibility and morality.

The foregoing speculative fantasy, if there is truth to its main features, would point to a sort of convergence between science and spirituality. It does not necessarily suggest an afterlife, but the dead would speak to us via time travelers who observe history through the window of a fifth dimension. It does not necessarily suggest reincarnation, but the ability to verify the truths and falsehoods of history would allow for a karmic-like self-correction that would be a dramatic past life therapy for the world. And yet, this fantasy, if true, would not be spirituality. Would it supplant spirituality and be the final and definitive victory of science over religion? I don't think so. Even the achievement of time travel to the past, while immensely empowering, would leave holes to be filled in those who suffer from a sense of soullessness. And while the reconciliation of past wrongs would benefit humanity it could not in itself be a cure for all who suffer when the suffering is beyond simple cause-and-effect; wisdom deeply embraced then becomes the only cure. But let us go even further and suppose that the grandfather paradox is incorrect, that the past and the future can actively meet and allow travel between the past and the future, so that even those who are about to die could simply skip to the future and receive their cure…but this is now becoming, even for this writer, ridiculous! I will not place a wager for any such total transcendence; but who knows?

Critics of mind-body dualism and theorists positing the reducibility of mind to empirical facts generally beg the question of the "hard problem" of defining what consciousness is by simply stating in so many words that *whatever* consciousness is, is ultimately reducible to scientific explanation. Explaining consciousness is going to require more than demonstrating how a living being or a machine might acquire the quality of consciousness. It is doubtful that understanding the science of *what enables consciousness* will produce an understanding of *what consciousness is*. In all likelihood, the only possible means of understanding consciousness will require a further convergence in the relationship between science and spirituality, mysticism *and* the "pseudoscience" of parapsychology that many scientific freethinkers love to deride. A co-evolution of consciousness and matter can be speculated. Mass-energy and consciousness are like two sides of a coin. Like mind and body, like the infant mind and the infant body and the communication between the two, evolution—material and conscious— develops in stages beginning with the organization of energy into subatomic, atomic and molecular compositions. We cannot with certainty say that there was a Big Bang but let us assume that it did in fact occur and that the universe was *born*. And the baby universe with its infant consciousness somehow formed the first wave or subatomic particle, and then the first atom, then the first molecule, and during this process even the "laws of nature" evolved or emerged, then the first gases, the first liquids, solids, galaxies, suns, planets, DNA. And from all of these things finally life too was born. And like the miraculous first step or the first sentence that a baby utters the universal conscious mind begins to evolve, gradually, beginning with the Big Bang, the entangled memory of subatomic particles and the *trauma* of its birth. On this basis, the universe is conscious and conscious- ness is as much a part of the universe as suns, planets and our very bones. If we will ever understand consciousness it will be through a unity and a fusion of hard science with the spiritual, the mystical and the parapsychological.

Oh mystical reverie! Could there be a reconnection of time and mind and space? What might come to pass by the fusion of science and spirit? Might human destiny include the reunification of the past with the present and, if only in spirit, with the living and the dead? Ah, this is only a dream that many have dreamed and, as you know well, I am a dreamer. But is not science now able to monitor our dreams?

II.49

Pascal's Wager

In his incomplete and posthumously published *Pensées* (1671) Blaise Pascal suggested that since knowledge concerning the truth or falsity of God's existence is impossible to ascertain with any certainty, belief in God's existence is nevertheless justified in the form of a wager. In modern terms, the wager might be described as a risk-benefit analysis:

> Let us weigh the gain and the loss in wagering that God is. Let us estimate these two chances. If you gain, you gain all; if you lose, you lose nothing. Wager, then, without hesitation that He is.[127]

Pascal was attempting to reconcile his deeply rational mind with his equally deep spiritual and religious faith. Contrary to the rigidly inflexible mentality of freethinkers this is a highly rational approach because, as Pascal argues, it is unwise to arbitrarily dismiss that which we cannot disprove. We cannot prove or disprove beliefs that are grounded in non-empirical or non-scientific methods such as revelation or mystical insight. However, Pascal fails to build a sustainable or meaningful bridge between faith and reason.

Pascal's first problem concerns the nature of what it is that he is wagering on. The question, "What is God?" must first be answered because until an answer is provided the wagerer doesn't know on what he places the wager. Pascal defines God theistically in terms of the familiar supreme being of the Bible. But clearly, the existence of God is not an either/or proposition because beliefs in God vary widely. For example, official Catholic doctrine (in Pascal's time as in the present) rejects belief in reincarnation; therefore, would a wager that both 'God' and reincarnation are existent realities rob the wagerer from his hope for gain? Let's consider the far more radical case in which a particular person's conception of 'God' has been influenced by a Satanic upbringing, which taught that Satan is the true ruler of the universe and that Evil is the only path to salvation. What if the Satanist believes that 'God' is subordinate to Satan and that He seeks to overturn Satan's rule and, therefore, his belief in God could end with the eternal disfavor of the Devil. In this devilish set of circumstances, basing your decision in terms of Pascal's wager calculated by the "odds" would suggest that you should believe in Satan and act in accordance with Satanic principles and ritual! By adopting the arbitrary logic of his wager Pascal would have no choice but to conclude that it would be foolhardy to bet against Satan because, clearly, he would derive maximum benefit by siding with him. Perhaps you say that this argument is absurd, but in retort I say that by linking eternal bliss to a wager that is made dependent upon a particular definition of that which is, admittedly, unknowable will guarantee absurd consequences.

For my part, I will freely and happily wager that God, if She or He or It exists, rewards those who devote their lives to *doing good for its own sake* and base their actions on a deep appreciation of love and an even deeper quest for understanding the meaning of love in the unfolding of human life. The notion of expecting everlasting reward for merely believing in a particular conception or doctrinally forced definition of God is and would, from my perspective, be an astronomical affront to God. The Wager suggests a supremely vain God, and one that is equally shallow in his reprimand or eternal rejection merely because some of his mortal creations disbelieve in his existence. But does belief in any conception or set of beliefs concerning God have *any* import whatsoever compared to the enormous blessings that are gotten by those whose only goal is to act with good intention, rational intelligence and conformance with "love thy neighbor as thyself."

Given the circumstances and the religious culture of his day, Pascal's wager may have been reasonably good medicine for a culture requiring the fear of eternal damnation (or the denial of eternal salvation). Pascal's logically articulated wager to help nudge thoughtful persons in a spiritual or ethical direction was perhaps good medicine. But while this may or may not be a defense of Pascal, his wager cannot work in our contemporary age. This rationalization is much like the one advanced in rationalizing the biblical God's terror tactics unleashed upon Abraham by commanding that he sacrifice his son, Isaac (§II.38); both rationalizations, however, offer no assistance to people in the modern day. Deeply spiritual and moral action can never be grounded in *fear* of God but only in the love, compassion and moral strength that a belief in God, while unnecessary, may inspire. But is believing in something done out of fear—as exemplified by the acceptance of The Wager, courage? Nonsense! A courage based only on fear is nothing but doublespeak; it is weakness, not courage.

It would be most strange if the Supreme Ruler of the Universe should have such an ultra paper thin skin that he requires a continuous, nauseating "Praise God!" or "God-fearing" and all forms of constant and obsequious praise, and who with Divine hubris will smite or eternally condemn anyone insufficiently obsequious. Praise the Lord! I would be willing to wager an infinite sum on an infinite being who has a much thicker skin, but my infinite dearth of funding saves me from making the wager. Better yet, if I had the infinite dough I would joyfully place my bet on the side of the Overman, or at least on a dialectically self-empowered, selfless and self-interested Overman (as opposed to Nietzsche's unbalanced version). Nietzsche's "God is dead!" remark is a rhetorical device to spur humanity to overcome itself, and I wager on the Overman to provide the overcoming that God would praise! I wager that a God who may have created us in his own image would have done so in order that we be noble creatures who would act with a devotion for good, for compassion and for self-realization of our greatest potential, in love, without fear or dependency on obsequious worship and idolatry. I wager on the side of a God who condemns not only the worship of idols but also the idolatry that profanely converts even him into, merely, another idol. And is it not idolatry that has promoted war in the name of religion and in the name of God?

But should human knowledge someday transcend the barrier of time we may each need to contemplate a very different sort of wager than Pascal's. I propose here a wager that is not an impossible metaphysical calculation but, rather, a calculation of humanity's potential in the virtual infinity of time. While some criminals and morally corrupt individuals may be able to evade justice and prevent the discovery of truth in the present, they may be unable to hide from the future. The premise being set here is less farfetched than Pascal's. A wager based on linking eternal bliss with a particular belief in a deity requires an arrogance and presumption of faith. On the other hand, wagering on the eventuality of some sort of time travel based on humanity's technological and intellectual development is a vastly more likely bet than Pascal's wager because, a) it would based on a projection of human development that does not entail knowing the mind of God and, b) the wager need not state how time travel will be achieved but only that it will be realized even if only in the distant future. 'Distant' could be one hundred years, one thousand years, many thousands or tens of thousands of years, more? But I submit that my wager on the future eventuality of time travel and its ramifications for justice is a wager worth making. "Wager then, without hesitation!" The prospect of time travel and potential intercessions from the future may give wrongdoers something other than an eternal barring from the Heavenly abode to think about. Death may be an all too shallow place to hide. Are you willing to wager against humanity's future and its terrestrial court?

II.50

The Meaning of Faith

Faith is a leap to a level beyond ordinary trust. Faith in oneself comes with the power of positive thinking and is the heart of freedom and overcoming. It can produce incredible acts of courage, amazing athletic feats in the height of competition, the will to create and invent, decisiveness and motivation. And for many, faith in oneself is a basis of spirituality that can glorify the potential for individual greatness that resides in the heart of every human being; it can also be the subjective link to a sense of the mystical. The Buddhists call this the true self, and for many others it is simply the ineffable sense or faith in what is traditionally referred to as one's soul.

Faith in others extends to groups or organizational associations. You join a young startup company because you believe in its mission and you are impressed with the principal owners and the management team. You had an opportunity to earn more money by working for other firms but you have faith that this young company is the path to your success. Unfortunately, the success hoped for does not materialize. Perhaps you have lost your faith in the fledgling business and also perhaps in those who managed it. But it is also possible that even though the enterprise was not successful, your faith in those involved in the business will remain unshaken and you would work with the same group again if future opportunities should arise. Part of faith is in the integrity and intelligence of a person or an organization that learns from error and overcomes past failure.

There have been connections between faith in God and faith in nations. The link has often been unfortunate, because faith in country and faith in God have at times been disastrously conflated in order to justify the most ungodly acts of senseless war, death, suffering and destruction. Confusing faith in nation and faith in God has the most heinous potential. Lincoln knew this well; he humbly prayed that his leadership be on God's side, he did not have the temerity or audacity to pray that God be on his. Who are we to divine the mind of God and thereby justify wanton acts of death and destruction! However, faith in a great nation can be warranted when it is founded on the belief that the government, leadership and citizenry are dedicated to an unbounded love that guides conduct along a path of dignity, moral intentionality and virtue. Faith in a nation must, most of all, be a humble faith that acknowledges the potential for error and the consequences of the misguided use of power. If faith in a nation is morally invested, it will be in the potential for true greatness that becomes possible when the national will is dedicated to the expression of loving intention in all dealings with its citizenry and with other nations. Faith by its very nature must always be steeped with humility. Because faith is a leap beyond the knowable, with great humility it acknowledges that sometimes good intentions fail, or our actions may not always be "on God's side" but with resilience and courage we can make things right.

We can see how faith is a belief in an active principle whose unpredictability is its strength for rising to the occasion and mastering situations in which set rules and prescribed solutions may not apply. However, faith can extend beyond individuals to dogma and ideology. Ideology seeks to supplant true wisdom by substituting broad precepts and theories as the basis of faith. Many millions have died for their faith in particular ideologies. Faith in radical capitalism fills the American airwaves ad nauseam as its proponents preach the gospel that their currently in vogue conservatism will solve all economic and social problems. Marxist-Leninist ideologues still promote their version of a reign of terror that they would call justice. Religious extremists are seen promulgating an exceedingly cruel subjection of women as a virtue, or displaying more concern with scriptural prophecy than lasting peace. In ideological faith we see the glorification of the mindless stupidity of some who dance around in praise of their sinful dogma and sacrilegiously Praise God! Praise the Lord! Praise Allah! And this is their faith. It is as if God were an insecure despot in need of constant praise lest he unleash his jealous venom. It is time to leave ideology in the dustbin of history so that we may finally begin the long march of true freedom from the shackles of dogma.

What does faith in God mean? This can be a very open question. To some, God can even be the very idol that the God of the Bible condemns, but if you are to have *faith* in God then idol worship is likely to be a faith easily lost. Your idols will be swiftly shown to be the blocks of stone, wood or rigid and breakable ideologies that they are. But the various faiths in the God of the great religions, also, need to be sustainable by more than ideological doctrine that is continually crammed into the brains of believers from childhood until death. While there is no escaping that we all have belief systems, they do not require dogmatic conformity or coercion in order for us to appreciate their value. Does faith in the power and ultimate victory of good over evil sound like dogma? Tenets concerning good and evil can, in religious ideology, be attached to specific conceptions or beliefs in God, but this is not *my* faith in the power of good over evil or any notion of God. My interpretation of the concept of God is informal, but since no one has ever defined God in a manner satisfactory to all believers it may be used in its generality, which I take to be a transcendent principle, essence, mind, spirit, consciousness, creator that is in some manner an underlying force in the universe and of life. But faith built upon ideology is ideology and nothing more, and faith in an ideology is not a faith in God. Faith in a religion is not faith in God but only faith in an ideology. Faith transcends any doctrine and it consists of feelings as much as of belief. Faith in God cannot pretend to be scientific or it will be something that it is not. Faith in God is attached to the Good and to morality and right conduct, but this alone does not comprise faith or explain it. Faith in God is most of all a deep form of conscious belief that merges with subconscious feeling and conviction, often with great intuitive force, concerning the Oneness of which morality and the Good are primary expressions. Faith in God, when stripped of all ideology and doctrine, is the ever evolving consciousness of what is good versus that which is not good or in the worst case evil, and that by virtuous striving we may believe or feel that our faith inches closer to God's consciousness and its expression of love in the world.

Faith in moral and ethical progress is faith in the ability of human beings and all rational beings to be in harmony with the universe. This faith may be consistent with classical Taoism, Stoicism, mysticism and other mystical or spiritual systems. Living in harmony with the universe without ideology is always an open question. Harmony can ultimately be defined by its moral coherence and yet the degree of its actualization will always be disputable. An entrepreneur's life can be more harmonic and morally coherent than that of a monk, and any prejudice towards one over the other is dogma pure and simple. Religious beliefs in Heaven or Nirvana cannot be validated or confirmed in this life, and the slippery loopholes of theology insulate it from refutation. But *faith in theology is an ideology; it is not faith in God.* Faith and any particular religion or set of religious doctrines is not a faith in God, but only a particular faith in an ideology that purports to know something about God. Maybe there is a spiritual validation of our lives or maybe there is none to be had but faith must transcend its unknowing. In our unknowing we can still have faith because faith in non-dogmatic and non-ideological principles applied with humility, dedicated to loving intention, and practiced with mindful openness to error and correction is the indomitable path to knowing that we have done our best. Faith in God cannot, in good faith, presuppose doctrines that pretend divine knowledge. Such a pretense would be un-philosophic and meaningless. But as with wisdom, faith has no final destination.

Appendix

Fig. 2

Perspectives of the Basic Ethical Dualisms
Configured by *I Ching* Hexagrams*

Major Self-Regarding Hexagrams

1	9	10	13	14	28	30	37

38	43	44	49	50	57	58	61

Minor Self-Regarding Hexagrams

6	12	17	20	21	25	31	33

35	42	45	47	53	56	59	64

Major Other-Regarding Hexagrams

2	3	4	7	8	15	16	23

4	27	29	39	40	51	52	62

Minor Other-Regarding Hexagrams

5	11	18	19	22	26	32	34

36	41	46	48	54	55	60	63

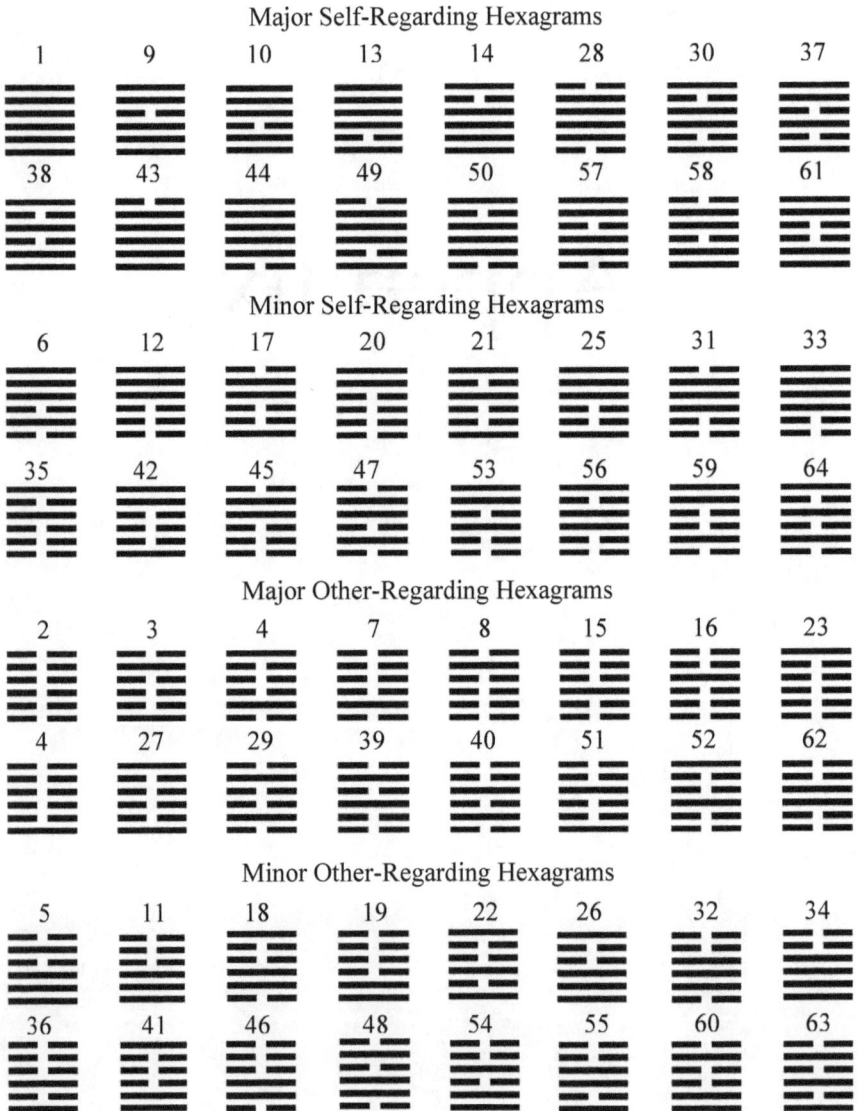

*Numbers reflect the sequencing assigned in the *I Ching*. (Images courtesy of
Ben Finney. Source: http://en.wikipedia.org/wiki/I_Ching_hexagrams)

Fig. 3

Text of Notarized Affidavit by Harvey Fletcher
See document image on next page.

I, Harvey Fletcher, being of sound mind, at the age of 94, on this 25th day of May, 1979, in the City of Provo, Utah, do make the following declaration of my own free will, to wit:

According to my memory, in the year 1928, while I was employed by Bell Telephone Labs in New York, I was invited to Utah by officials of the Mormon Church with the approval of my employer to observe a demonstration of a device invented by T. Henry Moray of Salt Lake City, Utah. The device was contained in a small wooden box about 18" x 24" x24" long, which I, personally, inspected and determined that it was connected to no prime mover but only to an antenna and a ground.

The electrical load on the device consisted of 12 clear 75 Watt 110 Volt light bulbs and a 500 Watt electric flat iron, also 110 Volt. When the antenna and ground were connected, and certain adjustments made by the inventor, internal to the box, the loads were electrically operated. I was permitted to inspect the interior of the box and certain of the schematic drawings pertaining to the circuits involved in the device. I was not permitted to inspect a plug-in unit which was removed and held in the palm of the inventor's hand which he stated was the most proprietary part of the apparatus.

I did not know how the device functioned and do not know today, but I do know that it did function for the several hours of time that I observed it. I could discern no batteries, and could observe no other known methods of inducing electric power into the box or its loads.

Signed this 25th day of May, 1979.

Harvey Fletcher

(see image of original document below)

Fig. 3 (continued). Harvery Fletcher's signed affidavit.

DECLARATION

I, __Harvey Fletcher__ , being of sound mind, at the age of 94,
on this 25th day of May, 1979, in the City of Provo, Utah, do
make the following declaration of my own free will, to wit:

According to my memory, in the year 1928, while I was employed
by Bell Telephone Labs in New York, I was invited with the
approval of my employer to observe a demonstration of a device
invented by T. Henry Moray of Salt Lake City, Utah. The device
was contained in a small wooden box about 18" x 24" x 24" long,
which I, personally inspected and determined that it was
connected to no prime mover but only to an antenna and a ground.

The electrical load on the device consisted of 12 clear 75 Watt
110 Volt light bulbs and a 500 Watt electric flat iron, also
110 Volt. When the antenna and ground were connected, and
certain adjustments made by the inventor, internal to the box,
the loads were electrically operated. I was permitted to
inspect the interior of the box and certain of the schematic
drawings pertaining to the circuits involved in the device.
I was not permitted to inspect a plug-in unit which was removed
and held in the palm of the inventor's hand which he stated was
the most proprietory part of the apparatus.

I did not know how the device functioned and do not know today,
but I do know that it did function for the several hours of
time that I observed it. I could discern no batteries, and
could observe no other known methods of inducing electric power
into the box or its loads.

Signed this 25th day of May, 1979.

                                    _Harvey Fletcher_____
                                      Harvey Fletcher

STATE OF   UTAH   )
                  } ss.
COUNTY OF UTAH   )

Subscribed and sworn to before me this 25th day of May, 1979.

                                    _____
                                         Notary Public
                                    Residing in Salem, Utah

My commission expires
16 April 1983

Courtesy of T. Henry Moray Foundation.
This document is currently available for viewing or download at:
http://thmoray.org/images/affidavit.pdf

Endnotes

1. Alan Watts, *Taoism: Way Beyond Seeking* (Boston: Charles E.Tuttle Co., 1997) p. 75-76
2. Friedrich Nietzsche, *Thus Spoke Zarathustra*, trans. Walter Kaufmann (New York: The Modern Library, 1995) p. 94
3. Immanuel Kant, "On a Supposed Right to Lie because of Philanthropic Concerns" in *Grounding for the Metaphysics of Morals*, trans. James W. Ellington (Indianapolis/Cambridge: Hacking Publishing Company, 1993) p. 65
4. Douglas Hofstadter, *Gödel, Escher, Bach: An Eternal Golden Braid* (New York, Vintage Books, 1979) p. 17-19
5. Friedrich Nietzsche, trans. and ed. Walter Kaufmann, *Beyond Good and Evil* in *Basic Writings of Nietzsche* (New York: The Modern Library, 1992) p. 205-206
6. Dave Elman, *Hypnotherapy* (Glendale, CA: Westwood Publishing Co., 1964) p. 16
7. Ibid., p. 27
8. G.W.F. Hegel, trans. J. Sibree, *The Philosophy of History* (New York: Dover Publications, 1956) p. 99
9. Roland Barthes, trans. Stephen Heath, "The Death of the Author" in *Image – Music – Text* (New York: Hill and Wang, 1977) p. 146
10. Ibid., p. 145
11. Jean-Paul Sartre, trans. Bernard Frechtmann, *Existentialism and Human Emotions* (New York: Citadel Press, 1985) p. 33
12. Ibid., p. 32
13. Ibid., p. 17
14. Immanuel Kant, *Foundations of the Metaphysics of Morals*, trans. Lewis White Beck (New York: The Bobbs-Merrill Company, 1969) p. 21
15. For further reading, see Stephen Darwall, *The British Moralists and the Internal 'Ought': 1640—1740* (Cambridge: Cambridge University Press, 1995)

16. Oliver Sacks, *An Anthropologist on Mars*: *Seven Paradoxical Tales* (New York: Alfred A. Knopf, 1995) p. 114-115

17. "The impossibility of violating the duty of self-love is already presupposed by the supreme commandment of Christian morals, 'Thou shalt love thy neighbor as thyself,' according to which the love that each cherishes for himself is assumed beforehand as the maximum and the condition of all other love."Arthur Schopenhauer, *On the Basis of Morality*, trans. E.F.J. Payne (Indianapolis/Cambridge: Hackett Publishing Company, 1995) p. 58-59

18. cf. Darwall, *The British Moralists and the Internal 'Ought': 1640—1740* p. 128-130

19. Ludwig Wittgenstein, *Philosophical Investigations*, trans. G.E.M. Anscombe (New York: The Macmillan Company, 1953) para. 580

20. William James, "The Moral Philosopher and Moral Life," in *The Will to Believe and Other Essays in Popular Philosophy* (New York: Dover Publications, 1956) p. 201

21. Arthur Schopenhauer, *On the Basis of Morality*, p. 172

22. Friedrich Nietzsche, trans. and ed. Walter Kaufmann, *On the Genealogy of Morals* in *Basic Writings of Nietzsche* (New York: The Modern Library, 1992) p. 455

23. Friedrich Nietzsche, trans. and ed. Walter Kaufmann, *Ecce Homo* in Basic Writings of Nietzsche (New York: The Modern Library, 1992) p. 729 (Nietzsche is quoting himself in *Twilight of the Idols*).

24. Friedrich Nietzsche, trans. and ed. Walter Kaufmann, *Genealogy of Morals* in *Basic Writings of Nietzsche*, p. 558

25. Friedrich Nietzsche, *Will to Power*, editor Walter Kaufmann, trans. Walter Kaufmann and R.J. Hollingdale (New York: Vintage Books, 1967) p. 291

26. Friedrich Nietzsche, *Genealogy of Morals*, trans. and ed. Walter Kaufmann, in *Basic Writings of Nietzsche* (New York: The Modern Library, 1992) p. 555

27. Isaiah Berlin, *The Crooked Timber of Humanity* (Princeton: Princeton University Press, 1990) p. 12

28. William James, "The Moral Philosopher and Moral Life" in *The Will to Believe and other essays in popular philosophy,* p. 209

29. Isaiah Berlin, "Two Concepts of Liberty" in *Four Essays on Liberty* (Oxford: Oxford University Press, 1969) p. 126-127

30. For an illustration of substituting the Star of David hexagrams for the *I Ching* hexagrams, see: http://kairos.laetusinpraesens.org/bagua_0_h_6

31. Aristotle, *Prior Analytics,* trans. A. J. Jenkinson, in *The Basic Works of*

Aristotle, Richard McKeon, ed., (New York: Random House, 1941) I 1, 24a26-29.

32. William, James, *A Pluralistic Universe* (Lincoln: University of Nebraska Press, 1996) P. 218-219

33. Immanuel Kant, *Foundations of the Metaphysics of Morals*, trans. Lewis White Beck (New York: The Bobbs-Merrill Company, 1969) p. 75-76

34. Ibid., p. 84

35. Robert Macintosh, *Hegel and Hegelianism* (Thoemmes Antiquarian Books: Bristol, 1990), p. 216. [A reprint of the 1903 edition.]

36. C.G. Jung, Forward: *The I Ching*, trans. Richard Wilhelm (Princeton: Princeton University Press, 1977) p. xxiii

37. Friedrich Nietzsche, *Beyond Good and Evil*, p. 330

38. For reading on the subject of the Amerindians and their loss of the lands they occupied, see Stuart Banner, *How the Indians Lost Their Land: Law and Power on the Frontier* (Cambridge: Harvard University Press, 2005)

39. Warren Earl Burger, *Wisconsin v. Yoder*, 406 U.S. 205 (1972)

40. William O. Douglas, *Wisconsin v. Yoder*, 406 U.S. 205 (1972)

41. Wing-Tsit Chan, *A Source Book in Chinese Philosophy* (Princeton: Princeton University Press, 1963) p. 189

42. Michel Foucault, *Madness and Civilization*, trans. Richard Howard (New York: Vintage Books, 1965) p. 99-100, quoting from Robert James' *A Medicinal Dictionary* (French translation)

43. Ibid., p. 289

44. William James, *Pragmatism* in *Pragmatism and The Meaning of Truth* (Cambridge: Harvard University Press, 1978) p. 35

45. Milton H. Erickson, *Life Reframing in Hypnosis: The Seminars, Workshops, and Lectures of Milton H. Erickson*, vol. II, ed. Ernest L. Rossi and Margaret O. Ryan (New York: Irvington Publishers, 1985) p. 205-206

46. Friedrich Nietzsche, trans. and ed. Walter Kaufmann, *Ecce Homo* in *Basic Writings of Nietzsche* (New York: The Modern Library, 1992) p. 747

47. Friedrich Nietzsche, trans. R.J. Hollindgdale, *The Anti-Christ* in *Twilight of the Idols* and *The Anti-Christ* (New York: Penguin Books, 1990) p. 98

48. Nietzsche, *Beyond Good and Evil*, p. 200

49. cf. Margaret Cheney, *Tesla: Man Out of Time* (New York: Simon & Schuster, 1981), source: p. 45-46, 63, 67, 72-74

50. Margaret Cheney, *Tesla: Man Out of Time*, p. 57

51. Friedrich Nietzsche, Beyond Good and Evil, p. 307

52. Herbert Spencer, *Social Statics* (New York: Robert Schalkenbach Foundation, 1995) p. 95

53. G. K. Chesterton, Illustrated London News (1924-04-19)

54. from Brian Josephson's webpages on the University of Cambridge website: http://www.tcm.phy.cam.ac.uk/~bdj10/articles/uninvite.html

55. Thomas S. Kuhn, *The Structure of Scientific Revolutions* (Chicago: The University of Chicago Press, 1996) p. 24

56. Michael Polanyi, *The Tacit Dimension* (Chicago: The University of Chicago Press, 1966) p. 65

57. Ibid. p. 71

58. National Cancer Institute at the National Institutes of Health http://www.cancer.gov/cancertopics/pdq/cam/milkthistle/HealthProfessional/page1

59. Barry Lynes, *The Cancer Cure that Worked* (S. Lake Tahoe, CA: BioMed Publishing Group, 1987) p. 54

60. Ibid. 105

61. Margaret Cheney, *Tesla: Man Out of Time,* p. 150

62. Anthony G. Holland, from "Rife-BarePlasmaExperimentsCompilation," posted on YouTube.com: http://www.youtube.com/watch?v=6rGrkz_8t5M

63. *From* "New Way to Kill Viruses: Shake Them to Death" by Michael Schirber, Courtesy of Live Science, livescience.com, http://www.livescience.com/7472-kill-viruses-shake-death.html

64. cf. Barry Lynes, *The Cancer Cure that Worked,* source ref: p. 60-61

65. A. Walter, "Royal Raymond Rife, A Timeline," *Educate-Yourself,* http://educate-yourself.org/cn/rifetimelinemay1998.shtml

66. cf. Barry Lynes, *The Cancer Cure that Worked,* source: p. 29, 60-61

67. cf. Barry Lynes, *The Cancer Cure that Worked,* source: p. 29-30, 96-99

68. cf. Barry Lynes, *The Cancer Cure that Worked,* source: p. 127-135

69. Barry Lynes, *The Cancer Cure that Worked,* 97-98

70. American Cancer Society, "Electromagnetic Therapy" (4/18/2011) http://www.cancer.org/Treatment/TreatmentsandSideEffects/ComplementaryandAlternativeMedicine/ManualHealingandPhysicalTouch/electromagnetic-therapy

71. *Wilk v. American Medical Ass'n,* 671 F. Supp. 1465 (1987), United States District Court, N.D. Illinois, E.D., September 25, 1987

72. Nature Communications http://www.nature.com/ncomms/journal/v2/n3/full/ncomms1211.html ; "Optical virtual imaging at 50 nm lateral resolution with a white-light nanoscope" (or search title at http://www.manchester.ac.uk/aboutus/search/)

73. Eurekalert "Microscope could 'solve the cause of viruses' " http://www.eurekalert.org/pub_releases/2011-03/uom-mc022411.php

74. Ibid.

75. A. Walter, "Royal Raymond Rife, A Timeline," Courtesy of Educate-Yourself, http://educate-yourself.org/cn/rifetimelinemay1998.shtml

76. Moray B. King, *The Energy Machine of T. Henry Moray: Zero-Point Energy & Pulsed Plasma Physics* (Kempton, Illinois: Adventures Unlimited Publications, 2005) p. 21

77. Jeane Manning, "Gunfire in the Laboratory: T. Henry Moray and the Free Energy Machine" in *Suppressed Inventions and Other Discoveries* by Jonathan Eisen (The Berkeley Publishing Company: New York, 1999) p. 450

78. Moray B. King, *The Energy Machine of T. Henry Moray*, p. 17

79. Jeane Manning, "Gunfire in the Laboratory: T. Henry Moray and the Free Energy Machine" in *Suppressed Inventions and Other Discoveries*, p. 451-455

80. Wikipedia.com http://en.wikipedia.org/wiki/Harvey_Fletcher

81. T. Henry Moray Foundation (thmoray.org)
For more information, visit:
http://www.thmoray.org or email: moray52@earthlink.com
cf. John E. Moray, *The Sea of Energy in Which the Earth Floats*, 2012 (first printed in 1930 as *Beyond the Light Rays* by T. Henry Moray)

82. Steven E. Jones, "What causes the anomalous excess heat? An hypothesis," Seminar given at the University of Missouri, October 25,2012.
http://pesn.com/2012/11/19/9602225_Steven_Jones_replica–Pons_and_Fleischmann _XS_
Heat_not_from_fusion/StevenJonesSeminarAtUnivMissouriOct2012.pdf

83. M. Ostrogorski, *Democracy and the Organization of Political Parties* Vol. II (New York: The Macmillan Company, 1902) p. 651

84. Alan Greenspan, "Gold and Economic Freedom" in *Capitalism: The Unknown Ideal* by Ayn Rand (New York: Signet, 1966) p. 107

85. Ibid.

86. Henry George, from the preface of *Progress and Poverty* (New York: Cosimo Classics, 2005) p. 5

87. Ibid. p. 240

88. Ibid. p. 255-256

89. Herbert Spencer, *Social Statics* (New York: Robert Schalkenbach Foundation, 1995) p. 112

90. Ibid.

91. Henry George, *Progress and Poverty*, p. 254

92. Ibid., p. 256

93. Ibid., p. 260-61

94. *The New York Times* (March 24, 2011), David Kocieniewski, "G.E.'S Strategies Let It Avoid Taxes Altogether." The article is also available

online at http://www.nytimes.com/2011/03/25/business/economy/
25tax.html?pagewanted=all

95. The only other legitimate forms government revenue, in addition to rental revenue, could perhaps be in the form of limited use fees and consumption taxes— but this would be a slippery slope that is best avoided.

96. Friedrich Nietzsche, *Thus Spoke Zarathustra*, p. 89

97. cf. Terry L. Anderson & Peter J. Hill, *The Not So Wild, Wild West*: *Property Rights on the Frontier* (Stanford: Stanford Economics and Finance, 2004)

98. Project Vote Smart. https://votesmart.org/public-statement/577124/reading-of-the-constitution#.Ufemuk6fybu

99. "During World War II, 212,000 of the 220,000 Jews who lived in Lithuania were murdered—the highest victim rate in Europe. A key factor was the widespread participation of volunteer local Nazi collaborators—a phenomenon which encompassed all strata of Lithuanian society from the clergy and intellectuals to its worst elements." -- in *The Jerusalem Post*, 05/01/2010 "No tolerance for false history" by Efraim Zuroff, http://www.jpost.com/Opinion/Op-EdContributors/Article.aspx?id=174425

100. Excepted from "Proposed Studies on the Implications of Peaceful Space Activities for Human Affairs," The Brookings Institution, source: The Enterprise Mission (enterprisemission.com) http://www.enterprisemission.com/images/brook-8.gif, p. 216

101. William James, *Pragmatism*, p. 42

102. cf. David Aaronovitch, *Voodoo Histories: The Role of the Conspiracy Theory in Shaping Modern History*, chapters 1 and 2 (New York: The Penguin Group, 2010)

103. David Aaronovitch, *Voodoo Histories: The Role of the Conspiracy Theory in Shaping Modern History*, p. 168-169

104. "...McCarthyism did more damage to the constitution than the American Communist Party ever did." – Ellen Schrecker, "Comments on John Earl Haynes', "The Cold War Debate Continues: A Traditionalist View of Historical Writing on Domestic Communism and Anti-Communism," in *Journal of Cold War Studies*, Volume 2, Number 1 (Winter 2000) http://www.fas.harvard.edu/~hpcws/comment15.htm

105. *9/11 Explosive Evidence – Experts Speak Out*, Architects & Engineers for 9//11 Truth (ae911truth.org).
A video is currently available for purchase online at http://www.ae911truth.org/ and also currently viewable on YouTube.com.

106. *9-11 Investigator*, First Edition 2010, First Edition, v1.2, page
Also available online: www2.ae911truth.org/events/so-cal-

tour/.../AEstreet_9_Inside2.pdf

cf. Jim Hoffman, "Building a Better Mirage: NIST's 3-Year $20,000,000 Cover-Up of the Crime of the Century." Currently available online: http://9-11research.wtc7.net/essays/nist/index.html

107. Ibid, p. 3-4

cf. Scholars for 9/11 Truth & Justice, http://stj911.org.

Also see Dr. Steven E. Jones' lecture:

http://www.youtube.com/watch?v=3pL0M5ST8jY

108. Ibid. p. 2

109. Ibid. p. 2-4

110. Ibid. p. 3-4

111. Karl Marx, *A Contribution to the Critique of Political Economy*, trans. S.W. Ryazanskaya, editor Maurice Dobb (New York: International Publishers, Inc., 1970) p. 21

112. Ibid.

113. Ibid.

114. Ibid.

115. Soren Kierkegaard, *Fear and Trembling*, trans. and ed. Howard V. Hong and Edna H. Hong (Princeton: Princeton University Press, 1983) p. 53

116. Ibid. p. 111-112

117. Friedrich Nietzsche, *The Anti-Christ*, trans. R.J. Hollingdale in *Twilight of the Idols* and *The Anti-Christ*, p.186

118. Marcus Aurelius, *Meditations*, trans. George Long (Chicago: Henry Regnery Company, 1956) p.145-146 (XI, 15)

119. Aristotle, *Politics*, trans. Benjamin Jowett (Oxford: Clarendon Press, 1885) bk. 1, 2, 1253a

120. People for the Ethical Treatment of Animals, http://www.peta.org/about/why-peta/why-animal-rights.aspx

121. Friedrich Nietzsche, *Thus Spoke Zarathustra*, p. 85-86

122. Ibid, p. 118

123. cf. Roland Barthes, "The Death of the Author" in *Image – Music – Text*

124. Friedrich Nietzsche, *Thus Spoke Zarathustra*, p. 12

125. http://www.hks.harvard.edu/news-events/news/press-releases/coexistence-in-israel-study by Todd L. Pittinsky, Jennifer J. Ratcliff, Laura A. Maruskin. ("Coexistence in Israel: A National Study" is available at http://dspace.mit.edu/bitstream/handle/1721.1/55715/coexistenceinisrael.pdf?sequence=1)

126. John Gribbin, *In Search of Schrodinger's Cat* (New York: Bantam Books, 1984) p. 230-231

127. Blaise Pascal, *Thoughts, Letters and Minor Works*, translators: W. F. Trotter (*Thoughts*), M.L. Booth (*Letters*), O.W. Wight (*Minor Works*) (New York: P.F. Collier & Son Company, 1910) Section 233 of *Thoughts* (alternatively, *Pensées)*

References

Aaronovitch, David. *Voodoo Histories: The Role of The Conspiracy Theory in Shaping Modern History*. New York: The Penguin Group, 2010.

Anderson, Terry L. and Hill, Peter J. *The Not So Wild, Wild West: Property Rights on the Frontier*. Stanford: Stanford Economics and Finance, 2004.

Aristotle, *Politics*. Translated by Benjamin Jowett. Oxford: Clarendon Press, 1885.

Aristotle. *The Basic Works of Aristotle*. Edited by Richard McKeon. New York: Random House, 1941.

Aurelius, Marcus. *Meditations*, translated by George Long. Chicago: Henry Regnery Company, 1956.

Banner, Stuart. *How the Indians Lost Their Land: Law and Power on the Frontier*. Cambridge: Harvard University Press, 2005.

Barthes, Roland. "The Death of the Author" in *Image – Music – Text*. Translated by Stephen Heath. New York: Hill and Wang, 1977.

Berlin, Isaiah. *Four Essays on Liberty*. Oxford: Oxford University Press, 1969.

Berlin, Isaiah. *The Crooked Timber of Humanity*. Princeton: Princeton University Press, 1990.

Chan, Wing-Tsit. *A Source Book in Chinese Philosophy*. Princeton: Princeton University Press, 1963.

Chesterton, G. K. in *Illustrated London News* (1924-04-19).

Cheney, Margaret. *Tesla: Man Out of Time*. New York: Simon & Schuster, 1981.

Darwall, Stephen. *The British Moralists and the Internal 'Ought': 1640—1740*. Cambridge: Cambridge University Press, 1995.

Eisen, Jonathan. *Suppressed Inventions and Other Discoveries*. New York: The Berkeley Publishing Company, 1999.

Elman, Dave. *Hypnotherapy*. Glendale, CA: Westwood Publishing Co., 1964.

Erickson, Milton H. *Life Reframing in Hypnosis: The Seminars, Workshops, and Lectures of Milton H. Erickson*, vol. II. Edited by Ernest L. Rossi and Margaret O. Ryan. New York: Irvington Publishers, 1985.

Fletcher, Joseph. *Situation Ethics: The New Morality*. Philadelphia: The Westminster Press, 1966.

Foucault, Michel. *Madness and Civilization*. Translated by Richard Howard. New York: Vintage Books, 1965.

George, Henry. *Progress and Poverty*. New York: Cosimo Classics, 2005.

Gribbin, John. *In Search of Schrodinger's Cat*. New York: Bantam Books, 1984.

Hegel, G.W.F. *The Philosophy of History*. New York: Dover Publications, 1956.

Hofstadter, Douglas. *Gödel, Escher, Bach: An Eternal Golden Braid*. New York: Vintage Books, 1979.

Hume, David. *A Treatise of Human Understanding*. Edited by David Fate Norton and Mary J. Norton. Oxford: Oxford University Press, 2000.

Hume, David. *Enquiries Concerning Human Understanding and Concerning the Principles of Morals*. Edited by L.A. Selby-Bigge. Oxford: Oxford University Press, 1966 (1902 second edition).

The I Ching: Book of Changes. Translated by Richard Wilhelm, Cary F. Baynes, and Hellmut Wilhelm. Forward by C.G. Jung. Princeton: Princeton University Press, 1977.

James, William. *A Pluralistic Universe*. Lincoln, NE: University of Nebraska Press, 1996.

James, William. *Pragmatism* in *Pragmatism and The Meaning of Truth*. Cambridge: Harvard University Press, 1978.

James, William. *The Will to Believe and other essays in popular philosophy*. New York: Dover Publications, 1956.

Kant, Immanuel. *Foundations of the Metaphysics of Morals*. Translated by Lewis White Beck. New York: The Bobbs-Merrill Company, 1969.

Kant, Immanuel. "On a Supposed Right to Lie because of Philanthropic Concerns" in *Grounding for the Metaphysics of Morals*. Translated by James W. Ellington. Indianapolis/Cambridge: Hacking Publishing Company, 1993.

Kierkegaard, Soren. *Fear and Trembling*. Translated and edited by Howard V. Hong and Edna H. Hong. Princeton: Princeton University Press, 1983.

King, Moray B. *The Energy Machine of T. Henry Moray: Zero-Point Energy & Pulsed Plasma Physics*. Kempton, Illinois: Adventures Unlimited Publications, 2005.

Kuhn, Thomas S. *The Structure of Scientific Revolutions*. Chicago: The University of Chicago Press, 1996.

Lynes, Barry. *The Cancer Cure that Worked*. S. Lake Tahoe, CA: BioMed Publishing Group, 1987

Macintosh, Robert. *Hegel and Hegelianism*. Thoemmes. Bristol: Antiquarian Books, 1990.

Marx, Karl. *A Contribution to the Critique of Political Economy*, translated by S.W. Ryazanskaya. Edited by Maurice Dobb. New York: International Publishers, Inc., 1970.

Moray, John E. Xlibris, Corp. *The Sea of Energy in Which the Earth Floats*, 2012.

Nietzsche, Friedrich. *Basic Writings of Nietzsche*. Translated and edited by Walter Kaufmann. New York: The Modern Library, 1992.

Nietzsche, Friedrich. *The Anti-Christ* in *Twilight of the Idols* and *The Anti-Christ*. Translated by R.J. Hollindgale. New York: Penguin Books, 1990.

Nietzsche, Friedrich. *Thus Spoke Zarathustra*. Translated and edited by Walter Kaufmann. New York: The Modern Library, 1995.

Nietzsche, Friedrich. *Will to Power*. Translated by Walter Kaufmann and R.J. Hollingdale and edited by Walter Kaufmann. New York: Vintage Books, 1967.

Ostrogorski, M. *Democracy and the Organization of Political Parties* Vol. II. New York: The Macmillan Company, 1902.

Pascal, Blaise. *Thoughts, Letters and Minor Works*. Translators: W. F. Trotter (*Thoughts*), M.L. Booth (*Letters*), O.W. Wight (*Minor Works*). New York: P.F. Collier & Son Company, 1910.

Polanyi, Michael. *The Tacit Dimension*. Chicago: The University of Chicago Press, 1966.

Rand, Ayn. *Capitalism: The Unknown Ideal*. New York: Signet, 1966.

Sacks, Oliver. *An Anthropologist on Mars*: *Seven Paradoxical Tales*. New York: Alfred A. Knopf, 1995.

Sartre, Jean-Paul. *Existentialism and Human Emotions*. Translated by Bernard Frechtmann. New York: Citadel Press, 1985.

Schopenhauer, Arthur. *On the Basis of Morality*. Translated by E.F.J. Payne. Indianapolis/Cambridge: Hackett Publishing Company, 1995.

Spencer, Herbert. *Social Statics*. New York: Robert Schalkenbach Foundation, 1995.

Watts, Alan. *Taoism: Way Beyond Seeking*. Boston: Charles E. Tuttle Co., 1997.

Wittgenstein, Ludwig. *Philosophical Investigations*. Translated by G.E.M. Anscombe. New York: The Macmillan Company, 1953.

Wittgenstein, Ludwig, *Tractatus Logico-Philosophicus*. Translated by D.F. Pears & B.F. McGuinness. Atlantic Highlands, NJ: Humanities Press. 1974

WEBSITES

Hoffman, Jim. http://9-11research.wtc7.net/essays/nist/index.html

Holland, Anthony G. "Rife-BarePlasmaExperimentsCompilation,"

YouTube.com: http://www.youtube.com/watch?v=6rGrkz_8t5M

Jackson, Jesse, Jr. Project Vote Smart. https://votesmart.org/ public-statement/577124/reading-of-the-constitution#.UFemUK6fYbU

Jones, Steven E. http://www.youtube.com/watch?v=3pL0M5ST8jY (lecture video)

Josephson, Brian. University of Cambridge website. http://www.tcm.phy.cam.ac.uk/~bdj10/articles/uninvite.html

Kocieniewski, David. "G.E.'s Strategies Let It Avoid Taxes Altogether." In the *The New York Times* (March 24, 2011). http://www.nytimes.com/2011/03/25/business/economy/ 25tax.html?pagewanted=all

Pittinsky, Todd L., Ratcliff, Jennifer J., Maruskin, Laura A. "Coexistence in Israel: A National Study." http://www.hks.harvard.edu/news-events/news/press-releases/coexistence-in-israel-study. (Complete document available at: http://dspace.mit.edu/bitstream/handle/1721.1/55715/ coexistenceinisrael.pdf?sequence=1

Schrecker, Ellen. "Comments on John Earl Haynes', "The Cold War Debate Continues: A Traditionalist View of Historical Writing on Domestic Communism and Anti-Communism," in *Journal of Cold War Studies*, Volume 2, Number 1 (Winter 2000). http://www.fas.harvard.edu/~hpcws/comment15.htm

Schirber, Michael. "New Way to Kill Viruses: Shake Them to Death" livescience.com http://www.livescience.com/7472-kill-viruses-shake- death.html

Walter, A. "Royal Raymond Rife, A Timeline", Educate-Yourself. http://educate-yourself.org/cn/rifetimelinemay1998.shtml

Zuroff, Efraim. "No tolerance for false history" in *The Jerusalem Post*, 05/01/2010. http://www.jpost.com/Opinion/Op-EdContributors/Article.aspx?id=174425

American Cancer Society. "Electromagnetic Therapy" *(4/18/2011)* http://www.cancer.org/Treatment/TreatmentsandSideEffects/ ComplementaryandAlternativeMedicine/ManualHealingandPhysicalTouch/ electromagnetic-therapy

Architects & Engineers for 9//11 Truth. http://www.ae911truth.org/

The Enterprise Mission. The Brookings Institution report: "Proposed Studies on the Implications of Peaceful Space Activities for Human Affairs". http://www.enterprisemission.com/images/brook-8.gif

Eurekalert. "Microscope could 'solve the cause of viruses'",

http://www.eurekalert.org/pub_releases/2011-03/uom-mc022411.php
National Cancer Institute at the National Institutes of Health.
http://www.cancer.gov/cancertopics/pdq/cam/milkthistle/HealthProfessional/
Page1
Nature Communications.
"Optical virtual imaging at 50 nm lateral resolution with a white-light
Nanoscope"
http://www.nature.com/ncomms/journal/v2/n3/full/ncomms1211.html
(or search title at http://www.manchester.ac.uk/aboutus/search/)
People for the Ethical Treatment of Animals.
http://www.peta.org/about/why-peta/why-animal-rights.aspx
Scholars for 9/11 Truth & Justice. http://stj911.org
T. Henry Moray Foundation. http://www.thmoray.org

Index